Praise for *On the Line*

"It is hard to imagine a more humanizing portrait of the American labor movement. Rendered with lyric, incandescent prose, *On the Line* is both deeply personal and profoundly political, with an acute sense for the ebb and flow of history. With this remarkable debut, Pitkin has given us a riveting and intimate meditation on power, class consciousness, and the true meaning of solidarity." —Francisco Cantú,
New York Times bestselling author of
The Line Becomes a River: Dispatches from the Border

"*On the Line* vibrates with . . . vital and potential power, and all the more so for the stumbles, falls, and bruises Alma and Daisy took together. It's one for the ages. Easily one of the best books ever written about American trade unionism. Reading it, I wept." —*Dissent*

"I started reading and couldn't stop. In an age of unchecked corporate power, *On the Line* is a timely and lyrical story of resistance, a behind-the-scenes portrait of labor organizing with all its hope and heartache. Candid, clear-eyed and utterly engrossing, Pitkin's writing couldn't come at a better—or more necessary—time." —Jessica Bruder,
New York Times bestselling author of *Nomadland:*
Surviving America in the Twenty-First Century

"An intimate and moving account . . . Enriched by Pitkin's sharp character sketches and sincere grappling with issues of class, race and privilege, this is a bracing look at the challenges facing American workers." —*Publishers Weekly*

"Intimate and touching . . . A much-needed spotlight on the daily struggles of a vulnerable population." —*Kirkus Reviews*

"Part memoir and part rallying cry, this is a gripping tale of the birth of a union today . . . Poetic, stirring . . . A heartfelt and persuasive argument for organized labor now more than ever."　　—*San Francisco Chronicle*

"[*On the Line* is] maddening, it's heartbreaking, it's inspiring, it's beautiful, and it seamlessly weaves Pitkin's and the workers' personal stories with labor history. It's one of the best labor memoirs ever published. You won't be able to put it down."　　　　　　　　　—*Jacobin* magazine

"Pitkin weaves a poetic narrative with a century of intertwining histories of union organization in the United States and its often-unsung leaders . . . An elegant chronicle out of the often-brutal realities of workers. Pitkin's literary innovation lends itself to a powerful message dissecting solidarity and the power of the collective . . . At once incredibly impactful and insightful, this is a lesson in history and humanity."
　　　　　　　　　　　　　　　　　　　　　—*Library Journal*

"Compelling. In this stirring debut, Daisy Pitkin deftly renders the intimate work of union organizing, demystifying the process as she takes care to ensure the focus remains on the workers themselves. Ultimately, *On the Line* is a ringing endorsement for the power of a union, and an essential read for anyone who's ever been inspired to fight for a better world."　　　　　　　　　—Kim Kelly, labor journalist and author of
Fight Like Hell: The Untold History of American Labor

"The first book I've read that gets into the messy, tangled weeds of organizing . . . Daisy overturns the gendered ways we think of organizing as a firmly political act removed from the organizer's personal life and identity and doubts. In doing so, *On the Line* opens up space for organizers to take our practice off the pedestal and open it up to reflection and critique."　　　　　　　　　—Aparna Gopalan, *Jewish Currents*

"Absorbing and lyrical . . . The organizing comes alive . . . Pitkin reminds us that ultimately our power lies in each other."

—Luis Feliz Leon, *Labor Notes*

"An excellent primer on labor organizing in addition to a gripping read. It shows just how difficult unionizing is in the US and how hard people have to work to overcome this broken labor system. It's especially relevant in the context of the current Great Resignation and reckoning with the nature of work in the US." —Sarah Neilson, Shondaland.com

"A sobering narrative that gives a human face to the plight of often-overlooked essential labor in the US." —*Booklist*

"Once in a while a book comes along that makes you feel the hard-won solidarity of a union organizing campaign and what it takes to build it. *On the Line* is such a book. Vivid and gripping . . . A must-read for anyone interested in the messy details and politics of union organizing in real-world campaigns." —*Convergence Magazine*

"Captivating . . . Remarkable . . . Beautifully written . . . An intimate look at the volatile work of union organizing." —*Minneapolis Star Tribune*

"With vulnerability and complexity, Daisy Pitkin delivers a beautifully written cultural critique and memoir about labor organizing and labor history, resistance and surrender, the unbalanced landscape between herself and the laborers she represents, but mainly, it's about love. *On the Line* is underscored by an obsession with moths, creatures—like herself—that are beckoned by flames that ultimately harm them. Pitkin is a companionable force you want on your side of any fight."

—Kerri Arsenault, author of
Mill Town: Reckoning with What Remains

"Compelling . . . Unflinching . . . *On the Line* shows us that workers, alone, cannot change the hand-to-mouth economy that traps them. For that kind of systemic change to happen, we need radical solidarity."

—Beth Alvarado, *The Los Angeles Review*

"Pitkin's book captures the drama and transformative power of labor organizing better than any book published in the United States in years. With so many powerful narratives generated by similar union campaigns in American history . . . we should have many more books like hers."

—Micah Uetricht, *The New Republic*

"Brilliant, evocative. Pitkin's journey through the trenches of the American class war is at once personal and universal, devastating and hopeful, raw and elegant. I am grateful that she chose to share it with us. I am awed that she wrote it so beautifully." —David Hill, vice president, National Writers Union, and author of *The Vapors*

"Highly moving and a fine piece of nonfiction . . . The gripping story of a labor struggle."

—*Pittsburgh Post-Gazette*

"The marathon course and quotidian tasks of the union drive alone would make for a worthy read, but as Pitkin's memoir unfurls, *On the Line* metamorphosizes into something greater . . . Her story and Alma's are saturated in heartbreak and offer no easy answers, yet the two keep finding their way back to the fire, to something more than just anger keeping it lit—something like the difference between taking power and building power."

—*Red Fault*

"*On the Line* will change the way you think about work that is hidden."

—Jody DiPerna, *Pittsburgh Institute for Nonprofit Journalism*

"A riveting, elegant, and intimate masterpiece. *On the Line* passed the great book test for me when I set it down for the last time and marveled and grieved in its beauty and sorrow, while understanding that my view of the world had changed."   —Todd Miller, author of *Storming the Wall: Climate Change, Migration, and Homeland Security*

"A stunning, luminous debut about what drives people to rise up for change. Pitkin tells a captivating personal story, as well as an essential cultural one, unveiling the cruelty and injustice of industrial laundries, the erosion of the right to organize, and the hard-won persistence of women who have fought for nearly a hundred years for safety and justice in the workplace."

—Alison Hawthorne Deming, author of *A Woven World*

On the Line

TWO WOMEN'S EPIC FIGHT TO BUILD A UNION

Daisy Pitkin

ALGONQUIN BOOKS OF CHAPEL HILL   2023

Published by
Algonquin Books of Chapel Hill
Post Office Box 2225
Chapel Hill, North Carolina 27515-2225

an imprint of Workman Publishing Co., Inc.
a subsidiary of Hachette Book Group, Inc.
1290 Avenue of the Americas
New York, New York 10104

Printed in the United States of America.
Design by Steve Godwin.

The publisher is not responsible for websites (or their content) that are not owned by the publisher.

The Library of Congress has cataloged the hardcover edition of this book as follows:
Library of Congress Cataloging-in-Publication Data
Names: Pitkin, Daisy, [date]– author.
Title: On the line : a story of class, solidarity, and two women's epic fight to build
    a union / Daisy Pitkin.
Description: First edition. | Chapel Hill, North Carolina : Algonquin Books of
    Chapel Hill, 2022. | Includes bibliographical references. | Summary: "The story
    of two dedicated women, a labor organizer and an immigrant laundry worker, coming
    together to spearhead an audacious campaign to unionize one of the
    most dangerous industries in one of the most anti-union states—Arizona—and offering
    a nuanced look at the modern-day labor movement and the future of workers' rights"—
    Provided by publisher.
Identifiers: LCCN 2021052739 | ISBN 9781643750712 (hardcover) |
    ISBN 9781643752976 (ebook)
Subjects: LCSH: Laundry workers—Labor unions—Arizona. | Laundry workers—Labor
    unions—Organizing—Arizona.
Classification: LCC HD8039.L32 U668 2022 | DDC 331.88/1671309791—
    dc23/eng/20211108 LC record available at https://lccn.loc.gov/2021052739

ISBN 978-1-64375-339-3 (PB)

10 9 8 7 6 5 4 3 2 1
First Paperback Edition

In memory of Eleazar Torres Gomez

In honor of every person who works in danger today

But mostly we're forgetting that we're dead stars too, my mouth is full of dust and I wish to reclaim the rising—

to lean in the spotlight of streetlight with you, toward what's larger within us, toward how we were born.

Look, we are not unspectacular things.

—ADA LIMÓN, "Dead Stars"

Unions are such a pain in the ass, really. Anyone who has dealt with a union understands. . . . But unions, Americans may finally be coming to realize, are absolutely essential to democracy.

—JANE McALEVEY,
*A Collective Bargain, Unions, Organizing,
and the Fight for Democracy*

A Note from the Author

This book is a work of nonfiction and, in part, a memoir, which is to say that, while it relies heavily on historical sources and notes and legal documents, it also relies on my memory and personal interpretation of events. I have reconstructed this story, timeline, and dialogue to the best of my ability. Some minor scenes have been compressed in the interest of space. Names and identifying information for some people have been changed in order to protect their privacy.

Any royalties from this book will be shared with Alma, la polilla mayor.

CONTENTS

1: Las Polillas

THE FIRST WEEK I arrived in Phoenix, I started to dream about moths. We were sleeping only a few hours a night, if at all, preparing the organizing campaign at your factory—gathering names and addresses of your coworkers and then scouting their residences so we knew which had fences with locked gates, which had snarling dogs in the yard, which had multiple units, making it uncertain on which door we'd need to knock when the time came. We mapped your coworkers in this way, at their homes scattered across the city, trying to put together a plan that would make it possible to talk to a majority of them about forming a union. A "blitz," we called it, to get a hold of as many people as possible in a day or two, before the company you worked for could figure out what was going on.

During this time, the other organizers and I were staying at the Days Inn on East Van Buren Street, an aging midcentury motel nestled between a used-car lot and a strip club called Blue Moon. I would wake up in the strange room not knowing where I was, not remembering having fallen asleep. I left the TV on a lot—the sound of it made slipping in and out of awakeness a little less jarring. The moths never arrived in the dream. That is, I didn't see them flying in from somewhere else. I didn't see them land on my body. They covered me suddenly, as if they had always been there. I'm prone on the grimy floor at the foot of the motel bed. I open my eyes. Lift my head. Look down at my body. Every cell of skin is carpeted with moths. Every inch gray-white-brown. Scaly. Dusty. Fluttering.

Years later, when I was long gone from the union because I had gotten so tired and sick and sad over watching (and causing, I know) what we had fought to build come apart, and I had somehow decided that feeling these things made it okay for me to stop organizing, I was working at a bar in Tucson that switched from having their towels and napkins cleaned at a small union laundry to a bigger, regional nonunion laundry. I had taken this job in part because it was a world away from the union campaigning I had been leading all across the country, or so I thought, but of course, bar rags need to be washed. I protested the switch to the manager and then to the owner and the landlord and even to one of the bar's investors when she came in for a glass of wine, but the nonunion laundry was cheaper, and I wasn't in contact with anyone at the union anymore and didn't have the standing with my coworkers at the bar to organize any sort of fight. One day, the new, nonunion laundry's driver showed up to empty the dirty-linen locker out back, and I recognized him as one of the drivers who'd fought against the union at your laundry during our campaign there. He was one of the nastier ones, and I could still see him, sweaty and red-faced, yelling "Bitches!" and "Cockroaches!" and a litany of other slurs from his truck window as he drove past us in the parking lot where we handed out our leaflets. He didn't recognize me, or he didn't say anything if he did.

Later that week, I went to the emergency room with a high fever and a hot throb in my back. I'd been to the hospital three times in two months, each time requiring a dose of morphine in order to withstand the hurt of infection, and once, the passing of kidney stones. As the nurses pushed the drug into the IV, my face grew heavy, my head hummed, my body stiffened and shook, hypothermic, as the refrigerated drip entered my bloodstream. This was eight years after we launched the campaign at your laundry. Three and a half years since we had spoken. And still I thought of you, Alma, as I asked for one blanket and then another and another. I thought of you as the nurses pulled them from a metal cabinet in the corner of the curtain-enclosed stall and shook the thin material open in the air space above the bed, as the blankets fluttered down, each one adding a layer to the thickening cocoon that enclosed my body. I thought of you and of Santiago, and Analía, and Antonia, and Reina, and Cecilia. That hospital, University Medical Center, contracts linen service from your industrial laundry. You touched those blankets. You touched the sheets on the bed, the pillowcase, the gown I wore. And after I was released, the linens that composed this cocoon would be placed into a plastic trash bag and loaded into a blue rolling bin with other linen-filled trash bags, and the bin would be loaded onto one of your factory's laundry trucks—a big one, an eighteen-wheeler— along with many dozens of other blue bins, and the truck would make its way up the I-10 from Tucson to Phoenix, and the bins would be unloaded into the soil-sort department, where you would likely be working, and the plastic bag would be ripped open by someone working the front of the line, who would probably not be you but might be Santiago, and the linens would travel down the conveyor belt to the position where you probably would be working, and you would touch them again.

I was alone in the hospital that night. And though you and I spent years together sealing ourselves off from any mention of fear, I will admit that I was afraid. Afraid that no one seemed to know what was causing the infection, afraid that it would spread to other parts of my body. The near contact with you, via the rough fabric of sheets and blankets that belonged to neither of us, was a comfort. I remembered how your laugh was sharp and loud when you were afraid. From inside the cocoon of blankets, I heard it.

The next day, at home and feverish on the couch, I started writing this to you.

I scribbled a timeline on a scrap of paper, but it overfilled to nonsense—with notes, and notes about notes, and corrections to notes—so I covered the coffee table with paper, five sheets taped end to end. I made more notes and threaded them together with winding arrows, pointing to a central throughline. A map of the three years we spent together organizing industrial laundries in Phoenix: the time you crashed the car while I was trying to teach you to drive; the time you taught me to dance in Antonia's living room; the day you were fired for leading the work stoppage at your factory; you, over time, telling me about losing your son, and me telling you about my mother. I was just about his age. You were just about hers.

I was trying to remember what happened, to parse how we got to that moment at the peak of the union's rupture, eyes locked on each other from opposite sides of Local 2732's glass front door, the people with you pushing and yelling and pounding the windows, the people with me barricading the doors with their bodies to keep you and them out, the two of us still and silent among the swarm.

I was still new to the union in 2003, when we launched the campaign at Sodexho—the sprawling multinational multiservice corporation that owned your laundry factory—and you had never been through a union fight either. So we learned together.

Just a few weeks before I got to Phoenix, an organizing director for UNITE (the Union of Needletrades, Industrial, and Textile Employees, one of the scrappier organizing unions in the United States), a white woman in her late twenties, came to Tucson to interview me, also a white woman, twenty-five. I had just moved there with my then girlfriend to get away from Washington, DC, where an airplane had flown into the Pentagon, and a pair of snipers had been shooting people at gas stations and grocery-store parking lots, and anthrax was being sent around in the mail.

The union was headhunting experienced organizers, which I sort of was after a few years of working on international solidarity campaigns, organizing protests at Gap stores across the country to support striking denim workers in Guatemala and the like. This was important work, but it was indirect. The stores where we would distribute informational leaflets and sometimes argue with mall security guards (whose jobs were also shitty with bad pay) about how close we could stand to the racks of clothes made by the workers we meant to support were thousands of miles away from those workers and the sweatshops they were fighting to change. I think I wanted to be closer to a fight, to put my body in the way of something, without really knowing what that meant or thinking very hard about why I wanted it or what my relationship as an organizer might be to a union fight.

The director picked me up from my house at 10 p.m., the standard time for nightly meetings among UNITE organizers, though I did not yet know it. We went to a bar on Fourth Avenue to drink beer and talk about UNITE, about the ambitious industry-wide laundry campaign they wanted to run in Arizona as a test to see if it was possible to organize low-wage immigrant workers, most of whom were women, many of whom were undocumented, in a deep-red state. We both laughed a little and shook our heads at how fucking hard it would be, how much of a war, but then she told me more about the industry, about the conditions in commercial laundry factories; the way managers remove or disable machine safeguards in order to run production faster, the number of workers who get injured and sick and killed. By the start of the second beer, I already had a fire in my gut.

After midnight, we got into her rental car and drove to a Sears call center in South Tucson, another kind of workplace the union was considering as a target, because the industry was growing and work there was also hell. The director wanted to see if we could gather any information that might help in an organizing campaign, and though she did not say it, she also needed to assess my capacity for the more enterprising ways this information could be gathered. She killed the headlights as we pulled into the parking lot. At her signal, I got out and quickly pulled trash bags from a dumpster and stuffed them into the trunk until a motion-detecting light flashed high up on the warehouse wall. I froze when a security guard came out of the building, and before I could duck back in the car, the director had gunned it out onto the street. I sprinted after her for a few long industrial blocks to the spot where she was waiting to pick me up. We pounded cigarettes, holding their glowing tips up to small openings in the car windows, watching the embers catch in the rush of air around the car and then streak diagonally across the windows as she drove me home. *I don't think the guard got the plate number,* she said. *But, goddamn, he probably made us anyway.*

When she dropped me off, she said that someone from the New York office would call me in a few days to let me know if I'd gotten the job.

Two days later, someone from the New York office did call. He told me to pick up a rental car at the Tucson airport and drive the three hundred miles across the state of Arizona to Lake Havasu City. *Now,* he said. *Right now.* A laundry there had caught fire, and the workers had walked out. They were standing on the sidewalk in front of the factory.

When I got there six or so hours later, three other organizers had already arrived, from Phoenix and California. The factory was still smoking. An iron had caught fire, which happens regularly in industrial laundries, where machinery is often poorly maintained. The manager told the workers to keep working—to continue operating washers and presses and folding machines, even as the smoke grew thick around them. He stood between them and the door when they tried to leave, but one of the workers dipped below his outstretched arm and made it to the door, and the other workers, nearly one hundred of them, followed her. When they got outside, one of the workers said she had a cousin who worked in a union laundry in Las Vegas. She walked the few blocks home, called her cousin to get the union's number, then she called UNITE through its 1-800 hotline.

When I arrived, the nearly one hundred people were standing in small groups in front of the factory, making picket signs and affixing bedsheets to poles and chairs to block the gusting wind and signing up for picket duty and cooking shifts. They had handwritten a petition, listing dangerous working conditions and demanding that they be addressed. One of the organizers told me to pick up a union card, which someone in New York had faxed to a nearby hotel, and to make copies at the Kinko's in town. When I brought the copies back to the picket line, the worker who had dipped below the manager's arm, Mariana Rivera, gathered her coworkers and asked them to join the union. She stood on a chair and read the union card aloud in Spanish while one of the organizers stood with a small group of English-speaking workers and interpreted what she said. Mariana told them that they had been screwed for a long time in that factory—that they all knew the machines were not functioning as they should and that they were working too fast to be safe. She told them they'd really be screwed now if they didn't all go back in together, speaking with one voice. Every worker standing there signed a card, and they won the strike in three days, because not a single person crossed the picket line. The factory smoldered across the parking lot the whole time.

On the momentum of that uncommonly clean and expeditious win, I was sent to Phoenix to help prepare the initial wave of laundry campaigns there. On my first night, the director who had interviewed me in Tucson debriefed the team of organizers—Dario, who had been a worker leader at a laundry in New York City; Ana, who had come out of a garment factory to organize with the union more than a decade earlier; and Manuel, who had organized with farmworkers in North Carolina for a few years. After reporting the new information they'd gathered that day—worker names and addresses and some client information—we went to the motel bar. The debrief had been in Spanish, but at the bar the organizers spoke to me in English while we played pool, asking about my organizing experience and assessing, I imagine, what I already knew and what I would need to learn. I tried to respond to them in Spanish at first, to demonstrate, I thought, my desire and willingness to practice, but the absurdity and unfairness of asking them to parse and correct what I was saying—to teach me to speak on top of figuring out how to teach me to organize—was evident, and I gave it up.

I don't know how much beer or whiskey I or anyone else drank, but at 2 a.m. it was decided that we should drive to one of the laundries—the big twenty-four-hour one, Sodexho's Commercial Linen Exchange—to watch the shift change and to count the number of workers leaving from second shift and the number going in for third. We drove there and, each in our own idling rental car, sat spread out across unlit patches of the industrial lots adjacent to the factory. At 4:30 a.m., after watching all of the departments in the laundry turn over, we drove to the tiny union office, which was a room UNITE was renting from the AFL-CIO (the largest federation of unions in the United States) in its state headquarters, and which we hadn't yet filled with thrift-store couches and tables, but which had cartons of cigarettes piled in the corner and a fishbowl of loose NoDoz tablets sitting on a box of strike signs. We smoked and

compared the numbers of people we had each counted. Two of the organizers had snuck onto company property and—without getting made—
had pulled trash bags out of the dumpster. We cut them open on the floor
and riffled through the waste, looking for names of workers, names of
clients, anything that could be useful.

You were our first contact at that laundry because your husband was
the cousin of the shop steward (the person elected by their coworkers to
defend their collective bargaining agreement and represent them in deal-
ings with the boss) at the one union laundry in Phoenix, Mission Linen. I
knocked on your door with Manuel a few days into the preparation work
we were doing. It was one of the first times I'd been on a union house call.
I sat on the olive couch in your living room, looking at a photograph of
a teenager in a black cowboy hat, which rested on a small shelf among
candles and dried flowers. I didn't know yet that he was Julio Martín,
that he was your son.

You worked in soil sort, you said. I asked if you would describe your
work—I still had no idea what "soil sort" was, or what you were required
to do with your body there for ten hours a day. You rose from your chair
to demonstrate, maybe because you could tell by how poorly I'd asked
the question that I didn't speak much Spanish, and maybe because
laundry work is difficult to explain without miming the motions of the
massive machines that fill the factory. When you stood up, I was surprised by how tall you are, which I hadn't noticed when you greeted us
at your door.

You showed us how huge bags of linen—up to three hundred pounds,
you said—are pushed off the backs of trucks in rolling carts. The carts
are pushed into a "dumper" machine, which, like a garbage truck, picks
them up with metal arms and turns them over in the air. You reached up
to show us how the linen is supposed to fall on the soil belt. A person is

stationed there who is also called a dumper. On your shift, that person is Santiago, you said. You bent forward to show how he tugs open the bags of soiled hospital laundry with his thinly gloved hands. You showed how he pulls each bag's mass of sheets and gowns and towels apart. You said, *The company doesn't replace the gloves every day, so we have to rinse and reuse the ones they give us. Sometimes the gloves break open, and we have to keep using them anyway.* You said this in Spanish after turning to me and saying, *Sorry, no English* in English, and I, in return, waved my hands, awkwardly, I imagine, and said, *No, don't worry!* in English, which Manuel then had to interpret.

The linen moves down the belt, you said, and then you flicked your arms back and forth to demonstrate how you and the other sorters toss sheets to one bin, towels to another, gowns to a third, and so on. You said, *Sometimes there are syringes and scalpels, sometimes body parts, wrapped in the linens.* You said, *Sometimes they speed up the conveyor, and we don't have time to be careful. There is a lot of blood and puke and feces.* You said, *We don't get shoe covers, so some of us take off our shoes and drive home in our socks.* You said, *Our gloves are too big—they slip off our hands. Sometimes when they tear open, we have to handle the soiled linen with exposed skin.*

Manuel was a more experienced organizer and had his own gestures for explaining things. The union, for example, he symbolized with a fist. *Spread apart*, he said, *our fingers can be broken, but squeezed together—* his fingers clamped down and hooked under by his thumb—*we are stronger.* You nodded. Your grandfather had been part of the land struggles in Mexico; your father led copper mine strikes in Sonora. You said, *I know what it means to fight.*

We talked about what would have to happen next to prepare for the organizing drive at Sodexho. Unlike you, not everyone does know what it means to fight, at least not in the way most workers have to fight if they want to build a union in this country. We had to prepare secretly—*bajo el agua*, Manuel said—if we didn't want to get made before we even got a start. I remember that you narrowed your eyes at this, and at the time, I didn't know if it was a sign that you were steeling yourself in your deter-mination to fight or if you were wincing because you inferred a tinge of condescension in his voice, though I imagine now, after knowing you so well for those many years, that you were envisioning how this secret phase would play out—who we would talk to next; how we would reach the workers on other shifts and in other departments of the factory; the particular kinds of threats your bosses would make if we misstepped and our plan came leaking out from bajo el agua; who among your coworkers would fight anyway, even in the face of threats, and who would be too afraid to go on.

We talked about the "blitz," which was key to our model of orga-nizing. As groundwork we needed to build a list of all your coworkers: their names and shifts and departments and phone numbers and, most importantly, home addresses, Manuel explained. We would build a map of when they worked and where they lived, and then many organizers from UNITE's staff and workers from union laundries in California and Las Vegas and Chicago and New York, who had been trained in this kind of organizing, would come to Phoenix, and we would visit everyone—all 220 or so of your coworkers—over the course of a single weekend. That was our best shot, because even though your factory operated 24/7, most of the supervisors and the main manager and the HR representative were away from the factory from Friday evening until Monday morning. And though they would certainly get word of our organizing from the first house calls on Friday evening—because someone would call their supervisor, out of fear or to curry favor, and the supervisor would call the general manager, who would call the corporate contact he and the other managers of Sodexho's more than thirteen thousand worksites had been trained to call at the first whiff of a union—they might not be able to react in a concerted way during that slim stretch of time. In this way, your coworkers could decide whether or not they wanted to form a union in a space, however momentary, that was free from the company's intimidation.

I use these words here—*workers could decide whether or not* and *free from intimidation*—because these are the phrases unions use to describe a situation in which the level of unfairness and volatility is often so extreme it is difficult to capture through language, and so it is often reduced either to cliché—an *unlevel playing field*, an *uphill battle*, a *stacked deck*—or to this kind of tepid legalese: *Workers should be allowed to decide whether or not to elect a union to represent them under circumstances that are free from employer intimidation.*

These were not the words we used in your living room. You did not need for us to tell you that winning a union in your factory would be hard or that the system is rigged in favor of the company. People don't work in industrial laundries unless they have to. And there is no real space or time that is "free from intimidation" inside the dynamic of trying to build power to be used against your boss at a job you need in order to live. You already knew the company was going to fight. *They'll probably fire all of us*, you said, with the hard crack of laugh that I was hearing for the first time and can still hear now.

Manuel described this blitz method with a dramatic analogy that I found mesmerizing even through my shitty Spanish comprehension, and which I tried to re-create in visits with your coworkers in the weeks to come but could never quite make my own: *The company is like a sleeping giant. We know from experience that the only way to beat a giant in a fight is with many people all working together and a plan, and to do it while the giant sleeps. If the people aren't prepared for what the giant will do when it wakes, they'll get plastered to the ground by giant feet every time.*

Months later, during the actual blitz, you found a tamer and perhaps more elegant description to explain the urgency of the rapid-fire house visits to your coworkers. It was something like: *We're building a shield against the company's anti-union campaign, and we have to talk to everyone. Right now. Today. Call the people on your shift, tell them to open their doors, sign their cards, and come to the meeting on Sunday night. We have to have a plan to win come Monday morning.*

2: Fires

THE FIRST TIME I talked about the Triangle shirtwaist factory fire of 1911 was at a union training. I got choked up and had to bite down hard on the edge of my tongue to let go the catch in my throat. This was early in 2004, a year after we had sat together for the first time in your living room. I stood in front of twenty or twenty-five people—workers who were leading campaigns within the industries that were actively organizing in Phoenix: ironworkers, roofers, painters, and laundry workers.

This was the first day of a three-day intensive training, and I was supposed to give a short history of UNITE, which was an offshoot of the legendary International Ladies' Garment Workers' Union (the ILGWU), which was founded in 1900 and played a key role in the expanding labor movement in the 1920s and '30s. The short history I was supposed to recount was a story of dispersion, of a union chasing an industry from place to place around the world. Something like: At the turn of the century, the garment industry was centered in New York. Workers there organized around safety conditions and hours and pay. The industry moved to the South, fleeing unionization, and there, too, workers started organizing. So the industry moved to the maquila sectors of Mexico and Central America, and there, too, workers organized. So the industry moved to South and Southeast Asia, and now it's migrating into China. With the decline of garment production in the United States, the union turned its focus to other industries like commercial laundries, where workers faced similar dangers on similar machines, laundering fabric now manufactured halfway around the world.

The Triangle fire—the industrial disaster at the now infamous shirtwaist blouse factory—was not necessary to this narrative. The fact of the fire, the fact that hundreds of people, mostly women and girls, jumped eight or nine stories to escape it, the sound their bodies made on impact with the sidewalk—no one was expecting to hear about these things during a weekend training focused on how to conduct a union house visit. But by this time, we were a year into the campaign at your factory, and I had started thinking about the emptiness of that broader history, how it didn't feel anything like the work of organizing, how devoid it was of lives and bodies and of the often-gruesome reality of industrial work. And I thought of you, and of the other laundry workers who would be at the training—Rigoberto, Maria, Mariana, and Susana—who were fighting day and night to organize your factories and using the little vacation time they had to be at the training. Your fights, as with most laundry campaigns, were focused on health and safety— lives and bodies—because industrial laundries are gruesome places to work. Through these fights, you were demanding a seemingly simple thing: to work your eight- or ten-hour shift and come home unharmed. You wanted gloves that hospital needles cannot puncture. You wanted face masks to keep the blood and fluids from other bodies from entering your bodies. You wanted safety guards put back on machines where they had been removed. You wanted linen dust cleaned from the rafters to prevent fires.

You and the other laundry workers at the training knew about the fire at the laundry in Lake Havasu City, knew about the manager who tried to block the exit door, trying to force people to work through it. At the Triangle shirtwaist factory, just under a century earlier, the managers escaped through a doorway most workers couldn't access, which led them onto the roof. On the shop floor, one of the exit doors was locked—the company had grown concerned about workers stealing scraps of material or spools of thread or time in the form of unsanctioned breaks, so they locked the door and then single-filed workers through the only other exit at the end of the day, making them turn out their pockets and purses for a security guard. When the fire swept through the factory, the workers were locked inside. They made their way to the windows and then out onto the window ledges and then out onto the cornice of the building. Some of the workers jumped; some of them fell. The managers escaped to the roof and then climbed up and over to another building. From the safety of the roof next door, they could see bodies jumping/falling.

At the training, I wanted to talk about fires and about people; about women and mainly immigrant women, fighting in what seemed to be echoing moments at both ends of a century. I started by saying that one hundred years ago—even before the fire—garment workers were organizing in New York City, and that they were doing it, at first, shop by small shop. The only way to force companies to pay attention at that time—before workers had a federally supported process for holding union elections—was to strike, so the garment workers struck. They demanded better pay and shorter hours but also safer factories, to not have to rent chairs to sit in, to have sewing tables moved closer to windows to make it easier to see the needles, to be able to use the toilet when they needed to, to keep the factories clear of scrap fabric and piles of lint to stop the spread of fire.

That shop-by-shop strategy changed in 1909 when a worker named Clara Lemlich spoke out of turn at a union meeting and called for a general strike. The workers at the meeting rallied around her, and the next day they rose up into a strike that would grow twenty thousand strong. I described to my audience at the training, to you and the other worker leaders who were organizing among your mainly immigrant coworkers, how the public, particularly wealthy women, started to support the workers when they found out that girls and young women were being beaten to break the strike at sweatshops where the garments they wore every day were made. When they could no longer ignore that this brutality was happening right there in their city, blocks from their homes. When they realized that they could, if they chose, walk to the picket lines that wound through the garment sector of the city and stand in witness to the violence against the strikers. And I explained that thirteen weeks later, in part because of the support of the wealthy white women who had started bailing the strikers out of jail, but mainly because the strikers themselves had a blazing will to fight, most of the industry—in fact nearly every garment company except Triangle—acquiesced to the workers' demands. They gave raises. They capped working hours. They put some basic safety practices into place: fire regulations and fire drills and rules about the handling of scraps. I had learned the story of this strike months before, while sitting around in the motel room with the other organizers on the team, but had learned only the night before my talk at the training that the Triangle owners had held out, that they had refused to recognize the union and give in to any of these demands, and that the strike of twenty thousand garment workers was settled without their compliance.

I got through this part of the story—the 1909 uprising and its aftermath—calmly, matter-of-factly, and, I imagine, very earnestly, as one does when conveying an urgent lesson not rooted in personal experience but in a collective past. And that's how I felt about it, that the training was part of a long, nearly sacred tradition of teaching workers the skills they need in order to organize and win. But when I started talking about Triangle, the shirtwaist company that refused to settle with strikers and where, sixteen months later, the most violent factory fire in US history would kill 146 workers, my voice broke, and I had to stop talking for a few moments and stand there, embarrassed, in the front of the room, before I was able to continue.

The story of the fire was not necessary to the training, but it was important to UNITE—both to its idea of itself, its origin and significance, and as a reminder of the urgency and high stakes of organizing, of what can happen if we lose. The telling and retelling of the story of the fire, which is memorialized annually through a gathering at the former factory in New York and vigils at local union offices across the country, is purposeful. It's an easy conduit to the anger that often serves as an engine to a fight. And it works on me in exactly that way—reminds me how monstrously inhuman it is to disregard the lives of some humans so that other humans can eke a little more out of the world. But it does something else to me, too; it breaks me in a way that organizers are not really supposed to break, at least not the organizers I knew at UNITE, especially not at the telling of the stories we used to move others. It was not our place to be caught up emotionally in the work of organizing, outside of the righteous indignation that underlay everything we did. We were there to serve as guides; to help workers navigate *their* fights, which were not our fights; to win unions that were not our unions but belonged to the workers who had fought and risked and been moved to build them.

Most accounts of the fire, now housed in various archives, use similar language, even repeat certain phrases verbatim, probably because they stem from the same primary sources, as from bystander William Shepherd, whose statement was taken down by a reporter whom Shepherd called from a pay phone in Washington Square as he watched the factory burn. The statement appeared in newspapers nationwide after the reporter broadcast it via telegraph:

I learned a new sound—a more horrible sound than description can picture. It was the thud of a speeding, living body on a stone sidewalk.

Thud-dead, thud-dead, thud-dead, thud-dead. Sixty-two thud-deads. I call them that, because the sound and the thought of death came to me each time, at the same instant. There was plenty of chance to watch them as they came down. The height was eighty feet.

The first ten thud-deads shocked me. I looked up—saw that there were scores of girls at the windows. The flames from the floor below were beating in their faces. Somehow I knew that they, too, must come down, and something within me—something that I didn't know was there—steeled me.

I even watched one girl falling. Waving her arms, trying to keep her body upright until the very instant she struck the sidewalk, she was trying to balance herself. Then came the thud—then a silent, unmoving pile of clothing and twisted, broken limbs.

Though Shepherd's account was supposedly transcribed in real time, it was reported in past tense. This differs from the versions of the story cobbled together from statements made by workers who survived the fire, many of which are conveyed in present tense, though they were recorded after the fact, as if they are asking readers to see what they saw, to stand witness to the atrocity alongside them. Many of these archives are kept by organizations concerned with the industrial violence of today's factories and the continued vulnerabilities of bodies at work, the present-tense telling of the fire doubling as metaphor and implication. More or less, they read like this:

Near closing time on March 25, 1911, fire engulfs the eighth, ninth, and tenth floors of the Asch Building, occupied by the Triangle Waist

Company. Within eighteen minutes, it causes the death of 146 workers. The call to fire stations goes out at 4:45 p.m. There is one call and then another and another and another, four in all. Firefighters rush to the scene but are unable to save the workers who are locked inside. Smoke billows from the windows, then flames lash through them into the air above the street. Then workers appear on the ledges. Many jump. Others burn inside the building. Others die in the freight shaft, jumping after the elevator that has stopped returning. Others are crushed in the collapse of the building's one fire escape, which bottlenecks with bodies because it does not reach the ground. Inside, only a few buckets of water are on hand to douse the flames. Outside, firefighters' ladders do not reach above the sixth floor, their hoses do not reach the ninth floor, and their safety nets rip like paper under the weight of falling bodies.

I had been nervous the night before the training—it was the first I'd ever helped to facilitate. I would be the youngest person in the room, one of only four women, and the only person not fluent in Spanish. I stayed up late, going over what I wanted to say, reading and rereading what I could find on the internet about the fire, practicing the words out loud. I scribbled notes and threw them out. I made bullet points and threw them out as well. Finally, I decided to trust that I would know what to say in the moment.

When I slept, I had the moth dream again. The residue from their scales was ash. Their charred bodies clung to my body. They were not burning exactly, but smoldering.

This conflation sticks with me still. Sometimes, in a kind of synesthesia, when I see a moth in the world, I smell smoke.

My reaction to my own telling of the story made the trainers from the other unions uncomfortable. They kept their distance for the rest of the day, as if they were afraid of contracting my too-thin skin. That night, during a palpably tense debrief, they rightly advised me to leave out any details about the fire the next time I ran a training. It was hard to listen to, they said, and I had taken more time than allotted, so we'd had to rush through some role-playing at the end of the day. *People don't learn to organize through emotional outbursts*, one of the trainers said. By then, I had the upwelling under control enough that his terseness did not bother me, and the prickling shame of his reprimand felt justified. Organizing is a system, rational and teachable. There are five steps to a house call. There are plant maps and worker assessments. We collect data and analyze it. We build timelines, set clear goals, and then calibrate our tactics accordingly.

I believed in this system (I believe in it and teach it still today). But I'm not sure the trick of moving people without being moved, of telling stories meant to evoke emotion that I, the teller, was not meant to feel, helped to make the union (or me, or anyone) any stronger. After all, unions are built on solidarity, and solidarity is a form of closeness, maybe even intimacy, a network of deep connection that rewires a splintered collective. By definition it is "unity or agreement of feeling or action." *Feeling* or action. What would it mean to build a union on both?

It was November 22, 1909, one year and four months before the Triangle fire, when Clara Lemlich stood up in the large meeting hall at Cooper Union and moved for a general strike. She was twenty-three years old. She spoke at first from the floor, where hundreds of workers had stood for over two hours listening to speakers—union leaders, all of them men, calling for cautious, deliberate action, trying to talk angry workers down from walking out of the city's garment shops—their measured approach stemming from the belief that women workers were unorganizable, unwilling or simply physically unable to stick out a strike.

Clara interrupted Jacob Panken, a union organizer who had just begun to speak. She spoke in Yiddish, in a voice that seemed too loud to be pouring from her small body, the size of which is a detail important enough to appear in nearly every recorded version of this story. The women around her hoisted her onto the platform and she bellowed words that she could not have known would be read and reread long into the future: "I have listened to all the speakers. I would not have further patience for talk, as I am one of those who feels and suffers from the things pictured. I move that we go on a general strike!"

Decades later, in 1965, a graduate student studying the mass strike that followed, which has come to be known as the Uprising of the 20,000, wrote to Clara, and Clara, who was then seventy-nine, wrote back. Clara's letter is the only written record of the meeting in her own words:

> Suddenly a young girl in the audience asked for the floor. When she was given the floor she said, "I make a motion that we go out in a general strike." The entire audience rose to its feet. Men threw their hats in the air, women waved their handkerchiefs.
>
> The girl who made the motion was called to the platform. . . . [The] chairman of the meeting, raised the right hand of the girl and made her repeat the famous Jewish oath: "May my [right] hand wither from [my] arm if I betray the cause I now pledge." The following day 20 thousand waistmakers came out on strike.

Clara refers to herself in the third person, "the girl," as if writing from the middle distance between what actually happened and the union parable the story became, as though she's witnessing the meeting from the outside, or witnessing her memory of the meeting through the filter of someone else's telling of the story.

* * *

At the end of the three-day training, we held a kind of graduation. I and the other facilitators handed out certificates to the workers who had participated, and then we all sat together and ate beans and rice from El Pollo Loco. We joked with one another about the funny things that had happened during our long days together: Gaspar confusing *inoculation* with *vaccination*, which stuck and became the name with which we referred to that step of an organizing conversation in which we prepare workers for the company's threats by anticipating them; the histrionic role-play one trainer had put on during a things-you-should-not-say section of the training; the ongoing teasing about my terrible gringa accent; and other inside jokes. We were leaving the training prepared to launch separate fights across the city and in different industries, but we'd be there for each other, in solidarity, we promised. And we were. For the next several years, we showed up at each other's rallies and strike lines, marches, and meetings.

When we'd finished eating, I asked if anyone had a final question or announcement, guessing someone would respond with another joke or an exaggerated call for me to just wrap it up already. For a moment, no one said anything, and then you raised your hand, Alma—a formality that brought a sudden seriousness to the room. You asked a question that stays with me still, though I don't hear it in your voice or even in Spanish anymore—it comes as a memory of my own translation. You were wondering about *the will to fight*, a phrase I had used in my story about the shirtwaist strikers in 1909. *Las ganas de luchar*, I had said, and those were the words you used, too, when you asked. You wanted to know what drives some people to fight while others don't, or don't want to, or can't. *Everyone is afraid*, you said. *So what is it that pushes some people across the threshold of fear? Is it all rage?* you wondered. *Is it courage? Are the ones who fall down in their fear too afraid or just not angry enough?*

* * *

By this time, early in 2004, you and I had started calling ourselves Las Polillas—The Moths. At night in the motel I was reading a book about Las Mariposas, the Mirabal sisters, who worked clandestinely to oppose the Trujillo dictatorship in the Dominican Republic and were nicknamed The Butterflies. We joked that we were their ugly cousins, grinding out our organizing one house call at a time in the dust of south Phoenix, so driven by the will to fight that we were bludgeoning ourselves against the porch light.

In the years after I left the union, my fascination with moths grew. I ventured out at night to look for them, curious about their strange nocturnal lives, in which they become most active after dark but then spend their time swarming around sources of light. I started reading about their biology—it seemed a good way to miss you.

Among the things I learned is the nerve-racking fact that there is no definitive answer as to why moths are attracted to light, though people have wondered at the ill-fated-ness of the habit for a long time. Since Shakespeare's *The Merchant of Venice* in 1596—"Thus hath the candle singed the moth"—references to the mothy death drive as simile for human behavior have appeared in countless poems, novels, pop songs, even advertising campaigns. As is true of most idioms, *like a moth to flame* is shorthand for something harder to describe, in this case an irresistible, often irrational, attraction to someone or something that has the potential to lead to the desirer's downfall. Most idioms work as shorthand because there is cultural agreement on their meaning. But interpretations of the relationship described by *moth to flame* seem to contradict each other; some placing agency with the moth as the active seeker of the flame, and others with the flame, luring the moth to its death.

We know that moths use transverse orientation, a kind of celestial navigation, to find their way—in as much as they do—in the dark. They orient their bodies to a source of light through a series of instinctive muscle contractions. As information from the light changes with the moth's movement, its muscles react immediately and in concert with each other. The leading theory regarding their attraction to light is that moths have been unable to adapt this navigational strategy to human-made points of light, that, by design, moth flight works as a function of distance. They confuse our porch lights and campfires for the moon and then collide with them because they've evolved to know that orienting around the moon's light will help them get somewhere, though not ever to the moon itself.

While many lepidopterists—those scientists who study moths—support this theory, it irks me. Moths are sophisticated creatures that have evolved the capacity to abruptly and wholly transform their bodies in the second half of their lives. After repeatedly growing too big for its skin and undergoing a series of molts, a moth caterpillar in its final stage surrounds itself with a single-stranded spun cocoon. There, in this quiescent home, the caterpillar denatures itself, its body releasing enzymes previously used to digest food to now instead dissolve itself, melting away all of its existing tissue. The process is holistic: one creature becomes another creature entirely. "If you were to cut open a cocoon or chrysalis at just the right time," reports an article in *Scientific American*, "caterpillar soup would ooze out."

But the content of this pupa is not entirely amorphous. Certain highly organized groups of cells, imaginal discs, survive the digestive process. "Imaginal" because they biologically foresee the imago, the adult moth—that dusty, scaly, nocturnal, thick-bodied, feathery-antennaed, ready-to-fly, freshly-alive-again thing.

In 2012, archaeologists in South Africa discovered the remnants of the oldest known campfire and dated it back one million years. If the leading moth-to-flame theory is correct, then moths have had one million years of human fires, of localized light, to adapt their navigation and have failed to do so. How has nature not selected out the trait of mistakenly burning oneself alive?

I was taken aback by your question at the end of the training: What drives a person to fight? I'm not sure if my surprise had to do with the timing of the question, there at the end of an intense three days, or if it was because I know you (knew you) enough to know that you were asking because it's something you'd been thinking about since I had mentioned the will to fight, something you wanted a serious answer to, not a canned response. While the intensity of the company's anti-union campaign over the last year at your factory had made you angry, made you want to fight harder, it had terrified some of your coworkers, who would no longer open their doors when we knocked.

I listened and nodded as one of the other trainers said something about struggles needing leaders and about it being the job of those leaders (*Of you, here in this room*, he said) to be courageous and to lead their coworkers through their fear. If I had tried to answer then, I think I would have said that people who fight and people who don't aren't very different from each other, or that the difference has less to do with anger or fear and more to do with vision—that some people can't imagine or haven't yet imagined what good a fight will do, can't see a version of the world that doesn't yet exist.

Now, having thought and thought about this question since you asked it in 2004, I wonder if the will to fight is unrelated to vision or imagination, if instead it's a kind of metamorphosis, a state of being so ravenous for change that *you* are changed. The tightening skin tightens around the neck and body of the caterpillar, which is already walking around with parts of another, future body tucked inside. The you before the fight denatures you, exploding into newness out of necessity. ("He must shed that tight dry skin, or die," writes Nabokov of a caterpillar in its final stage.)

3: Las Polillas

YOU WERE BORN on an ejido in Álamos, Mexico, you told Manuel and me that first afternoon in your living room. After you said that word, *ejido*, you turned to me, assuming that I hadn't understood—I hadn't—and said, generously and slowly, *Es como un pueblito donde se hace todo junto, como una cooperativa*, which I only sort of understood. (It's like a little town that works together, like a cooperative.) The ejido didn't really function as a cooperative anymore, you explained. By the time you were born, it was just your family there working the land.

In your house, two months before the blitz began, you promised to help build the lists we'd need. You sat next to me on your couch, spelling out the names of the people who work with you on the soil-sort belt. You helped me draw a diagram of the department in a small notebook I'd brought along. You drew a line horizontally across the page to represent the conveyor belt, and then wrote *d* on the right-hand side of the page—for *dumper*, you said. Then you drew a line from the letter to the start of the conveyor. Sitting this close, I noticed for the first time that you have makeup tattooed around your eyes, and though I knew it was not the time to ask, I wondered about the logistics of the procedure—how badly it had hurt, how long it had taken. I tried to imagine myself enduring the puncture of a needle on the tender edge of my eyelid and could not.

You dashed the line you had drawn eight times, one for each work-station on the conveyor belt. On your wrist, you wore a bunch of thin-banded metal bangles, a kind of trademark, though I didn't know it yet, and they jangled together as you made the marks. The heaviest position is "el uno," you said, finger on the dash next to the dumper, because the person working there throws the big hospital sheets. This is when you stood to demonstrate—the belt moves in front, you said, standing but leaning down a bit, miming the motion of the conveyor with both hands. The speed at which your hands moved surprised me. *That fast?* I asked, and you nodded and hardened the *S* on *Sí* for emphasis. You demonstrated how the person working in that first position picks sheets up off the automated belt, hands not moving in tandem but opposite each other, doubling the pace of movement and, I supposed, the number of sheets that it is possible to throw in a given stretch of time. You gestured that the sheets are thrown across the belt to bins on the other side. I tried to imagine doing this for an eight- or ten-hour shift. I tried to imagine doing it during the heavy season, which in Arizona was underway—it was February, and the snowbirds had already arrived in droves to wait out the cold months back home, upping the traffic at hospitals and clinics across the state. You told us that the factory had moved thirty-five thousand pounds of soiled hospital linen that day. You were animated, energetic, even "fired up," as I wrote in my notebook when Manuel and I got back to the car. But you must have been tired, too.

El uno is the hardest position, but that's not where you had worked that day. The positions, you explained, were assigned based on a mix of supervisor favoritism and physical ability. That day, you had worked "el cinco," which was hospital gowns. Gowns that were often, as some had been that day, covered in various forms of bodily excrement. This is when you told us that the gloves were too thin, that you had to rinse and reuse them day after day, that you didn't have shoe protection, that sometimes there are fluids bags and IV drip lines and surgical tools left wrapped in the sheets and gowns. At the end of the line was "el ocho," a sort of prized workstation, where only the smaller items, like hand towels and washcloths, are left on the belt to be sorted—easier but still not easy, you said. The woman who works there most days had started a round of prophylactic antivirals just the day before, after a hypodermic needle, which had been folded into a washcloth, pierced her hand.

You wrote the names of your coworkers next to their typical positions, mapping who talks to whom, who likes and dislikes whom, who trips up the line by working too slowly or by missing pieces meant for the bins at their station, who tells sexist jokes and gets away with it because he drinks beer with the supervisor after work. You had some of their phone numbers on a scrap of paper you kept tucked in a kitchen drawer. I wrote them carefully in my notebook and you checked them over to be sure I had them right. You told us about the bulletin boards, stationed throughout the factory, where department leads sometimes hang lists of the workers on their shifts. *There is a list of soil-sort workers from the second and third shifts hanging right now on the board just inside the plastic flap doorway that separates the soil side of the factory from the clean side*, you said. You described the location in such detail it was as if you were visualizing your plan to steal it. *I'll take it on the way to the bathroom*, you said.

When we were finished talking, you walked us out onto your front stoop, into what must have been the waning golden hour, which in Phoenix winter is long and lovely. You shook my hand, and the firmness of your grasp surprised me. Thinking about it now, I imagine that you caught my gaze and nodded once, as I would learn was your habit when leaving a home or a meeting where something important had been decided. I remember that you glanced quickly down the street and toward the apartments across it, as if checking for neighbors who might be nosing around their yards, might be wondering why two people in their twenties, one of whom was white, had driven up to your house in a brand-new car. Manuel said not to worry, that we'd knock on some other doors, too. He showed you his clipboard with a stack of fake surveys, about road conditions or neighborhood traffic or some such thing, that we would fill out with a few of your neighbors, to make it seem to anyone who had noticed us that our visit had a more benign and civic intention.

That is how we met on my second or maybe third day in Phoenix. And the next night, it rained—harder than is typical for February in the desert. I was at a bar with Manuel and Dario and Ana after our nightly debrief with the organizing director when the street outside flash flooded, as streets there sometimes do during the summer monsoon but very rarely do in winter. We stood stranded in the portico of the place until long after closing, watching the street fill with water and watching the water form little white heads at the intersection on the corner.

Perhaps it was this rain or the fecund explosion of growth that followed it that brought on the moths. It is hard to describe the immediacy and speed of new growth after a hard rain in that desert, but by the next morning, the barren ground had sprouted green shoots of all kinds. Yard vegetation and gardens now out from under the film of dust had come alive. Cacti and other arid plants bloomed with papery flowers in white and near-neon shades of purple and pink. The palms, most of which in south Phoenix typically look as though they are trying very hard to survive and failing, were green and tender, vivified, breathing.

It had been a mild winter, even in the mountains in the northern part of the state, and entomologists believe that the warmth, combined with the sudden flourishing of green vegetation, led to the large number of moths and other insects that descended on parts of Arizona that winter and spring. The "attack," as it was reported, began with an outsize crop of army cutworms, which molted as they grew, and marched en masse, and did not die off, because it was not cold. The worms then pupated, as they do, and emerged as an extraordinarily large flight of miller moths, so named because the dusty residue of their profusely shedding scales is reminiscent of the flour that coats the clothing of grain millers.

The moth flight didn't reach attack level until months after that February afternoon when we first met, not until early May—likely the very week you and your coworkers shut down your factory and announced to your bosses that you were going to form a union, whether they liked it or not. And so I had no way of knowing that an explosion of the moth population was in the works all around when I started having the dream. We didn't notice that the foliage at the motel and in your yard and in the yards of the neighborhoods we drove through and that lined the parking lots of the industrial warehouses were already teeming with cutworms. That year, the cutworms hatched in such enormous numbers one newspaper noted, "it looks like the ground is moving."

After conducting the fake survey to cover for our visit with you, Manuel and I drove back to the UNITE office, on the first floor of the AFL-CIO building, at the end of an open-air hallway, which our small team traipsed through at all hours. I imagine we were a strange sight to the union staff who occupied the other small offices on the hallway—mostly older white men, most of whom left their doors open on nice days to welcome airflow that the smallish midcentury windows, which opened only a few slanted inches, didn't allow. We'd had the office less than a week, but these "business representatives," as I learned to call them, most of whom worked for building-trades locals, had seen us leaving our office in the morning, exhausted, just as they were arriving. We'd already pulled a U-Haul up to the front gate of the building and unloaded a Goodwill couch and chairs and coffee table. The business representatives, who did the good work of grievance handling to ensure the integrity of union contracts among the various kinds of construction workers they represented, were always friendly, always waved or waved back at us when we walked by.

What I didn't understand in that first week, or maybe even for the first month, is that most unions in Arizona—as is true of locals in a lot of places—were not (and are not today) organizing unions, meaning that they do not organize nonunion workers. They either grow via enrollment in their apprenticeship programs when demand for labor in their trade goes up, or they shrink. And in nearly every year since the mid-1970s, they have shrunk. There are a lot of reasons for their lack of interest in organizing the unorganized, ranging from the fact that organizing in conservative right-to-work states—in which people who are not union members can work hard-won union jobs—is fucking hard and it takes a lot of resources, to the fact that many nonunion workers, especially in the building trades in Arizona, are Mexican or Central American and the white elected leaders of the locals know that the likelihood that they will continue to be elected to their positions after a major demographic shift in their rank and file is slim to none.

When I learned that there are unions that don't organize nonunion workers, I was appalled. And I'll admit that I thought this made UNITE a better union, made us, its organizers, superior in some way to these business representatives and the locals they staffed. After all, I thought, if unions are not organizing, then they aren't building power, and if they aren't building power, they are most certainly ceding power to bosses and their corporations, to industry.

Now, when I think about what seemed at the time a very clear understanding of unions and power, I feel mostly perplexed. Of course it is better to organize than not organize—that is not the question. But I no longer subscribe to that top-down theory, nor do I think of power as a finite sum, a thing that is acquired by wresting it away—however forcefully—from the powerful, as if the work of organizing were akin to cleaving an orange, or as if the substance of solidarity were the same as the substance of oppression. What I mean is that I no longer think that worker power originates with the boss, or that workers come by it by taking it away from the company where they work. Worker power is built and waged through an entirely separate system.

The union we built in Phoenix was a wholly original force. Its power was not stripped away from Sodexho or the other laundry companies or the managers who oversaw production. It was built, piece by piece, through the everyday tasks and exchanges that comprised our organizing. We made leaflet copies at Kinko's. We drove in circles around the city. We packed and unpacked the folding chairs for our committee meetings. We knocked on thousands of doors. We asked people to trust us, and they did. We stood together in the parking lot, running department meetings from midnight until 4 a.m., and listened as the moths plinked their bodies against the floodlights.

When Manuel and I got to the union office at the end of the breezeway, we walked through the door on which we'd hung a cardboard UNITE sign, then through the small front room where the couch and chairs and coffee table were, to the back room, where the organizing director sat in front of a laptop, which was stationed on a table we had borrowed from the AFL-CIO office upstairs. While Manuel and I were collecting information to prep the campaign at Sodexho, Ana was working on CleanCo, a hospitality laundry, which washed sheets for hotels and bars and restaurants, and Dario was working on another hospitality laundry, ACE. We planned to blitz all three companies simultaneously sometime at the end of April, about ten weeks away.

We reported the information we'd gathered from you—the names of your coworkers and their phone numbers—and we gave them preliminary ratings—a number from one to five—according to how you described them and whether or not you thought they might support the union. The director entered this data into the spreadsheet she was keeping. In a separate database, she added the names of the two or three hospitals you knew to be the big clients of the factory, which would be important later, when we got into the thick of the fight.

As we debriefed the house visit with her, she pressed Manuel hard on why he had trusted you so much, why we had given away the whole playbook of the campaign before testing how serious you were about supporting the union, before waiting to see if you would steal that list of worker names from the bulletin board or not. Manuel kept saying, *I trust her, I trust her,* and *Don't worry. We're not going to get made.* The director didn't ask me—I was new, and she didn't know if I was any good at reading a person, the way organizers learn to do—but I trusted you, too.

The next day, I followed laundry trucks in my rental car, trying to build the list of your factory's clients so we could pressure them to pressure the company not to violate your right to organize and to bargain an agreement in good faith when we got to that point. We needed to assemble the names of all of the biggest clients, along with the names and addresses of at least 85 percent of your coworkers, before moving on to the blitz. First, I traced the path of one of the big semis from factory to freeway until it hit the Gila River reservation, south of the city, and then I turned back, figuring the truck was headed for University Medical Center in Tucson, which you had already named as one of the company's major accounts. "Fotografía" probably played on 106.3, the Spanish pop station, as I circled back. I probably sang along, loudly and badly, in the hope it would help me to learn Spanish more quickly.

From the parking lot of the empty office building across the street, I waited for the next truck, letting it travel down Broadway Road and out of sight before pulling onto the street to follow it. I stayed as far back as I could, as the director had shown me when I rode along with her, but as the truck crossed into the heavier traffic of central Phoenix, I had to ride its bumper not to lose it. At a red light, I was sure the driver was looking back at me through the truck's rectangular side mirror. He changed lanes in the next block, and I changed with him, though I knew I should have begged off at that point to be safe. A few blocks later, he pulled into a gated lot at St. Joseph's Hospital, and I noted the time of the delivery in my notebook.

I didn't sleep much that night, up sweating in the motel bed, the relative quiet of the late hours intensifying my worry that the truck driver had seen me, until, in my mind, it was a barefaced certainty. I spun through what would happen next: Even if the driver hadn't been trained to look out for union organizers following his truck (as many of them have), he would surely tell his boss about the weirdness of being followed, and the boss would know what it meant. I imagined the company calling a meeting the next day, telling workers they'd close the factory if anyone talked to the union, or maybe they'd veil the threat in some way: *A union will cost us a lot of money. We'll have to make cuts.* Unions have to weigh organizing targets and strategies against available resources—especially smaller unions, like UNITE. We couldn't afford to start fights we knew couldn't win, not while there are so many nonunion laundries to organize. I imagined having to tell you that I'd fucked up, that I'd gotten us made while following a truck, that there would be no union in the factory after all.

I didn't mention the bad follow to any of the other organizers or to the director, and after a couple of days with no word or indication of disaster, the dread I'd been cultivating subsided.

That week, you called the union office: you had the list. I drove to your house straightaway. You beamed as you opened the door. *I did it,* you said in English as you handed me a tightly folded piece of paper.

You started coming into the office on some evenings and on your days off, anxious, I think, to start the blitz. You did not drive, so I picked you up at your house, and we drove to the office together, mostly in silence the first few days, or with 106.3 on the radio. And then, slowly, we started talking. The little Spanish I knew from high school and the months I'd spent in Central America—half dropped out of college, half chasing a woman I loved who was in Nicaragua, falling in love with someone else—was improving. I could understand more of what you said. I could say about half of what I wanted to.

At first, you asked questions I could answer in one or two sentences: I was born in Ohio, out in the country. I lived on a farm, but my parents didn't own the farm. I have three brothers. I am twenty-five years old. I asked, *¿Y tú?* after answering each of the questions, grateful you were asking them so I could simply ask them back without having to string the words together. I already knew that you were born on a farm in Álamos, Mexico, that your big family lived there, spread out over two houses. You grew mostly beans, but also kept horses and cattle and some other animals. Later, you moved farther north in Sonora and worked in a maquiladora. In your family there were twelve children, three of whom died when they were very little, and nine of whom lived.

Your first evening in the office, you sat on the couch. I was embarrassed by how much it stank of cigarette smoke—*Lo siento*, I said, *huele horrible*—even as I smoked more cigarettes in the next room. You called through the phone numbers we'd been collecting, making offers of free shampoo samples—one of a few tricks we used to gather addresses. This one we'd learned from Ana, who had learned it from another organizer on another campaign somewhere across the country. The workers on the other end, or their children, or whoever in the house happened to pick up the phone, gave you their address as a destination for the shampoo samples. We added the addresses to our lists, which we were getting closer to completing every day.

We carefully expanded our contacts inside the plant, too. We didn't want to blitz without a group of workers—five or six maybe, including you—already committed to the fight, who would ride along with the organizers, asking your coworkers to join with you to build your union. You took Manuel and me to meet Santiago, who was your neighbor and the dumper on your shift, and whom everyone called Chino, which, still, after asking you many times over the years, doesn't make sense to me as a stand-in for *curly-haired*, which is how you described the origin of the nickname. You trusted him with the secrecy of our work, and so Manuel and the director and I did, too.

He lived in a small structure with a warped tin roof in the backyard of a slightly larger house, where no one seemed to live. Inside, we sat on plastic chairs and talked for a few minutes about the posters he had hung on his walls of a baseball team in Acapulco, his hometown. Manuel asked him about growing up there, about when he left home, when he came to the United States, how long he'd been working at the laundry, after which you cut to the business of the visit. You asked him to show us his stomach, and he stood up from his chair and lifted his shirt to uncover a swollen mass arising from the area above his belly button. *It happened at work*, he said, poking the hernia with his finger, *but the company keeps saying, no, it must have happened somewhere else*. He moved his shirt back into place, sat down again, and crossed his arms over the bulge.

We shook our heads together for a moment, all four of us: a mute, collective seething. Then we talked about the union and the blitz and the fight in the factory that we knew would follow. Santiago said we needed to talk to Pollo, a wash worker who fit the way Manuel was describing "a leader"—the other washers liked him, went to him for help when there were problems with the machines or with paychecks or with the schedule. *And Pollo is mad*, Santiago said; *he will be ready to fight*.

So we went to Pollo's apartment together. It was the first house visit we did by ourselves, just you and me. On the ride there, I asked if you knew why he was called Pollo, if it meant the animal, a chicken, and you told me it's a nickname for people who follow a coyote across the border, that this Pollo has a limp from something that happened when he crossed, that the name stuck with him because the limp is a constant reminder.

Pollo's building was sparse, surrounded by barren dirt on one side and a potholed parking lot on the other, one among the vast legion of beige apartment buildings in Phoenix made out of particleboard and cracked, peeling stucco. We climbed cement steps to the second floor and knocked on the door. Pollo opened it, squinting out from the dark room into the sun. He wore boxers and an undershirt and looked as if he'd been sleeping. He recognized you, of course, but then looked at me and came rushing from the apartment out onto the landing with us, closing the door behind him.

He told me much later, after years of never letting me into this apartment, that many people live there, and that some of them might think I'm from Immigration, to which I asked, *Could you tell them that I'm not?* to which he answered, *Yes, but it wouldn't matter.* And I think of this often still, the likelihood that, in my moving around Phoenix and later Flagstaff and Fresno and Vista and Compton, and other cities where laundry workers include people who are undocumented, my presence at someone's front door caused a spike in the current of fear many people are forced to live in every day.

We stood close to each other, the three of us, perched in that small space at the top of the stairs, and you told him you thought the factory needed to change, that you were tired of being treated like a machine, tired of working in such dangerous conditions, and doing it for a company that didn't care if you got sick or hurt. You introduced me as an organizer from the union. *A big union,* you said, *in laundries all over the country.*

Pollo was nodding along sort of numbly, not looking at us, still half-asleep. I read his posture as disinterest, annoyance even, and in my worry that we had contacted the wrong person at the wrong point in the campaign, I felt the same dread from my reckless pursuit of the truck welling up again.

I asked Pollo about the "wash alley," the department where he worked, told him I'd never seen the kinds of machines he works on. He described the tunnel washers in the plant, using his arms to gesture. *As long as a bus*, he said. He described moving bags of linen from the soil-sort area to the wash department, explaining that the heavy, full bags are hooked to a system of rails overhead. The wash workers push them through the air, along the tracks, to the wash conveyor. Pollo is short, about my height, five foot three, so when he demonstrated reaching up to loosen the pull string on the bags, he rose to his tiptoes. He said, *The soiled linen, still full of asquerosidad*—foulness, a word I wrote down in my notebook when we got to the car and looked up later—*falls onto the belt, which runs it up and into the mouth of the tunnel washer.* He told us that he sometimes has to crawl into the tunnel, through hot, bleachy water that leaches the foulness from the linen, in order to clear jams. He said that the supervisors don't cut power to the machines when he's inside like they are supposed to. He made eye contact for the first time when he said this, angry about having to go into the tunnel in this way. He knew how dangerous it was, climbing inside the machine without following the lockout/tagout and confined-space standards required by the Occupational Safety and Health Administration (OSHA), which get skirted by some companies because they are costly in terms of time and production. *I make $7.80 an hour*, he said.

When the linen comes out of the tunnel's far end, it goes to "the cake," he said, using English for this term. After saying the word back and forth to each other, he could see that I was confused. He held up his finger, as in, Just wait a second. He stepped inside the apartment and came back with pants on and with a cordless phone, which he was using to call his cousin, who worked on "the cake prensa."

While I protested that we shouldn't talk to anyone else just yet, that we needed to keep things bajo el agua, the cousin, snidely nicknamed Pollito by the coworkers who knew them, came through the door of the apartment below. His arm was in a cast, and Pollo explained that he had been injured by this cake prensa, which I had started to glean was a kind of water extractor. *It presses the water out, compacting the linen into a giant, round cake*, Pollo said. *He shouldn't have been near that machine, but the linen got stuck, and he had to clear it,* he said. The cousin, who was shy and alarmingly young, stood at the bottom of the stairs and said nothing.

The wash and dry departments of industrial laundries are not the most injury-prone, but they are the most fatal, according to government statistics. By the end of March of 2003, as we stood there together on Pollo's landing, one worker had already been killed in an industrial laundry in Massachusetts, when a commercial washer started by accident and decapitated him. Two more would die before the end of that year. (Twenty-two others have died in the time it has taken me to write this to you.)

Pollo told us that to collect information on workers in the production department, where newly clean linen is moved from industrial dryers into what is really a series of stations in which the clean linen is ironed, folded, and packed for shipping, we should talk to Cecilia. So we did. Then Cecilia took us to meet Antonia, and Antonia took us to meet Analía, and between the three of them, it took just over a week to gather the names and addresses we needed.

Ana and Dario had been building lists, too, and had enough information to blitz their respective targets at CleanCo and ACE. The director called organizers from around the country—over a dozen of them—and told them to get flights to Phoenix for the last weekend in April, about two weeks away. We wanted to launch sooner, now that we were ready—every day we waited was a risk—but that was the quickest we could get enough people into town to do five hundred house visits in two days, which is what it would take for us to talk to the workers at all three factories before the companies would start to hit back.

The two weeks proved to be too long at ACE, where managers discovered that we had been talking to one of our contacts there. They shut down production one day and called the workers to a meeting. I don't know what happened during the meeting because no one from the factory would talk to us afterward, but the boss marched workers out of the plant and onto the sidewalk in front of it, where the company had hung a nylon banner on the wrought-iron fence that surrounded the property: NOW HIRING ALL POSITIONS, it read in English and in Spanish.

Dario was parked across the street. He saw this procession, saw that the company sent workers home early that day to punctuate their message. None of the workers he'd been talking to called him back that day. None would open their doors. So by that evening, the director decided to scrap the campaign there, to focus the blitz on Sodexho and CleanCo. (As of July 2021, ACE was still the largest nonunion laundry in Phoenix.)

The weekend before the blitz, we needed to rest. We'd already been sleeping in short, broken patches, and from the blitz on, the campaign would get more difficult, the director said. I remember this because the way she said the Spanish word *difícil*—dee-FEE-sill—became a long-running joke on the team. It was not a joke meant to be aimed at her, whom we all admired, but a way of comically understating the shitty or ludicrous or otherwise out-of-control circumstances in which we would sometimes find ourselves. (Spending a day knocking doors that workers are too afraid to open: dee-FEE-sill. Receiving letters in the union office, signed by your coworkers under coercion, asking for their union cards back: dee-FEE-sill.)

She sent us all home for three days. Ana to Florida, Dario to the Bronx, and the director herself, home to Brooklyn. I had the shortest commute. I checked out of the motel and drove down to Tucson, leaving after the debrief on a Thursday around 11 p.m.

The I-10 runs fast that time of night, cars jockeying for position, easily going one hundred. I waited until I got to the edge of the city, where the Phoenix palms are overtaken by saguaros and creosote and ironwood, before allowing myself to flip from 106.3 to an English-language station. The switch was a relief. Words poured from the speakers. The ease and immediacy of turning their sounds into meaning made them cartoonish, saturated with something that felt like color. Inside the words, I located myself. I took a long breath and realized that I hadn't been breathing, at least not in that way, for many weeks.

The weightlessness of fluency was comforting. Inside that wave of relief, I wondered how English felt to you. Most of your life was (and remains, I imagine) in Spanish—most of work and the grocery store and your friendships and the days you spent babysitting your niece. But that nucleus of fluency is surrounded by a hard barrier of English—street signs and public transportation, government and medical forms, billboards, and the increasingly present and militarized police.

All around in the desert, the miller moths were emerging from their cocoons. Their soft bodies thumped against the windshield as I drove. I turned on the wipers and fluid to clear their powdery residue, but they clumped and smeared. I had to reposition myself in the driver's seat to find a clear line of sight. I don't know if the moths I dreamed were this or some other species. These ones were illuminated too briefly by the headlights before smashing into the window to get a handle on their color and shape. It was a dense eclipse, as a group of moths is sometimes called, like driving through a field of tiny dead stars.

At home that weekend, I did not rest as I was meant to do. I drank too much at the one lesbian bar in Tucson, Ain't Nobody's Bizness, and got kicked out for climbing on and falling off of a speaker. I went home and argued with my girlfriend until morning, accusing her of being too flirtatious with her coworker at the queer community center. I spent the rest of the weekend recovering and then drinking again and then recovering again. By Monday, I was ready to be back in Phoenix.

That Thursday before the blitz the other organizers arrived, over a dozen of them, pulled from their campaigns across the country for the weekend. You and Santiago and Pollo and Cecilia and Antonia and Raúl, a contact Manuel had made, were at the motel to greet them. The six of you signed your union cards together in the lobby that night, and then you committed to one another to form the organizing committee for your factory, the comité.

On Friday morning, we trained these newly arrived organizers on the specifics of your factory—the demographics of the workers, the structure of the plant, the names of your managers and supervisors and their particular brands of cruelty, the low wages and safety hazards. You took a sick day to help with the training. You told the organizers, *There is a lot of fear here, but there is a lot of anger, too. We'll see which one wins out.*

You and I were a team for the weekend, which made sense—I was still the newest organizer, and you were by far the strongest worker leader. We had assigned ourselves the task of talking to the coworkers of yours who would not be guaranteed union supporters, but whose support it would be crucial to have if we were going to win, people we had preliminarily assessed as threes or fours on our scale from one to five, but who we knew would move other coworkers to the union if they signed. This was a hard set of house visits, with people who, if they were going to sign at all, would probably sign only with you. The other members of the comité paired with Manuel and the fly-in organizers, and we gave them folders with house-call sheets, one for each worker assigned to their team, and then we "hit the doors," as we say.

The blitz itself is hard to remember. I don't think we slept. We barely stopped to pee or eat. We drank water out of gallon jugs we bought at the gas station, which got hot in the car while we were in someone's house. My Spanish was improving, but there were still things I could not say. You packed tamales to eat in the car between house visits and offered me one, but I could smell the pork in it. *No, thank you,* I said, *Soy vegetaria.* Which is an incorrect way of saying "I'm vegetarian." You told me much later that you had to bite your lip hard to keep from laughing out loud, because it sounded as though I were calling myself a vegetable.

We moved very fast. A worker would sign a card and then get in the car with us to go to another worker's house, that worker would call another worker over to her house, and we'd hold an impromptu meeting. Almost everyone we talked to signed a card, and all the while, we were mapping—who knows whom, who works where, who should we talk to next and then next after that. By Saturday, workers who had already signed were calling to direct us to the homes of workers who had not yet signed but wanted to. Workers were calling to ask us to pick them up at their homes and take them to the homes of coworkers who wanted to sign. It was a movement. It was wildfire. And by Sunday evening, when we held the first general meeting among your coworkers, the blitz had worked as it should; we had visited workers and inoculated them faster than the company could react, and two days in, a majority of your coworkers had signed union cards.

4: Fires

UNIONS ARE ESSENTIALLY working people standing together, in solidarity, to form collective power in the workplace and sometimes beyond. One root of this type of power in the United States stretches back to 1824, when in Pawtucket, Rhode Island, hundreds of girls—teenagers mostly, but some as young as seven—led what they called a "turnout," which would become the first factory strike in US history.

The girls worked at a dam-powered cotton mill, where their bosses had met the night before and decided to cut their pay by 25 percent while simultaneously extending their thirteen- to fifteen-hour workdays by yet another hour. The day after the bosses announced these new conditions, 102 workers blocked the mill entrances at start time. They held a meeting there, just outside the factory, in front of their bosses and the rest of the town. They resolved not to go inside to work, and by the next day, their turnout had spread to the other cotton mills in town. It lasted a week, until one of the mills mysteriously caught fire, in what was perhaps the first act of industrial sabotage in this country's long, rich history of industrial sabotage. The day after the fire, mill owners negotiated better hours and pay and safer conditions with the teenage strike leaders.

This root of the labor movement—the Pawtucket cotton industry—was closely intertwined with slavery, the multifaceted struggle against which forms another kind of root of the modern union, if you think of a union as a necessitated practice of rebellion and resistance and solidarity for collective survival. The mills were founded and funded in part by wealth generated by the slave trade and, in turn, they drove the demand for cotton that fueled the expansion of slavery on plantations in the US South. A large percentage of what was produced in Pawtucket was called "cheap cloth," and it was shipped back to the plantations and used to make clothes for the enslaved people who harvested the cotton.

Despite these strong and traceable lineages, many labor histories discount these founding struggles and instead begin around 1877, the year of the Great Railroad Strike, which signaled the beginning of a new kind of movement of workers fighting back against growing inequality and oppression in the midst of the American Industrial Revolution. These workers joined together to form unions, which are and have always been the only significant institutions representing the rights of working people in this country.

The Uprising of the 20,000 was part of a wave of strikes that blew the top off of whatever had been containing the remaining rage and militancy of workers during the Gilded Age, a time that, until around the turn of the twenty-first century, marked the greatest level of economic disparity in US history. One response to this period of great and growing labor strife was a legislative one—the National Labor Relations Act of 1935.

The NLRA was created as a system to manage industrial conflict. It, through the government agency it precipitated, the National Labor Relations Board (NLRB), supports labor organizing through its power to compel employers to recognize unions and bargain over working conditions. The NLRB represented a significant shift in the government's stance with regard to unions: from repression to what has been called "integrative prevention." The legislation marked a turning point in union density, too—membership shot up, because the government was suddenly regulating and protecting workers' rights, and the strike wave that led to its passage died down as strikes became more limited to the bread-and-butter issues of wages and benefits that arose during contract renewal fights at already union worksites.

Of course, the NLRA is not what gives workers the right to organize. Working people have the right to assemble and can withhold their labor with or without the NRLA. They had been doing so and winning since long before 1935, both in the United States and around the world. And, anyway, almost immediately after its passage, the protections that *were* established by the NLRA were peeled away.

In 1938, just three years after the NLRA's passing, the Supreme Court ruled in its Mackay Radio decision that while workers could not be fired for striking, they could be permanently replaced. Under the Mackay doctrine, as it came to be called, if workers struck for economic gains like raises and improved working conditions, the employer could hire permanent replacements—scabs, as they are otherwise known—and then not have to give the workers their jobs back when the strike was over. For workers, the difference between the terms *fired* and *permanently replaced* was of little importance if both meant they were out of a job. After a short curve of learning how to wield this new crushing tool, bosses realized that, since they can hire scabs to keep production moving during a strike, there is little incentive to reach an agreement with current employees at the bargaining table.

Despite the modest protections of the NLRA and the active threat of the Mackay doctrine, workers in the mid-1940s launched another massive strike wave, which included over five million workers at public utilities and in industries like coal and steel, meatpacking, and auto manufacturing. In 1946 in Pittsburgh alone, 120,000 workers went on strike. This time, instead of passing legislation that would calm strife as it had in 1935, Congress did the opposite. In 1947, it ratified the Taft-Hartley Act, or the Labor-Management Relations Act, even over the veto of President Harry S. Truman. This vile law establishes a litany of constraints on union activity. It prohibits certain strikes and boycotts. It limits union political power by banning federal campaign contributions. It allows states to pass right-to-work laws, which were first championed by Jim Crow architects as a way to prevent the coming together of Black and white workers into the same unions.

Despite the blow, union membership hovered at about 30 percent until around 1960, when the bread-and-butter unionism of the labor movement's increasingly conservative leadership morphed into a stale, bureaucratic business unionism, and, frankly, stopped organizing workers. The social justice unionism of the more progressive pockets of the labor movement—which had its own system of roots leading all the way back to the Knights of Labor, which was formed in 1869—made some gains in farmworker organizing and through efforts to fuse civil rights and labor rights, as with Martin Luther King Jr.'s campaign for striking sanitation workers in Memphis in 1968. But through the 1970s and '80s—both because of unions' general failure to organize and because of the pressures of globalization and the growing corporatization of the Democratic Party—union membership was in free fall.

In 1981, President Ronald Reagan summarily fired striking air traffic controllers and busted their union, the Professional Air Traffic Controllers Organization (PATCO), a loud announcement that the federal government had taken a decisive stand against unions. Seeing an opening to drive down labor costs, employers in unionized industries adopted aggressive tactics to rid themselves of unions. Union busting developed into its own industry, with an array of business consultants, law firms, industrial psychologists, and private security strike management services. Union membership bottomed out.

By the time you and I were organizing industrial laundries in Phoenix in the early 2000s, both union density and protections for organized labor were nearly back to where they were when UNITE's precursor, the ILGWU, was formed one hundred years earlier.

As part of its fondness for its own lore, the labor movement loves to trace its lineages through the deep palimpsest of antecedent organizations and their mergers and the internal culture shifts they necessitated. Most unions in the United States are the products of the mergers of other unions. UNITE was the result of a 1995 merger between the International Ladies' Garment Workers' Union (ILGWU) and the Amalgamated Clothing and Textile Workers Union (ACTWU), which were both also products of mergers. ACTWU emerged in 1976 when the Amalgamated Clothing Workers of America (ACWA) merged with the Textile Workers Union of America (TWUA), and the ILGWU was formed in the year 1900, when seven small cloak and shirtmaker unions came together in New York City.

ACTWU was a fiery organizing union, mainly because it inherited that culture from ACWA, a union which was the result of an internal revolt and secession of progressive members of the United Garment Workers (UGW) against that union's conservative leadership. The roots of that revolt lead back to the 1910 general strike of Chicago, when more than forty thousand workers, mainly women, inspired by the Uprising of the 20,000 in New York a year earlier, went on strike and stayed on strike despite the male leadership of UGW accepting an inadequate settlement from the garment bosses and then ordering the strikers back to work.

In retaliation for this insubordination, the leadership of UGW attempted to disenfranchise the women and their locals at the union's 1914 convention, so the locals led an exodus, taking with them nearly all of the union's women members—two-thirds of its overall membership— and formed their own union, the ACWA. The fledgling union was led by Sidney Hillman, who was an elected leader at UGW but whom the insurgent women had petitioned to head the union because they trusted him. He'd been a rank-and-file leader during the 1910 strike, and he was the fiancé of Bessie Abramowitz, one of the original worker leaders of that strike. The split was nasty, and the UGW retaliated. It spent the next years raiding the new union, furnishing strikebreakers and cozying up with struck employers to sign crap contracts behind the backs of ACWA leadership.

The ILGWU, UNITE's other predecessor, had its own internal strife, which predated and inspired the Chicago women. It grew rapidly during its first four years but then stagnated because its leadership was interested only in organizing the men who worked as skilled cutters and pattern makers (the union was composed of workers who made ladies' garments, not "lady" workers, or at least, not yet), and they did not want (and did not think it was possible) to organize the women, who were quickly being brought in from tenement sweatshops to the industry's new factory floors, and who made up the vast majority of workers in the industry.

The union men said of the women that they were unreliable soldiers, that they'd scab a strike for a penny raise, that they'd leave the union as soon as they found a husband. This did not sit well with the women, who were working long hours in hot, dim, crowded conditions, who were cheated out of pay, who were sexually harassed and sometimes assaulted by bosses and their male coworkers, who were not allowed to go to the bathroom, who were searched every day on their way out of work, and who were dying by the hundreds in fires and other industrial accidents. They were ready for a fight. And in 1905, Clara Lemlich and other leaders of these women workers chartered their own local, the ILGWU Local 25.

The men still did not recognize the women, telling them they could not hold decision-making meetings without the presence of higher-ranking

electeds, but then the electeds would not agree to meet and would hold
their own meetings in secret. Clara would sometimes learn about these
meetings to which she had not been invited, and push her way into them.
"Ah, then I had fire in my mouth," she would later say. After months of
pressure and protest and proving that they could organize, the women
forced the ILGWU leadership to officially recognize Local 25.

During my time with UNITE, I knew nothing of PATCO or Pawtucket.
I knew nothing of the Homestead Strike or McKees Rock or the Atlanta
Washerwomen Strike or Mary Harris "Mother" Jones. I did not know
that the Collar Laundry Union, led by Kate Mullany, organized and
struck commercial laundry workers—and won—way back in 1864. I
knew almost no labor history beyond the few stories that were of myth-
ological importance to UNITE, the stories I was trained to tell in the
manner they were told to me: the Triangle fire and the Uprising of the
20,000, the legislative victory that was the National Labor Relations Act,
and then the neutering of that victory with the passage of Taft-Hartley,
ACTWU's epic public boycott of the textile manufacturer J. P. Stevens in
the 1970s and the birth of the corporate campaign.

I didn't think to look beyond this lore, to look at the other roots giving life to what we were growing, because during those years I didn't
have time to do anything that wasn't immediately useful to the campaigns we ran. By contrast, after I stopped organizing, life was suddenly dull. I had time on my hands but no intention of using it to think
about unions. Instead, I languished in Tucson. I read a lot. I slept more
than is healthy. I adopted a dog and took him on long night walks
through the sodium glow of the small city's "dark-sky" lights, which I
noticed did not attract insects in the way the floodlights of your factory did. I enrolled in art classes at the local community college, and
the reading I'd been doing about moth biology folded into elaborate

projects, for which I went into the mountains that surround Tucson and collected moths.

At first, I did not know how to catch them. I did not know how to immobilize them or freeze them or relax them for pinning. I learned how to do these things from books I found at the library, where one day, as I rummaged through the stacks, I encountered another kind of book about moths: *The Story of Silk* by John Feltwell, the cover of which is backgrounded by an image of a silk tapestry depicting a flowering, fruiting tree and foregrounded with a close-up photograph of a silk moth in its muted, furry-bodied glory, standing atop a cocoon already laden with eggs. I know from reading this book, which details the life cycle of silk moths, that the moth had emerged, or eclosed, just hours before, that she had spread her wings, which were still damp from the soup of her body, that she shivered until they dried, that she emptied her sex pheromones into the air in a powerful incantation, and laid her eggs while she waited for the nearby males to respond. I know that, in being chosen to hatch in order to breed, the moth had broken through, and therefore rendered unusable, the silk thread it had spun. Though it was no longer of monetary value, the production of the thread had served its biological purpose, and instead the moth's eggs—her reproduction—became her contribution to the silk farm's production.

But even as I strayed, even as I looked into moths as a method for looking *away* from unions and their fights, they led me back. In this book, I learned about the painstaking process of silk making. I learned that silk moths have been domesticated for five thousand years. Over this period, they have lost the ability to wander more than a few inches—as silkworms, they lay writhing, many dozens thick, in the lipped wooden beds provided by their breeders. As imagoes, they can spread their wings but they cannot fly. I learned that it takes two thousand cocoons to make a single dress, that in order to unravel the silken thread that composes it, each cocoon is boiled, to cleanse it of the soupy matter inside, then brushed gently on the outside until the end of the silk filament is located.

I learned that Lyon was the silk-producing center of France, and that there, as in other silk cities across Europe, most of the care and breeding of the moths was done by women, from carrying the eggs around in special sacks between their breasts to keep them warm, to feeding fresh mulberry leaves, day and night, to the newly hatched silkworms, to providing carefully hand-constructed twig tents for the fully grown worms to climb inside and spin their silky enclosures. All of this work, called sericulture, was done in magnaneries, which were structures ranging from large stone buildings at the edge of town to smaller structures: a barn or a shack or simply a covered area on the roof of a house.

The work was ritualistic, based on myth and superstition as much as on collective and intergenerational knowledge: It was believed that the presence of iron helped the worms to feed, so iron objects were placed throughout the magnanery, or the silkworm beds were wired to an iron sink. It was believed that the worms thrived around sweet smells, so every day the women sprinkled the floors with vinegar and then covered them over with fresh lavender and rosemary and thyme. It was believed that violent noises could kill the worms or cause them not to feed, so if there was thunder, a live coal had to be carried through the magnanery to calm them. These rooms were not quiet, though. According to Feltwell, the sound of thousands of caterpillars chewing is akin to a torrential rain.

I was interested in the constant, deliberate, abiding nature of this work—the plucking and shredding of mulberry leaves at the right age and size for each instar of the worms, the just-so construction of the twig brooms, which would house the cocoons, the quiet feet of the workers—these other moth women—against the floors of the rooms where the worms fed.

It was in Googling images of the still-standing magnaneries of Lyon that I learned these women workers fought, too. They joined in the Canut revolts, which are sometimes described as the first working-class rising of industrialization. The Canuts, named after the French word for the silk bobbin, were silk weavers, who lived with their families around the edges of their giant looms, their cooking and sleeping spaces crammed into the corners of high-ceilinged workshops.

In the 1830s, they got tired of bankers and traders fixing the price of silk at lower and lower rates, and they rose up. The first revolt happened in October of 1831, when the Canuts spilled out of their workshops and occupied the city, holding off the French army, at least for a while, with bayonets and barricades. The town magistrates reported walking through the rows of workshops, unable to find a single loom spinning.

The second Canut revolt happened in April of 1834, during the early weeks of spring, which are the most sensitive in the life span of the silk moth. The year's worms had hatched from their eggs. They needed to be fed new mulberry buds at two-hour increments, like newborn children. No record I can find describes what happened to them when the women walked out.

5: Las Polillas

IN THE WEEKS before the Sunday night meeting that served as the culmination of the blitz at your factory, I had, almost in passing, asked you about the photograph hanging on your wall. I noticed the flowers underneath it, but I didn't understand that they were marking the space as a memorial. You said, *That's my son, Julio Martín García Lopez, who died two years ago from violencia de la calle.* You said his full name. You said it with a bite to your tone, which I understood then as a signal that you did not want to say more. We had just exchanged some sort of small talk and were on our way through your door, heading to the union office, or maybe to Santiago's or Pollo's, already wrapped in the mode in which we would remain together for years, the perpetual freneticism of organizing. Thinking back on that moment, I am no longer sure you were asking me not to ask. And I wonder now what you thought when I said nothing.

When you spoke to your coworkers that Sunday night, just ten or so hours before you went back into the plant to face the company's fury at what you had started, I watched as you asked the others—provoked them, really—to fight with you. You did this as you did most things, with a spare sort of might. In that moment, I tried to form an image of you grieving and could not do it.

I recognize now that this is shameful. Portraits of strong women (may this be one, among the other things it might be) often don't allow for

much outside a narrow image of strength—stoic, invulnerable, uncomplicated—and in this way, strong women are required to double the weight
they carry and double its erasure. And I still didn't know you, at least not
well, didn't know the way that grief and rage and love and grit can press
down into each other and become part of the same glowing ember. Plus
there was the terrible fact of doing this at all, of trying to paint grief, or
whatever flimsy idea I had about it, onto another human, onto you, in a
moment when you were radiant with another kind of power.

I wonder if you knew all of this, and knew that it was why I did not
say more about your son, because I didn't know much about the relationship between grief and strength, because I needed you to play a certain
role on the campaign. And you didn't say more then, either, because you
needed to play the role, too. You wanted to win.

Earlier that evening, we stood together at the entrance to the meeting
hall. You greeted your compañeros and pressed union buttons into their
palms as they came through the double doors and made their way to the
rows of folding chairs. There was an electric hush, with which we were
not yet familiar, but which we now know as the same feeling that pre-
empts the first general meeting of every campaign. We talked about this
feeling once, about how nothing else compares.

The hall was a bigger space than we needed—room for five hundred
when we had about one hundred in attendance. People stood in small
groups, like satellites, around the rows of folding chairs we'd made in
the middle. They nodded in acknowledgment to each other and spoke
very quietly or not at all. As new people arrived, they would look ner-
vously around the space before approaching one of these small groups.
They would shake hands in the way that people sometimes do when the
level of formality of a gathering is unknown or has not yet been established. In a factory that operates the way yours does, 24/7, with teams

of workers rotating through breaks and lunches, many of them had never spoken to each other. They were meeting people they had likely seen in the parking lot in the early morning or late at night and maybe had crossed paths with at the punch clock or in the bathroom, but once the factory swallowed them up at the start of their shift, it was hard to talk to anyone who didn't work in their immediate area. Now they were introducing husbands and wives and boyfriends and children and babies who had come with them to the meeting. For many of the people in the room, this was the first time they had seen each other in plain clothes, instead of the hospital scrubs and hair nets they were required to wear to work.

I was in charge of the sign-in, which meant that I circulated clipboards among the workers as they arrived, asking them to write their full names and addresses and phone numbers so we could clean up and complete our lists—being able to communicate quickly was an imperative that I understood only theoretically until the very day after this meeting. A few of the workers could not read or write, and you would say, *Está bien, compa*, placing your hand on their shoulder and asking for their information so I could write it down. Some workers didn't know their addresses and instead described where they lived. I would write things like third door in the pink apartments two houses from corner on 25th and Tamarisk.

When the meeting began, the organizing director welcomed the workers to UNITE. Manuel whooped in the front of the room to encourage an energetic response, and you and your coworkers applauded politely. Manuel said, *No, no, no, compañeros*, and then repeated the director's phrase while placing more emphasis on the words in a way that broke them open to reveal their urgent significance: "Bienve*nidos* a UNITE!" We all clapped a little harder, and Manuel's whooping was taken up by a few of your coworkers.

The director was concise in her description of the union. Some version of: We are the international union of laundry and garment workers. Thousands of immigrants formed our union to fight for safer working conditions and better pay. They rose up after a gruesome factory fire in New York City almost one hundred years ago. They fought for and won safer factories, better pay, and a voice at work. *Those workers would be honored by your courage to join them,* I remember her saying.

And then it was my turn. I said, in my improved but still-not-great Spanish, that a majority of the workers in your plant had signed cards in just forty-eight hours, to which everyone in the room cheered and you started a "Sí, se puede" chant that crescendoed finally into the whooping Manuel had been angling to hear. Then I echoed the inoculation we had already played out in house calls over the weekend—that we had a long way to go before winning recognition for the union, a longer way still to a collective bargaining agreement that would lock in negotiated improvements, that the fight had not yet begun. That the managers and supervisors were probably at this very minute in a meeting or on a conference call, deciding what to do about the budding union, deciding how they were going to try to break it, how they were going to try to break you.

In inoculation, it's important to get it right. Anticipating the bosses' lines of attack, getting ahead of them by saying "This is what they're going to say," can undercut their power, can make the managers and supervisors into caricatures of all the managers and supervisors who have opposed worker organizing since the beginning of time. Correctly predicting their backlash helps to position organizers as trustworthy guides who have seen the boss campaign before and who know how to steer workers safely through the shitstorm.

The figure of the guide is not without its complications. It is generally the guide who decides where to go, for example. If there is a guide, then there are followers, guidees, a flock, even. Can you follow a guide to freedom? What is the difference between guide and leader? Between guide and shepherd? What is the difference between guide and *coyote*? It is a capacious role, with space aplenty for power to roam.

At the meeting, I talk about Good Boss/Bad Boss/Sad Boss as the kind of menu of tactics the company will draw from. I said some version of a thing I have now said thousands of times in meetings and house calls: *Good Boss* is when they buy off or try to buy off workers, with favors and fixes or even pay raises, to quell the anger that drives the organizing, to make it seem as though workers don't need a union after all. *Bad Boss* is when they terrify or try to terrify workers through threats, like plant closure and rumors like "Wherever the union goes, Immigration follows," so that fear overpowers the driving anger. *Sad Boss* is when they play the strange game of pretending to suffer a deep, personal heartbreak as the result of workers deciding to organize, in hopes that the workers' anger will be confused or blunted by empathy for the boss.

There was some laughter at this last idea. There often is. *Imagine John or Adam or another of the supervisors*, I said, putting on a weepy, childish face. The laughter was nervous but rippled through the room as it was meant to. People looked at one another and scoffed and smiled. I had lifted this joke from Dario, who had, I imagine, lifted it from the more experienced organizers who'd trained him. It worked. The crack in the facade of the all-powerful bosses that had first appeared over the weekend of house visits now deepened. The atmosphere in the hall shifted as workers sat together in this collective levity, imagining these more puerile versions of their imperious bosses.

Then Manuel talked about Sodexho, about its obscene wealth, about its notoriety as a low-wage company. He talked about our "plan to win," which is what we called the portion of a union meeting where the next steps of the campaign are delineated. That night, the plan was a kind of introduction to labor law and the messy, unpredictable process for having a union election via the National Labor Relations Board. Manuel delivered some version of: We want to give as many of your coworkers as possible the chance to join the union over the next few days, then we'll go as a group—all of us here and anyone else who wants to join—to the labor board to file an election petition. We do not know when the election will happen. If the company thinks they'll win, they might settle on a date in the next few weeks. If the company thinks they'll lose, they can drag their feet, using the law to challenge us at every step, putting the election off to give themselves more time to try to turn you against each other and the union.

You spoke next. You stood in front of the room and told your coworkers to stand up out of their chairs, to look each other in the eye and promise to stay in the fight for one another. You promised to stay in the fight "hasta las últimas consecuencias." The eye contact you made with your coworkers, one by one, was sharp and forceful, as if you were stitching yourself to them, writing yourself into whatever they were imagining might happen next.

Then you pinned your UNITE button to your shirt, and then most of your coworkers pinned their buttons to their shirts, and then the meeting was over. It was around 9:30 p.m.—time for the third-shift workers in the room to get to work.

After the meeting, we went into our office, which was adjacent to the big hall. Ana and Dario and the organizers who had blitzed CleanCo over the weekend were coming back from the first general meeting among those workers, which had been held at a borrowed Teamsters hall on the other side of the city and which had not been as well attended as ours, though we had expected it to be better attended on account of the factory not being a twenty-four-hour operation, as yours was. The whole team, including the fly-in organizers who had not yet flown back out, crammed onto the couch and chairs and sat cross-legged on the floor. We checked our attendance lists from the meetings against the lists of people who had already signed union cards, and in that way, we had an idea which people the companies had sent to spy.

We filled in our wall charts, the massively enlarged worker lists we'd pinned up around the room, sorted by shift and department, which wall-papered the office. The columns of names and addresses were followed by check marks, noting whether or not a person had signed a union card, and those marks were followed by numbers, one through five, rating our assessment of each worker's level of support for the union. Then there were blank columns, in which we would track meeting attendance and participation in the demonstrations and factory-floor actions we would plan in the weeks to come. The charts were a visual display of momentum, enabling us to watch as support for the union grew or stagnated or collapsed over time.

During this post-meeting debrief you seemed quiet, deflated after the rush of being in a room with so many of your coworkers for the first time. There were a lot of blank spaces on the charts. You sat on the edge of the couch, drumming your heels on the floor. You pointed at a blank space next to the name of a worker who had promised to be there and to bring two other coworkers who also hadn't come.

Most of the organizers soon left for the airport to catch overnight flights or for the motel to sleep before catching their flights in the morning. You moved around the office, scanning the wall charts while I helped the director make a leaflet on the laptop, then you stayed quiet in the car, though you insisted on coming with me to Kinko's to copy the leaflet and print more union cards, because it was on the way to your house.

I remember the smell of that copy shop, some mixture of candy and burnt ink and carpet cleaner, where we developed a ritual of choosing the paper color for our leaflets based on the content of the message. The ritual likely started that night, though I don't remember what color we chose that first time. At the register, the kid who we would see behind the counter most nights as the campaign rolled forward, who didn't speak Spanish but who I think wanted to greet you kindly, said, *Hola, señorita*, and you nearly burst, but you held your laughter until we got to the car. It was not even objectively funny, calling an adult Mexican woman a diminutive form of a title in a language one does not speak. It was the context and timing, really—we both knew you had just become the center of a disruption of deeply instituted power—and we were bone-tired, and so once we started laughing we could not stop. I laughed so hard I couldn't see to drive, so I pulled the rental car over to the side of the street, hazard lights blinking, until we could catch our breath and calm down.

When we got going again, we drove the rest of the way without talking. I still had all night outside the plant ahead of me, as third-shift workers had been harder to find at home and awake over the weekend, and we had not talked to enough of them.

You had a war to face in the morning. And though you were ready for it, the knowledge that your bosses had likely met that very night to plan their response, that they had likely talked about you—by name—weighed heavily on you. We pulled up to your house, and I think I wished you good luck, and I think you said, *A ver qué pasa*, and then you got out of the car.

I got to the factory sometime around midnight and parked on the street, next to the paper-shredding warehouse that shared its parking lot with the laundry. I didn't need to be there until 2 a.m., but I knew that if I went back to the motel room, I would fall asleep, and that if I did, I'd probably oversleep an alarm. So I parked there, next to the factory, and turned the AC on high to stay awake. The parking lot was dark, with only two or three light poles that illuminated the asphalt in small, disjointed pockets—a safety issue we'd heard about over the weekend from workers who had to come and go from their cars at night. I watched the maniacal circling of moths in these pockets of light as I sat in the car not sleeping.

At two, Manuel pulled his rental car up behind mine, flashing his lights to let me know he was there. I got out with our leaflets and union cards, and a banner that you and I had painted the week before in an unused section of the motel parking lot, kneeling on flattened cardboard boxes over a twin bedsheet in the sun. We painted sí SE PUEDE, AHORA O NUNCA, UNITE, and when we finished, we both had red and blue paint on our fingertips and elbows and jeans.

That night, Manuel and I walked into the factory parking lot. For the first time, we were in plain view of anyone who might have been in the front office. We stopped at a picnic table on a gravel island at the edge of the blacktop. One of the floodlights buzzed overhead. The campaign was now above the water and in the open. Anyone in the factory could see us. We tied the banner to the picnic table, but it hung unevenly, folding over itself in a way that obscured most of the words we'd painted. The moths plinked as they bashed their bodies into the metal and glass of the light fixture.

Raúl, the worker leader Manuel had recruited, and another of the night-shift washers told us they would try to bring their coworkers outside for a meeting. We could hear the bell ring from the parking lot, letting the soil side of the factory out. At first, Raúl came through the exit door with just four or five other workers—not nearly as many as we had hoped to see—and Manuel turned toward me with a silent but emphatic *Fuck.* But then other workers started to trickle out of the factory, joining us in groups of two or three, until there were about forty people gathered together around the table.

I stood on the bench and delivered a rapid-fire version of the talk from the earlier meeting while Manuel and Raúl talked one-on-one with workers and passed around union cards and leaflets. The same live-wire tension from the first meeting was there, but now, in the vulnerability of open campaigning, it coursed along over a current of unease. After a few minutes, the night manager and production supervisor came out of the factory and walked over to the group. Manuel saw them coming and walked toward them with his arms outstretched, telling them that this was a union meeting, that it was protected activity under the law, that they were not allowed to surveil workers engaged in protected activity, and so on. The manager said that she wanted to see who was present, and then she and the supervisor stopped and backed away a little and took notes on a pair of clipboards while they scanned the faces of the workers. Ultimately, the interruption succeeded as I imagine they'd planned, and the group who stood with us diffused quickly into the dark parking lot.

I went back to the hotel to sleep for a while—in my clothes, on top of the sheet, TV blaring, because after so many days of constant talking and gathering, meeting and organizing people, it was uncomfortable to be and feel totally alone. The dream moths shivered in unison on my body, dusting my skin with their residue.

At 6 a.m., the director and Manuel and I were back in the parking lot to distribute our leaflets as you and the rest of first shift prepared to go en masse into the factory. We stood together with maybe fifty of your coworkers. We chanted, "El pueblo unido jamás será vencido" and "Sí, se puede," and the modulated rhythm of our chanting, of our voices sounding in unison, bounced off the factory walls and ricocheted in the space around us. You stood in the middle of the group, and the bodies in the crowd around you grew larger than their bounds, touching each other without touching, the interstitial space shimmering in the open light of day. The world and its capacity expanded all around us. This feeling, where it comes from, is the part of this story that matters most.

¡Con ánimo! you shouted in a way that perfectly countered the inherent cheesiness of such slogans, and then you led the group into the building.

That day, the company hit back, fast and hard. By 8 a.m., La Sandra, as you called the human resources manager who had a mean-big-sister hold on a handful of the women who worked there, started calling workers into the office, one by one and in groups of two or three. (Adding the article *La* in front of her name made it a nickname that poked fun of both her position and her disposition.) La Sandra began these meetings by telling workers that if there was a union election, and if the union won the election, wages and benefits would be frozen. She said that negotiations, if they happened, could take a long time. She asked workers if they knew how the union organizers had found their houses. She mentioned the union meeting the night before, to impress, I imagine, upon the people in the room that she knew all about it.

Saying these things, only some of which were illegal to say, was a calculated maneuver, one which she had likely been coached through by Sodexho lawyers, whose job it was to steer the company through the wide-open loopholes of the National Labor Relations Act—which still, even in its extremely watered-down current state—holds that employers cannot threaten workers in this way. Calculated because even if the union could later prove in court that the company had made illegal threats, the violation would cost them nothing. At most, they'd be ordered to "cease and desist" from violating the law and to temporarily post a notice informing employees of the order to a bulletin board in the lunchroom. I imagine they held that up against what they stood to gain through this intimidation and did not think very hard about the risk—there was none.

La Sandra warned her "captive audience"—the legal term for these intimidation meetings—that the cards they had signed were "a blank check." Then she played a video titled *Little Card, Big Trouble,* in which a group of actors playing workers in some unknown workplace sat around a conference table in a dark room and talked about union dues and lay-offs, and factories and whole industries going out of business. The video was in English but dubbed into a very formal Spanish that you and the other members of the comité made fun of for the rest of the long, searing summer.

After the video, the plant manager, El Mero Mero, as you called him, which translates to Head Honcho or maybe Big Boss, made an appearance at the meetings and performed Sad Boss with aplomb. According to his own testimony months later, he told you and your coworkers that he "was saddened and hurt by the employees' conduct, that in his twenty-eight years with the company he had never seen anything like it, and he could not understand why it was happening to him, and that he was surprised that his workers, whom he considered to be his friends, had reached out to a third party and not to him with whatever problems they had, that he had always been there for them." He would then walk out of the meetings, somber, seemingly on the verge of tears.

When El Mero Mero had finished, La Sandra pivoted from Bad Boss to Good Boss, or at least, Benevolent Boss. She told workers not to worry, that she could help them get their signed union cards back. She invited them to her office if they wanted her to do so. In her office, she handed out form letters for them to sign and told them they should sign the letters right there and then so there would be a witness—La Sandra herself—to their demand that their cards be revoked. A judge later wrote of this stunt, "Here, [the manager] did not merely advise employees of their rights, she encouraged them to contact her to find out how to get their cards back and when they did so, collected their revocations. . . . [T]he procedure permitted [the manager] to observe whether employees availed themselves of the opportunity to revoke their cards."

The company would later admit to holding over two hundred of these meetings. You calculated the number at closer to five hundred, with each worker attending at least two versions of the same loosely scripted show. And many workers did sign the letter, and their letters flooded the mail in the union office and then, later, at the labor board for weeks. Challenged on its behavior years later, Sodexo (by then spelled without the *h*) would issue a statement insisting that it does not intimidate workers involved in union organizing. The company said: it "believes that our employees have the absolute right to make that decision freely, in an informed manner, and in an atmosphere that is free from interference, intimidation, harassment or coercion."

Running commercial laundries is only one part of the operations of Sodexo, which is a colossal corporation headquartered near Paris that operates in eighty countries. The company now admits that plant managers in Phoenix acted improperly but calls what they did in 2003 to you and your coworkers an "outdated matter." In a 2010 report, Sodexo insisted that it "will not discriminate against any employee [who] engages in union organizing activities" and that it has taken "appropriate measures" to ensure that managers in Phoenix would follow the labor laws in the future.

At break time that Monday, you came out of the factory. Manuel and the director were out on the doors, visiting workers from other shifts who we were still trying to reach, tracking down the people who had dispersed from the picnic table the night before. I was there waiting for you in my rental car, which I had parked in the shade of a palm tree and had inched forward every so often to chase the shadow as the sun moved across the sky.

I saw you walking across the parking lot, and I got out of the car to greet you. *It's not good*, you said, shaking your head. You hadn't sat through a captive-audience meeting yet, but the rumors stemming from them were having an effect on your coworkers. You'd heard about the video, that it was giving your coworkers the impression that the cards they had signed would cause "big trouble." But then you smiled—sly and serious—and pulled two newly signed cards out of your purse. *I told them it's a bunch of lies*, you said. You'd gotten them to sign in the bathroom.

The director and Manuel and I, along with Dario and Ana, who were kicking ass on CleanCo, kept holding nightly debriefs in our office at ten, in which we updated our wall charts, debated tactics, and made plans and leaflets for the next day. We talked a lot about the shoddy state of US labor law.

I went to the debrief that first Monday night angry and indignant and naïve, certain that we could take immediate legal action against the company, that we could file for some kind of injunctive relief to stop them from lying to and scaring people, stop them from forcing workers to sit through anti-union meetings while they were on the clock and had no choice about attending. And, yes, the director said, we would file unfair labor practice (ULP) charges at the labor board, because bosses still aren't legally allowed to threaten employees with reprisals for organizing, though proving that a threat violates the law is a high bar to meet because the part of the National Labor Relations Act, requiring employers to stay neutral during organizing campaigns, had lasted only twelve years before it was amended by the Taft-Hartley Act, which encoded into law a litany of things that unions were no longer allowed to do (certain kinds of strikes and boycotts and other tactics that had proven too effective for bosses and their lawmakers to stomach) and at the same time gave employers the usefully broad and vague legal right "to deliver anti-union messages in the workplace."

After the debrief, we went back to the factory. We ran shift meetings around the clock that night and the next day and the next night and the next day, even as the company was also running its meetings day and night inside the factory. The cops showed up every few hours, responding to calls from La Sandra and El Mero Mero, and each time they moved back the line over which we were not allowed to pass, pushing us farther and farther from the factory, until we were holding meetings on the sidewalk of the businesses across the street. And the wide, mostly dark parking lot that stood between us and the factory became the only space in which workers were not engaged in one kind of meeting or the other.

But you and Raúl and the other members of the comité worked hard against the company's message, and by Wednesday morning, we were at a solid majority on all three shifts. Through the cycles of shift meetings, we planned a set of actions to demonstrate to the company that you and your coworkers were building your union despite their threats, and that they would have to recognize it and negotiate a contract with you. At night we stood in the floodlights of the parking lot next door, and during the day in the shade of a tree at a small park a few blocks away. We hauled an aluminum easel and big paper flip charts back and forth between these two locations. In group after group, your coworkers committed to delivering the union cards en masse to the labor board office, and to rallying in front of the factory ahead of time, so the bosses knew we were on our way to file for a union election. On the easel, we made lists of key issues you and your coworkers wanted to resolve—safer conditions in the factory, less production pressure, better pay, affordable health insurance—and then passed a paper petition around and you each pressed it up against a coworker's back in order to sign. We made a plan to deliver the petition, to have a delegation of your coworkers, as large as we could manage, bring it to the factory's front office along with a message: this is what we're fighting for, and your threats and captive-audience meetings aren't going to stop us.

On Wednesday, we rented a bus, which pulled up to the parking lot during the first-to-second shift change. We blew red UNITE whistles and chanted as you and the rest of the comité and some of the stronger supporters boarded the bus, even as La Sandra and El Mero Mero and the other managers and supervisors and office employees watched through the office windows. The bus transported us from that universe of industrial factories and warehouses to downtown Phoenix, where the shiny glass-and-chrome buildings reached into the forever-blue sky of Arizona, reflecting and refracting and amplifying the already caustic late-April sun.

The bus parked at the Burger King across the street from the high-rise that housed the National Labor Relations Board. We filed off and down a pristine sidewalk lined with the lush, tropical landscape of that part of the city and into the HVAC chill of the lobby. It took many elevator cars to carry all of us up to the fourteenth floor. We waited for each other in the space where the elevators let us off and then went together through the double glass doors into the labor board office, where we crammed shoulder to shoulder in its small front lobby. As the organizing director completed the form to petition for a union election, you and your coworkers, still in your scrubs and shower caps, delivered a box of signed union cards as proof of your interest in forming a union. The box was too big to fit in the pass-through of the bulletproof glass that separated the receptionists' work space from the lobby, and the head receptionist—the nice one with red hair whom we would later get to know, and who would roll her eyes dramatically as the company lawyers walked by—had to come around through the office door to retrieve it.

On the bus back to the factory, you and I sat together, melting in our exhaustion into the seat even as the cool, constant adrenaline prickle of underdogging our way through the start of the fight had us wired and awake. You told me about the maquila in Sonora where you worked for four years in the 1980s, making electronics, some kind of transformers. I asked more about what you did there, and you said, *I don't know. I put one little piece of something into another thing.* You told me about the bakery there in Phoenix—your first job with a paycheck in the States— where a boss had hit on you and groped you before you threw a spatula at him and quit. Then you got your work permit and you went to work for Sodexho. On December 22, 1994. You remembered the date precisely. *I started at $3.75 an hour,* you said, raising your eyebrows to impress upon me the lunacy of this low figure.

I told you about a job I worked at a diner in Ohio, where I'd started washing glasses the summer I was eleven, and then bused tables and then made the toast and coffee and tea and then waited tables until I was sixteen. Most mornings, the owner came into the kitchen drunk and insisted on working the cook line. After years of hands on my waist, and unwanted shoulder massages, and towels whipped at the backs of my legs and ass, and his lips, weird and wet, on my cheeks and once on my neck, he asked me to take my shirt off. Right there in the kitchen, in front of my coworkers. And when I would not, he started throwing whole raw eggs at me, and the eggs splattered on the front of my T-shirt and then on my hair and back as I walked out through the pantry door. *I should have thrown a spatula!* I told you, wishing I had been brave enough to fight back instead of run, and we both laughed. But then you turned toward me a little and put your hand on my wrist. *You were young,* you said.

You told me you had not wanted to move to Nogales to work in the maquila, but the land around the ejido was drying up and could no longer support all of the families who lived there. I told you about the patch of land where I'd grown up—two dozen houses in middle-of-nowhere

Ohio—that it had been a swamp until people drained it for farmland, that every spring the water welled up and we would wait to see if the ditches would do their work in time to plant, which some years the flooding made impossible. And though you did not say it, the way you nodded your head at this made clear that the differences in our stories regarding lack and excess outweighed any idea I had been holding about the apparent commonalities of these farming communities where we each were raised.

I asked where Julio Martín was born, if it was in Nogales while you were working at the maquila—I still didn't know how old he was when he was killed. *No,* you said, folding into yourself. *He was five in Nogales. He would be your age if he had lived.* Then you turned to look through the window, and then I looked through the window, and we watched as the city gleam gave way to the anonymous corporate office strips near the airport and then to the sea of warehouses until we were back again at Sodexho. The bus stopped to let everyone out on the street, near the entrance to the parking lot, where there was a solitary palm, its wiry roots spilling out of the small square of dirt it was left to inhabit and onto the concrete that surrounded it. As if at one point they'd been liquid but had fossilized in the heat of the too-bright sun.

The next day, Thursday, was May Day: May 1, International Workers' Day. And you led the work stoppage in the factory. Our plan had not originally included shutting down production on the factory floor, but the delegation to deliver the petition had grown larger than we had anticipated—workers from every shift and department wanted to take part. So during around-the-clock meetings the day and night before, you and your coworkers voted to change the nature of the action—you would shut down the machines and walk away from your workstations in order to all go to the factory office together.

A group of off-duty workers met at the park down the street from the factory. They carried the AHORA O NUNCA banner we had made and the petition workers had signed during the shift meetings. They marched from the park down the sidewalk, across the parking lot, through an emergency-exit door, to which the alarm system had long been disabled, and right onto the production floor. They blew whistles to signal to everyone in the plant that the action had begun.

You were waiting at your workstation at the other end of the factory, and when you heard the whistles, you took off your gloves and the paper apron that helped shield your body from contamination, and then Santiago took off his gloves and apron, and then the others in your department removed their gloves and aprons. Together, you walked through the plastic curtain that separated the factory's soil side from its clean side to join the bigger group. When Antonia heard the signal, she was first to shut down her iron machine on the production floor. Then she waved her arms in the air, gesturing for her coworkers to join the strike, and, one by one, they shut down their machines, too. The whistling and chanting stopped as the group coalesced, and for a moment the factory was silent. *Quieter than I'd ever heard it*, you would say later. You could hear your footsteps against the factory floor as you and your coworkers moved toward the office.

There is a lot of confusion about what happened next. We know that you and the rest of the strikers made it to the office, either by marching around La Sandra, who tried to stop you, or, according to La Sandra herself, when Cecilia, who was sixty-four years old and not five feet tall, violently shoved her aside. We know that you and Raúl tried to deliver the petition to El Mero Mero, but he would not accept it, so you placed it on his desk, and he picked it up and threw it in a trash can. We know that La Sandra called 911. Twice. We know that she claimed she was calling to report being assaulted by Cecilia, but we know from the call tapes that she did not mention an assault and instead asked the police to come to the factory to break up a riot. We know that you said to El Mero Mero, who spoke only English, via Raúl, who interpreted, because he spoke a little English, *We are UNITE, and we are not afraid.*

And we know, of course, that you were fired. In front of the managers and supervisors and administrative workers. In front of all your coworkers.

During this action, I paced the small length of shade from the palm on the sidewalk and chewed the skin away from the sides of my fingernails. I asked Manuel, who also waited on the sidewalk, "How long has it been?" so many times that he laughed even as he continuously squeezed his hands into white-knuckled fists. The action took much longer than the ten-or-so-minute work stoppage we had carefully planned. We were waiting for Raúl, who was not yet on the clock for the day, to come back through the door to tell us what had happened, but instead it was you who came through the door first, though you should have been heading back to your workstation. You were smiling but also shaking your head. Angry, I could see even from across the parking lot. Your laugh cracked across the space between us. *At least now I have more time for house visits,* you yelled.

You were only partway to the sidewalk when Santiago and two of your other coworkers—Isabel and Maria—also came walking out of the factory. Your shift, and theirs, went on for another two hours, but when they'd tried to go back to the soil belt, El Mero Mero had chased them through the plant yelling, *No work for you, no work for you.* He held open the emergency door with one arm and pushed them out of the factory with his other.

The next morning, they fired Cecilia. Then they called Antonia into the office via an intercom announcement that sounded throughout the factory to give her a warning for being the first to turn off her machine.

There were two supervisors plus La Sandra and El Mero Mero in the room, and Antonia kept interrupting them to tell them that what they were doing was illegal, that they could not threaten her or discipline her for taking part in a union action. They gave her a second warning for interrupting them.

Antonia was crying and shaking when she got back to the production floor, and later in her living room, her face flushed as she remembered it. She knew people had seen her and thought it meant that she was afraid. She wasn't, she said. Crying is what her body does when she is too full of rage. She's always been that way, she said, since she was very small. She cried again in her living room when she told us this, and then she punched herself in the arm, hard enough for it to start bruising by the end of our visit.

After they gave the warnings to Antonia, they called in all of the other workers who had marched to the office, one by one, all day on Thursday and Friday and through the weekend, questioning them: about what they had done, and who had turned off machines, and had they seen Cecilia push La Sandra, and who had carried the banner, and did they know that you and Santiago and the others had already been "permanently replaced," and that this was perfectly legal and could happen to anyone who takes part in a work stoppage or strike.

We dug in for the hard work of holding ground. You were equal parts incensed at being fired and energized from not having to work the soil line ten hours a day. In the car, you pushed to visit one more coworker before stopping for food, one more coworker before stopping for the night. You wanted people to see you, to see your resoluteness.

Our visits were meant to assess and reassess your coworkers. We needed numbers. How many people would still open their doors to us after hearing the company's threat? How many would let us inside? How many would still sign a petition? How many were still with us, and how many were too afraid to go on? We "called the question," which is the way we talked about asking workers flat out if they were going to vote for or against the union in the labor board election. *It seems a little confrontational,* you said on our way to the first of these visits—you wanted me to do the calling of the question when we got to that part of the conversation. But then we were there, sitting on the couch of Beatriz Sanchez, talking with her about why she had signed her union card in the first place, and you looked her in the eye and asked her. You said, *Look, we need to know right now.*

On Monday, the labor board announced the date for the union election: May 29—still more than three long weeks away.

I picked you up in the mornings, and we would go to the office, and together with the director and Manuel, we divvied up lists of workers to visit. On most days, one of them would pick up Cecilia from her house and one would pick up Santiago from his, and we would knock doors until shift change, at which time we would meet on the street in front of the factory and hand out new leaflets that you and I had copied at Kinko's. Some of the leaflets were messages of support, from workers in union laundries around the country or from Phoenix community and student organizations. One leaflet was about pay—highlighting the fact that raises in your factory were capped at 4 percent and that most workers got either 0 percent, meaning no raise at all, or 1 percent, which, at current hourly rates, equaled about seven cents more per hour. These were annual raises, the only pay increases offered in the entirety of a year. A seven-cent raise at forty hours a week over the course of a year is only $145.60. The leaflet did this math. We printed it on light-green paper. *The color of US cash*, you said.

Most of the leaflets centered on the dire safety issues in the factory: that the company forced you to rinse the feces and urine and blood and other fluids from your gloves and reuse them day after day, instead of providing you with new ones; that production quotas would go up often and seemingly at random; that the iron machines—huge systems of hot rollers, into which one group of workers fed damp sheets on one end of the factory while another group of workers caught them when they were spit out on the other end, sometimes burned the fingers and hands of the "catchers." One leaflet about burns had a picture of Cecilia's hand, the back of which had a small scar, which puckered and waved like a topographical map, the skin shining softly like liquid. We had originally chosen red for this leaflet, but the color obscured the detail of the scar, so we printed it instead on crisp, flat white.

There was only one entrance to the parking lot, so that is where we stood to distribute the leaflets. The laundry trucks passed us on their way out, trailers packed with clean, ironed folded linen for the hospitals and, on their way back in, filled with thousands of pounds of soil. Under NLRB rules, laundry truck drivers rarely qualify as part of the same bargaining unit as the workers inside the factory, so we hadn't included them in our meetings, and they were steeped in the company's rhetoric. It made them vitriolic. They gunned their engines as they passed us, or they pointed their cabs toward us and revved, or they lay on their horns long and hard, blasting us with sound. A few of the drivers spit at us through their open windows or threw Wendy's or Del Taco wrappers. The worst of them, the one I would see years later at the bar in Tucson, leered grotesquely and growled foul things. Sometimes as he approached, we would yell the words at him before he could spew them. "Bitches!" we'd shout in English, and then laugh.

Once we knew the date of the election, most of our work shifted into calculating, with absolute certainty, how the vote would go, so that we could better target our house calls and engineer an effective get-out-the-vote plan. We mapped everything on new wall charts: Who would vote yes and who would vote no. Which workers in each department on each shift held sway with which of the workers who were undecided or who had signed cards but were now afraid. Which workers were off on the day the vote happened, and who was picking them up at what time to bring them to the factory to vote. Which workers would talk with which other workers to be sure they voted. We mapped how much coverage this network afforded, and identified who was left out and how should we grow the network to reach those people.

Then we assessed these maps, traced the structure of the union the maps delineated. Workers wore union buttons into the factory, and at lunch, members of the comité came out to the sidewalk with lists of who was still wearing the buttons and who was not. We collected statements from workers about why they were going to vote for the union and then took photo portraits of them. We stayed up for the better part of a night at Kinko's cutting and gluing and copying the photos and statements into crude booklets that members of the comité brought into the lunchroom in stacks. The buttons and photo books were tests, and we adjusted our assessments of workers, the likelihood they would vote for the union, accordingly.

We made a radio spot. You and eleven of your coworkers went to a recording studio downtown and took turns putting on the oversize headphones and speaking into the giant circular microphone, announcing your name and how long you had worked in the factory, and in which department you worked, and why you were voting for the union. We bought time on the radio station that played on the production floor. The first morning the spot played, workers came out to the shift meeting on the sidewalk bursting with laughter, reporting that La Sandra had run all the way from the office through the factory to unplug the boom box.

As required by law, the company sent us a list of employees it had deemed eligible to vote in the election, along with their addresses. The list was stacked with names we had never heard of, many of whom were ineligible to vote—a common diversion that companies employ in order to pull our time away from talking to the workers who would be participating in the election. We spent days driving to the addresses of these dozens of people, on a wild goose chase of the company's design, to whittle the list down by people who had not worked in the factory for many years, people who had never worked in the factory, and employees who worked on-site at the big hospitals as attendants in their linen rooms. We had not known that these linen-room workers existed. Not one of them would speak to us—the company had gotten to them first. And there were enough of them to swing the election, which was already going to be won or lost by a narrow margin.

Two days before the labor board's secret-ballot election, a rumor spread through the plant that the company had installed hidden cameras in the lunchroom so they could see who voted for the union. And by some extraordinary "coincidence," as La Sandra later called it in court, the rumor was timed perfectly with the actual removal of old surveillance cameras from the lunchroom, where the voting would occur, and the drilling of small holes in the ceiling, where apparently the company planned to install new cameras at some future time.

This had an effect. Some of the quieter supporters were suddenly not opening their doors to us, though we knew that someone was at home. We could hear the TV or radio switch off. We could see the blinds shift as someone peeked through the window. One of your coworkers, Julia, who had signed a card during the blitz, finally came to the door on our third or fourth try. Her hands shook as she said, over and over, *I'm sorry, I'm sorry, I'm sorry.*

When this happened, you would turn quickly away from the door, a forced nonchalance barely masking your agitation as we returned to the car. *What are they so afraid of?* you would say, seething. *Are they afraid* things will get worse? And: *How could things get any worse—people are burned and stuck with needles, and their arms are crushed?* And: *Are they worried the company will stop giving us their seven-cent raises?* And: *Why do they believe anything the company says?* And: *How are they not more angry?* And: How are they not more angry. And: How are they not more angry?

I did not have any answers, and I think you took my wordlessness—my awkward "I know, I know"—for dispassion.

Why do you even do this work? you demanded to know in the car after yet another of your coworkers hid behind her door. *Why do this*, you said, *instead of some other job you could have gotten?* You didn't say "you, a white person, you, a person who went to college." You didn't say "you, a person who has nothing to lose in this fight, who is, in fact, being paid to organize the fight, instead of hoping to hang on to her job despite the fight, or hoping to get her job back after it is won." But I understood. You were pointing directly to a sort of slipperiness, or a fissure, that had gone unaddressed, one that perhaps had been brought into sharper view by the anguish of losing ground as we were, but one that I am guessing you'd had in mind since the first time I sat on the olive couch in your living room.

I said something about the fact that organizing workers is the only way to make real change in a world controlled by rich people who already have too much and still want more, and that's why I was doing it. And this is the truth, of course, or it is *a* truth. But we both knew it was not an answer to what you were asking.

Another truth is that I had not spent enough time thinking about the fissure between staff organizers and the workers we help organize, or the disparity at its heart. Most staff organizers, like me, came in from outside the union rank and file—which was okay, most people seemed to believe, because we were skilled, or becoming skilled, in fighting highly organized corporations, which is a very hard job. We justified our presence in the union as a necessary intervention, required by the professional skill set we provided. And it was not my job to think about the structure of the union, to wonder about its fairness, or what shape it might give to power, or its ability or not to precipitate internal democracy. My job was to organize your coworkers and win. My job was to organize you.

I had also not thought about the disparity between our roles in the fight because the pace of campaigning allowed little room for anything outside the daily, hourly, minute-by-minute work of moving people toward the union in order to win. In fact, I had only noticed the disparity at all when I grappled with the slippery language organizers use to describe campaigning, the way pronouns shifted depending on the presence or absence of workers. I learned early on to say that it was *your* fight, *your* union, that we were there to help guide *you*, to fight alongside *you*. But in the late-night debriefs or at the motel bar afterward, the *we* staff organizers used referred to us alone, and the prepositions in our speech did a lot of heavy lifting. *We* were going to grow the union through organizing. *We* were going to build power *for* workers. *We* were going to win the campaign against the company, or *we* were going to lose it.

I want you to know that I was not dispassionate during these weeks. I was not unaffected. We were losing ground, in real time, and our failure to win would have consequences: Your coworkers, and you—if we were able to win your job back—would continue to work unprotected from the grievous dangers of the factory. It would be even more difficult to win at other laundries in Phoenix after losing at yours. The union would likely scale back on resources for red-state organizing if the campaigns seemed unwinnable, and tens of thousands of laundry workers around the country would remain unorganized.

* * *

At the motel bar on the night before the election, which was four weeks after the work stoppage, four weeks after you'd been fired, Ana and Dario and Manuel made bets on what the vote count would be—a tradition, they explained, a way to test how good each organizer's read was, how skilled we each were at predicting the strength of the union campaign versus the power of the boss's intimidation. It was one hundred dollars to buy in, but they wouldn't take my money. *Just hang on to it this time*, Ana said. *It's still your first election.* Manuel had us winning by one vote, Dario by five, and Ana had us losing by twenty.

We got to the factory while it was still dark out the next morning. Third shift would vote first, before they went home. The NLRB sent two agents to carry out the election, and they built a small cardboard structure in the corner of the lunchroom to serve as the voting booth. The director and Manuel were the union's representatives inside the factory, along with workers on each shift who had been elected by their coworkers to witness the process. They spent the day seated at a long folding table next to La Sandra and one of the workers who had been most vocally opposed to the union, who were there to witness on behalf of the company. I was not allowed to go inside until the vote count. You, having been fired, were not allowed to go inside at all.

We stood at the parking lot entrance, checking names off our list of people who had committed to vote for the union, making sure each one showed up for work and then, at the end of their shift, confirming with them that they had voted. We ate lime freeze pops out of a cooler someone had brought and drank orange Jarritos from the gas station down the street. We rested in the shade during the stretches when no one was coming or going. We held ice from the cooler to our necks and wrists. We talked about music, and I remember trying to describe riot grrrl to you, and you wrinkling your forehead and telling me to bring you a CD sometime (later, I did). You told me you liked banda, norteña, anything with a little rhythm and an accordion, that the Spanish pop station we'd been listening to in the car, 106.3, drove you crazy (we never listened to it again).

We talked about the weather, the lack of rain since winter. We talked about the moths, that they were everywhere, that it was hard to open a door without letting one inside.

In the late afternoon, we went to pick up a worker who had given birth just three days before—we needed every possible vote. We borrowed a car seat from Cecilia on the way, so that we could transport the baby. I had never installed a car seat before, and by the time you and I wrestled it into place on that one-hundred-degree day, we were both dripping with sweat. We went to pick up the worker and her baby and the baby's older sister, who both slept a little on the way to the factory, the baby in the car seat and her sister curled into her mother's lap. When we got to the factory, the worker did not want to bring her baby inside. Too much contamination, she said, so you took the baby onto your shoulder and whisper-sang to her in the passenger seat while her mother went in to vote. The baby slept in your arms, and when her mother and sister returned, we decided not to wake her while we waited. We sat together in the car's AC for what felt like a long time.

When the voting was over, the baby's mother and sister and I left you there, rocking and singing, to go inside for the count. It was my first time inside the factory. It was my first time inside any factory aside from the tomato cannery and Ford stamping plant near the farms where I grew up, and though it was a space I had diagrammed and mapped and stood outside of and tried very hard to picture and understand, I was disoriented as soon as we entered the cool, quiet, nearly empty front office. I followed the mother around the front desk and through a doorway, into the hallway where the bathrooms are, and then through another doorway, into the lunchroom.

The board agents counted the votes one by one, announcing "Yes" or "No" for each, and I tallied them in two columns in my notebook. I sat with the director and Manuel as we watched the nos pile up faster than the yeses.

When one of the agents announced, "No union wins," La Sandra and two of the other managers, who had brought pom-poms to the factory that day in anticipation of their celebration, climbed onto the benches of the tables where you and your coworkers ate your lunches every day and performed a choreographed cheer that I imagine they had practiced together in the office in the lead-up to the election.

Years later, in 2010, Human Rights Watch, a nonprofit that investigates abuses all over the world, issued a detailed report accusing Sodexo of a great number of misdeeds, including improperly holding captive-audience meetings and threatening workers that they could be fired for engaging in union activities. The company replied that, in effect, what happened at your plant was an aberration, and that generally the company is fair to labor, even pro-union. The company claimed that Human Rights Watch had latched on to "an exceptional and outdated set of circumstances to . . . paint a false picture of [the company, which] strives continuously to improve its methods for ensuring compliance with its policies."

6: Fires

I DON'T KNOW what the women of the magnaneries in Lyon thought about their silk moths. I do not harbor any illusion that they were devoted to the rapacious worms or scaly imagoes beyond keeping them alive. After all, the point of cultivating them was to glean silk, the one thing they were capable of producing, aside from another generation of moths, and then to sell that thing—the silky cocoon burned free of their bodies—in order to keep themselves and their families alive. This required an intimate understanding of the mechanisms and cycles of silk-moth birth and feeding and excrement and molting and metamorphosis and sex and death. Intimate, but not, I imagine, sentimental. Practical, even inside the ritual and fableistic superstition to which their breeding and care gave way. But in the way the care and slaughter of animals on the small farms where I grew up seemed a world apart from the heavy machine work of plowing and planting and reaping the fields, I like to believe that the fact of the writhing aliveness of the moths, so different from the inanimate machinery upon which the women may have worked in other industries—even in other parts of the silk industry—added up to something, some meaning in the work that was not monetizable or suited for sale.

Across the English Channel from France, in 1848, just as the Canut silk workers launched their third armed revolt in under twenty years, amateur lepidopterist R. L. Edleston pinned a rare dark moth into his already impressive collection. The specimen was a new form of the peppered moth, the first soot-black one of the usually spotted species known to have been collected. Edleston lived in Manchester, where small row houses, like the one where he resided, were intermingled with factories that piped smoke into air that was already so smoke-filled it blocked the sun, all day, every day, in a kind of Dickensian nightmare. At the time, as much as fifty thousand pounds of industrial fallout was deposited annually on each square mile of the city. From the 1840s to the 1960s, a walk around the block in Manchester would coat your skin and hair and clothes with a black film of fetid gunk.

In its original white-and-black form, the peppered moth is delicate and ornate, like a still image of a starling murmuration on the evening of a bright day, or like the dark branches of cedars interred in snow, or like braille. In her book on the sordid story of the science on the species, *Of Moths and Men*, Judith Hooper writes of the moths in this form, "When I saw the real thing at Oxford's Hope Entomology Department, dead, pinned and displayed like a jewelled pendant against a dark velvety background, I was taken aback by its beauty. The dark markings etched on the pearly wings had the understated elegance of certain Japanese textiles, compared with which all those vivid tiger moths now seemed gaudy and immodest." By contrast, the black-bodied, or melanic, form of the peppered moth, which emerged after several generations of living in and surviving the factory soot, is often described as drab or unremarkable. "It is hard to see how the inky-black melanic form, *carbonaria*, could appear lovely to anyone except a nineteenth-century entomologist desperate for an exotic variant," Hooper writes.

But the moth I saw pinned in an oak-and-glass case was lush: a deep, yawning black, with a few pinpoints of silver, chroming their way through the dark. As I looked over the two forms in the display, it was difficult to remember that the creatures were of the same species, difficult even to understand what *species* might mean in the face of such dramatic difference. The lepidopterist who showed them to me at Pittsburgh's Carnegie Museum of Natural History explained that the population of peppered moths in cities like Manchester in early industrial England morphed from the light-bodied form to the dark-bodied form over the course of just thirty or forty years. And that when factories were forced to start cleaning up around a century later, the moths morphed back just as quickly. It would make them the clearest, most observable proof of evolutionary adaptation ever put forth.

I remember learning about these moths in high school, remember seeing the images of the two forms side by side in textbooks. My rural high school had one biology teacher, who was a strict creationist (and also the county's best taxidermist, whose classroom served as his showroom) and who warned that the textbook would tell us some horseshit about this moth being a golden example of evolution, but that if we looked at the photos and didn't see God's splendor, we were going straight to hell. And that is essentially how the story of the peppered moth has gone, twisting this way and that to serve competing narratives about the moths and the mechanisms behind their color shifts and about the lepidopterists and their eccentricities and faulty experiments.

In 2003, while you and I were grinding out house calls to organize your laundry, running shift meetings at night under swarms of our own moths, the peppered moth was at the center of a controversy. In Judith Hooper's book, published a year earlier, she challenged the series of experiments that had positioned the moth as living proof of the theory of natural selection, claiming that Bernard Kettlewell, the moth collector who spent the mid-1950s investigating the mechanism behind peppered moth adaptation, had faked his experiments, which had supposedly led to the conclusion that the dark-bodied moths were twice as likely to survive on soot-covered trees as those of the lighter form, supporting the notion that the moths had adapted to the darker color because it allowed them to camouflage against the industrial muck. But instead of releasing equal numbers of both moth forms into the woods, observing where they would land and recording if and at what rate their predators would find them, as Kettlewell claimed to have done, he actually adhered the bodies of moths to tree trunks, proving little more than the fact that birds will happily feast when presented a buffet of dead moths. Or so the skeptical Hooper's argument goes.

She further alleges that Kettlewell and his amateur affinity for moths had all along been supported and exploited by Darwinian zealots, like Oxford zoologist E. B. Ford, whose main interest was the general scientific acceptance of evolution, which is precisely what occurred as a result of the experiments. Despite several published critiques of Kettlewell's work from various scientists over the years, once the story of peppered moth evolution had been told and repeated and believed enough times, it became unquestionable, too sacred to biological science to trouble.

It wasn't until Hooper's more journalistic take on the mess of bad science at the heart of Kettlewell's work that the famous photos of black-and-white peppered moth pairs began disappearing from high school textbooks, a process which was helped along by fervent creationists, who, encouraged by Hooper's takedown, went to town on Kettlewell's work and its blind acceptance among most scientists, declaring it proof that evolutionary science is nothing more than a system for indoctrinating the naïve and the godless.

Of Moths and Men takes as much interest in the lepidopterists of this saga—the "moth men," as they sometimes called themselves—as it does in the moths themselves. Hooper portrays them as eccentric nerds, cartoonishly driven in their work. "Some moth men," she writes, "have the stunted social skills of the more monomaniacal computer hackers, going about with misbuttoned shirts and uncombed hair, spouting taxonomic Latin." In her final chapter, Hooper writes: "As I looked into the world of moth-hunters, I sensed I was in the presence of a powerful compulsion I did not understand. There seemed to be something primal about this intimate communion with creatures so phylogenetically distant from ourselves. Lepidoptery was obviously addictive, a fever of the mind contracted, mainly by boys, on the verge of adolescence, and the consoling powers of moth-hunting on the lonely, the unloved and the bereaved seemed self-evident in the personal stories of the scientists I learned about." She notes elsewhere that girls and women tend toward butterflies.

R. L. Edleston was unlike most collectors of the mid-nineteenth century in that he was also a textile worker—a calico maker—and not a wealthy man with access to the leisure time most collectors relied on to amass their moths. His method of collection is unknown, but he likely had his own sugaring recipe, some favored mixture of beer and sugar, as most moth men did. He likely spent an afternoon painting the syrup onto trees and then went out again at night with a lantern to find the shellacked trunks swathed in moths. After he pinned this first specimen, dark-bodied peppered moths started showing up in collections across England, and taken together, they form a spatiotemporal map of the moths' transition corresponding to the spread of industrialization and the presence of black soot in the air.

Hooper notes the sugaring recipes of other famous moth men, including renowned literary lepidopterist Vladimir Nabokov, who crafted his own syrup from molasses, beer, and rum. In *Speak, Memory*, he writes, "Through the gusty blackness, one's lantern would illumine the stickily glistening furrows of the bark and two or three large moths upon it imbibing the sweets, their nervous wings half open butterfly fashion, the lower ones exhibiting their incredibly crimson silk form beneath the lichen-gray primaries." Hooper notes that, here, Nabokov is describing an underwing, a drab little everyday moth—gray or brown, built to blend in with anything. At rest, these moths are entirely unremarkable. But when they spread their forewings, they blaze with color, the underside of their wings coral or fuchsia, saffron or incarnadine, bright enough to shock a predator, to buy enough time to either nose-dive to the ground and hide or fly away. In flight, the underwings flicker through the air like tiny flames.

After *Of Moths and Men* was published, entomologist Michael Majerus came to the peppered moths' (and Kettlewell's) rescue, railing to anyone who would listen that the book was "littered with errors, misrepresentations, misinterpretations, and falsehoods." He conducted an elaborate six-year experiment, for which he released 4,864 moths into a rural garden, the largest number of moths by several magnitudes ever observed in a peppered moth study. He did not live to see the publication of his results, which definitively proved that camouflage and bird predation are, in fact, the overriding explanation for the rise and fall of melanism in moths, and which restored the peppered moth as the clearest example of Darwinian evolution in action. His vindication was published posthumously, in 2012, just as I was reading *Of Moths and Men*.

I had, of course, been rooting for the moths, and in my admittedly peculiar alliance with them, their exoneration as harbingers of industrial trouble was gratifying.

But even in my amateur kinship with the moth men (I am an organizer, not a scientist), I could see Hooper's point about them and about the strangeness of the lepidopterists' lust for these small nocturnal beings. While I find myself bound to the moths in my dream, I wouldn't have taken any interest in them if they hadn't come to me first.

What compels me about the battle over the peppered moths is not even the moths, per se (though they are there, a kind of ambient heart of the story), but the fight for control over what they are supposed to mean, how stories about them evolve alongside their bodily forms.

We know what Clara Lemlich's story is supposed to mean, at least when it is told in its most distilled and widely reported form. *Small firebrand of a girl spontaneously rises from an audience of thousands to call for strike, and tens of thousands follow her to the street* is a narrative so tightly compressed that it leaves no space for anything other than awe, no room in which one might conspire to similar action. When decontextualized from the hard work of movement building that both made it possible and necessitated it, Clara's defiance of the union leaders and her call for strike becomes a fluke, a miraculous act, an unreplicable disobedience. I imagine this is part of the aim, conscious or not, of telling the story this way. This version of the story says: radical action—especially when taken by immigrant women or women of color (recall the treatment of civil-rights activist Rosa Parks)—requires superhuman courage and a miracle of timing. It says: this is not really how unions are built, through spontaneous moments of high drama, which, of course, is true.

Even Clara seemed to live in a state of astonishment at the story. According to an interviewer from *Jewish Life* magazine who spoke with Clara in 1954, she did not like to talk about herself. When pushed to do so, she would squint coldly at the floor, as if she were looking at a very small thing from a great distance. Clara was warmer, more alive, when she talked about the women with whom she fought and the meaning of the fight itself. As the magazine profile read: "'That is what you must write about!' The small woman with the vivid eyes would still rather talk about the strike's meaning than her part in it. They used to say that you couldn't even organize women. They wouldn't come to union meetings.

They were 'temporary' workers; they would always undercut men. Well, we showed them!'"

Through time and recontextualization, Clara's organizing has been recoded from strategic and hard-won to spontaneous, even accidental. But as she was hoisted onto the stage, Clara's ribs were likely still sore. As she inhaled, filling her lungs in order to yell out over the crowd of thousands, she must have felt the tenderness of still-healing bones, still-bruised interstitial muscle. When she raised her right arm—to ask that her hand wither if she were to turn against the cause she pledged—and as she held her arm in the air and watched thousands of other arms rise along with hers, her body likely ached.

She ached because the mass meeting at Cooper Union, where her famous speech occurred, happened in the eleventh week of a strike Clara was already leading, among hundreds of workers at the three largest shirtwaist factories in New York City: Leiserson's, the Rosen Brothers, and the Triangle Waist Company. The meeting happened ten weeks after the companies had hired a man to follow her on her way from the picket line to the union office, ten weeks after he closed in on her from behind and beat her so badly he broke six of her ribs and left her bleeding in an alley. The meeting happened nine weeks after she went back to the picket line, still swollen and broken, and stood on an overturned crate to yell to her fellow strikers that she'd rather starve quickly than starve slowly, and so she would stay on the picket line even if they came to beat her again.

And this was after she had already been arrested seventeen times and had been lectured by judges that women and girls are meant to do as they are told and that she was—in her very manner of being—acting against God. And the meeting happened as her own local's strike fund had dwindled to nothing and after she had gone to higher-ranking officials in the union to ask for support in expanding the strike to all six hundred or so shirtwaist factories in the city, and the leadership of the union counseled her to end the strike because some of the women were getting tired of the arrests and beatings and were afraid to live without strike pay and were returning to work, and, besides, Triangle and Leiserson's were churning out work with scab labor at nonunion shops elsewhere in the city. And it was after she had gone to the Women's Trade Union League (WTUL)—an upper-class suffragist organization that promoted the "welfare of working women"—and asked them to observe the picket lines to help curb the violent attacks against the strikes, which they had done but which had not deterred the violence. And it was after WTUL had also hesitated at the idea of expanding the strike, telling Clara that she should go slow, that she should be more disciplined, less brash.

And it was after Clara and other Local 25 leaders had done the work on the ground at hundreds of other garment factories to establish organizing committees and to build support for a bigger strike. The meeting happened in a moment when Clara knew there was a will to fight among these workers, a will to strike. It happened in a moment when most, if not all, of the workers in the hall knew very well who she was, had heard her speak many times, and when they saw her raise her hand from the floor in front of the stage, they hoisted her up because they already knew what she was going to say, and it was what they had come to hear.

This is who she was when she spoke out from the stage. She was not a "frail little girl," an "anonymous wisp of a girl," as she was often characterized.

When she was ten, Clara would stow away to read in the crossbeams of the attic ceiling of her home in a small town in Ukraine. A neighbor caught her there once, perched like a bird, holding a Russian novel—by Dostoevsky or Turgenev or Tolstoy—that nearly outweighed her. When Clara realized she'd been seen, she begged the neighbor not to tell her mother, who kept a grocery store down the street, or her father, an Orthodox Jewish scholar, who had banned Russian in their home in protest of the fact that Jews were not allowed to attend the grade schools nearby. She had learned to read the language by paying Russian girls for lessons that she snuck away from housework to attend. And she had raised money for the lessons by also sneaking away, to sew buttonholes at a tailor shop in town. In order to ask for the lessons, she had to befriend the Russian girls, which she did by learning folk songs from the non-Jewish peasants who lived near her family on the outskirts of town and then offering to teach them to the Russian girls.

Instead of telling on her, the neighbor brought her more books and also political pamphlets, which she read hungrily for the next six years, in the attic or hidden away in the dark, quiet kitchen at night while the rest of the family was sleeping.

When Clara was seventeen, priests in the city of Kishinev led their congregants from Easter church services out onto the streets in a murderous riot targeting local Jews. In the pogrom's wake, Clara later said, some elders called for the organization of Jewish self-defense forces. But as survivors started to describe what they had witnessed—the bodies of Jewish children piled in the streets, the bodies, including those of babies, torn to pieces by the mob—her family, along with hundreds of thousands of others, fled from the region in 1903. They traveled first to England, where they waited for months to board a ship, and where Clara lived among the muck and haze and soot of unrestricted industry, among the same conditions that turned the peppered moth black, before sailing to the United States.

In New York, she was struck by how tired everyone seemed, both adults and children—how sunken-eyed their faces, how bedraggled their clothing, how hunched their bodies from bending down and over their factory machines. She landed in this world and wondered how anything would ever get better, she would later say.

Clara's mother had lugged a sewing machine all the way from Ukraine and managed to hold on to it through the long journey to England and then on the voyage to New York and then through the chaos of Ellis Island. With that machine, along with needles and thread borrowed from her new tenement neighbors, Clara found a job at the Gotham shirtwaist factory. She carried the machine to and from work on her back every day. Without it, she would not have been hired, or she would have been charged for using company supplies, as workers were charged for most anything they touched inside the garment factories—for needles and thread, for clothes lockers, for the chairs they sat in, for any damage to garments or bolts of cloth. They worked sixty-five hours a week in the slow season. They worked eighty-five hours in the high season; driven to produce new garments by changing weather in the spring and fall, they worked into the night, by gaslight, sometimes until dawn. "All week long, I wouldn't see daylight," Clara would later say.

The factories had no heat, and the workers were not allowed to leave their coats on, for fear that they would smuggle supplies out at the end of the day. The conditions were unsanitary. "That's the word that is generally used, though there ought to be a worse one used," Clara would later say. The toilets overflowed into the shop floor, and managers locked the doors so no one could leave to find a toilet outside. The workers got one bathroom break per day, and after that, if they could not hold their urine in, they had to let it out on the floor. The machines hissed loudly, the foremen yelled incessantly, and workers were fired if they spoke to each other on the clock. "Not only your hands and your time, but your mind is sold," Clara wrote in a 1912 guest article for *Good Housekeeping*.

Just months into her first job, Clara and her coworkers walked out over the company's pay system, which involved the workers keeping track of piles of tiny tickets representing their production. They were not allowed to keep the tickets on the sewing tables. They were not allowed to place them in their pockets. The company was betting that they would lose track of the tickets, and they did. Some of the girls who walked out were as young as eight. They worked in corners of the factory called "kindergartens," where they trimmed threads on finished garments for fourteen hours a day and where they had to hide in boxes on the rare occasion that an inspector showed up to enforce new laws prohibiting children from working at night.

Clara was not resigned to living her life as a piece of machinery, as she claimed the work was designed to make her feel. When her shift ended at night, she would walk to the public library, where she read through its vast collection of Russian classics. Then she would stumble home to sleep a few hours before going back to the factory in the morning. In her second year in New York, she joined a free night school, where she learned to read in English, and during lunch at the garment factories, she would read aloud to the younger girls from Dickens and Shelley and George Eliot and Thomas Hood. She started reading Marx in classes at the Rand School, too, and then formed a small fist of a study group that wandered the streets during lunch, to talk without their bosses being able to listen in.

That group called themselves "the fiery girls," and during one lunch break in 1905, they walked to the office of the *Jewish Daily Forward* to ask for advice on forming a union.

After the decision was made to strike at Cooper Union in 1909, after the workers gathered there raised their hands and recited the oath, a delegation of fifteen women (along with a man, appointed to lead them) ran to nearby halls to report the decision to the thousands of workers who had overflowed from the main meeting. In these halls, too, the strike was unanimously approved. In the morning, they went in to work at shirt-waist factories across the city. They sat at their machines and waited for the walkout to begin. At one factory, a sixteen-year-old worker named Rose Perr later reported that the women sat silently for what seemed a long time, that the room was alive with some kind of energy, but that no one moved until somehow they were all on their feet at once, without any one of them having taken the lead.

More workers walked out than the union had expected—fifteen thousand on the first morning alone. Clara and other Local 25 officers spent the first day frantically renting meeting spaces across the city to accommodate the number of bodies who had spilled into the streets. At each of these sites, strike leaders collected lists of worker demands, an exercise that, journalist David Von Drehle writes in his book *Triangle: The Fire That Changed America*, "was probably designed simply to fill time," since before the workers had finished compiling these lists of issues they would like to see resolved, ILGWU leaders had published their own demands, which included better wages and shorter working hours but mentioned nothing of safer working conditions or more sanitary factories. Clara and the thousands who had followed her out of their factories and into the streets learned of these demands at the same time and in the same way as their bosses, from reading them in the newspaper. At the end of this first day, the wealthy women of WTUL visited the meeting sites and ran workshops on the importance of polite and orderly picketing in order to gain the sympathy of the public. Within twenty hours, the strikers had been instructed not only on the demands for which they were fighting but also on how, precisely, they were to fight.

Despite these corralling forces, the strike was Clara's life. She stood on picket lines from 6 a.m. to midnight, when she and the other strike leaders met to make plans for the next day. In the first month, 723 people were arrested and 19 were sentenced to workhouses, including a ten-year-old girl who was tried without testimony. With a dry strike fund, Local 25 turned to the WTUL for help in paying bail and court fees, which averaged more than $7,000 per day. The wealthy women of WTUL backed the strikers and organized mass rallies at the Hippodrome theater, Carnegie Hall, and City Hall, in which the strike was connected to the suffragist cause.

This strike loomed large in the years that I worked for the union, a key event in its founding, a major plot point in the union's story of itself. The black-and-white images of young women—standing shoulder to shoulder in long dark coats with velvety dark hats, wearing white strike sashes, standing together in the bitter cold—hang on the walls of union halls across the country. I printed one such photo and hung it in our office in Phoenix. It stood in the background as we built our lists and plotted our fights over the years we worked together.

But for all of those years, I had the story of the strike wrong, at least in its chronology with respect to the fire. I had thought that the fire happened *first*—that these thousands of women had risen up because of the fire, that their strike forced the garment industry and all industries and the country as a whole to change.

But it was the strike that came first, a strike that was "called off unceremoniously" eleven weeks later. A strike that was deemed "successful," or "very successful," or "a massive victory," or "only partially successful," or "not a total victory," depending on the source. Three hundred thirty-nine factories signed contracts with the ILGWU, which included, according to the Jewish Women's Archive, "a fifty-two-hour week, at least four holidays with pay per year, no discrimination against union loyalists, provision of tools and materials without fee, equal division of work during slack seasons, and negotiation of wages with employees." JWA also notes that "by the end of the strike, 85 percent of all shirtwaist workers in New

York had joined the ILGWU." But some of the strikers' demands went unresolved, and some of the biggest factories, like Triangle, did not sign contracts at all. And some of the strikers would be fated to die in the fire there.

Many accounts credit the social and political capital of the WTUL with pushing bosses to settle with the union. Other accounts credit Socialist Party leader Morris Hillquit and John Mitchell of the United Mine Workers, who sat at the negotiating table with the garment bosses, bargaining over the working conditions of young immigrant women in an industry they did not know. The strikers themselves, many of whom were illiterate, many of whom spoke only Yiddish, and who, through the strike, had gained a reputation for being loudmouthed and unruly, were not invited to attend the negotiations.

Clara collapsed when the strike ended and went upstate to lie on a bed in the country house of a WTUL friend. When she returned to the city, weeks later, she found that she had been blacklisted—no garment factory would hire her. The ILGWU appointed her to inspect factories for safety or child-labor violations, a sanction the strike had forced through at some shops. But Clara would not or could not be quiet about her discontent with the terms of the settlement, and ILGWU leaders fired her. She then went to work for WTUL, soapboxing for suffrage, but did not last long there either—her speeches tended to stray from the script about voting rights to the lives and rights of women workers.

Three days before the Triangle factory burned in March of 1911, Clara cofounded a new organization for women workers organizing for the right to vote: the Wage Earners' League for Woman Suffrage. Among her small group of cofounders were fellow garment workers and organizers Rose Schneiderman and Leonora O'Reilly, and a laundry worker, Margaret Hinchey, who was organizing her coworkers in the quickly expanding industry of machine-powered laundries. The organization would be run by and for factory workers—a truly democratic organizing body, a new home for the fiery girls.

Eight days after the fire, the new organization helped to lead a protest at the Metropolitan Opera House, where in front of an audience that included the men who led the ILGWU and the women who led WTUL, Rose Schneiderman, who one report describes as a small woman who normally spoke barely above a whisper, gave a speech: "I would be a traitor to these poor burned bodies if I came here to talk good fellowship. . . . This is not the first time girls have been burned alive in the city. Every week I must learn of the untimely death of one of my sister workers. Every year thousands of us are maimed. The life of men and women is so cheap and property is so sacred. . . . Too much blood has been spilled. I know from my experience it is up to the working people to save themselves."

7: Las Polillas

WE LOST THE election by twenty-eight votes.

If fifteen more people had voted yes instead of no—each one taking a vote away from the company and adding instead to the union's tally—then the union would have had a one-vote advantage and we would have won. If only fourteen more people had voted yes instead of no, then the count would have been even, and the company still would have won. Under current law, a tie supports the status quo—no union.

Five weeks earlier, a clear majority of your coworkers had joined the union. If we had managed to hang on to fifteen more of them, if we'd been better at shielding them from the company's attacks in these weeks from blitz to election—the "critical period," as it's called—your union would have been certified by the NLRB that afternoon, and we would have moved into preparing for negotiations with the company, building the strength we would need to gain a decent contract. These fifteen people could not have included you and Santiago and Isabel and Cecilia and Maria, who were not permitted by the company to enter the factory, which is where the election took place. You did not get to vote.

Inside the lunchroom, no union was announced as the winner. I sat next to the director at a table in the middle of the room. Antonia sat across from us. She cried. A lot of the people around us were crying. I looked down at the tally sheet I'd been keeping and moved my pen over the paper, pretending to engage in some urgent note-taking, though I wrote nothing. I was ashamed but knew it was the wrong thing to feel. I was sad. I was worried. I bit my tongue to blunt these feelings with the brightness of that pain so as not to trespass onto the parts of the fight that were not mine. I didn't feel angry, at least not right away.

The room was full of people who five weeks earlier had told the labor board that a majority of them wanted a union, had in fact hand-delivered a box of signed cards stating that they wanted to join the union, that they were electing UNITE to represent them in negotiations with the company to better their working conditions. But under current law, a company is permitted to claim that the cards are not enough to determine whether or not the workers want to have a union, no matter how many employees have signed them. Under current law, companies are allowed to require workers to demonstrate that they want a union a second time, through a labor board–managed election, such as the one we had just lost. Under current law, during the weeks between the card signing and the election, the company is allowed to campaign against the union, including by openly expressing its opposition in mandatory meetings with workers, making negative predictions about what might happen if workers vote for a union, and telling workers that if they engage in an economic strike, they may be permanently replaced. All of this to say that union elections are not simply a matter of voting "union" or "no union," but deciding if the union you have already chosen to form is worth the war.

After La Sandra and her crew finished their pom-pom cheer, they cried and hugged and thanked the workers they knew had voted against the union. The director sat very still next to me. She made her face hard, unreadable. In a voice loud enough for everyone to hear, she assured Antonia and Raúl and Beatriz and the other members of the comité who had gathered around us that the fight was not over, that the company had broken laws that are in place to prevent employers from retaliating against unionizing workers, that we would file charges. Her movements were fluid and deliberate as she stood up from the table, collected her things, and walked out of the factory. I did my best to mimic her.

In the parking lot, you held the baby and watched through the rental car's windshield as we came out. You told me later that you knew we had lost the moment you saw my face. *White as a ghost?* I asked. *No*, you said. *Purple, bruised. You did not look like you.*

Santiago and Isabel and Cecilia sat in the shade of one of the mesquite trees that lined the parking lot. Cecilia was sitting at the base of the tree with her head on her forearms and her forearms on her knees. She had tailored her red UNITE T-shirt so that small strips of material around her upper arms and waist had curled into each other, forming a fringe, and as she rested like this, the fringe hung down from her arms like feathers. She didn't look up as we approached.

I don't remember taking you to your house that day, though I must have. I must have driven you there after the half hour or so that we stood around on the sidewalk while you calmly reassured your coworkers, who streamed out of the factory feeling defeated, that we'd see El Mero Mero and La Sandra in court. I don't remember what the other organizers and I did that evening—if we went to the office to debrief or not, if we ate food or not. Later that night, the team congregated in Manuel's room and swigged whiskey out of a bottle, instead of going to the motel bar, which had been our ritual. We got very drunk. We smoked packs of cigarettes. Ana went to bed at some point, and I don't know why, but the rest of us decided not to sleep. We crushed NoDoz and snorted them in lines and were awake all night.

Manuel and Dario and the director told stories about fucked-up campaigns they had worked on across the country—bosses buying off workers, and calling Immigration to deport workers, and hiring people to

stalk and beat up workers. They told stories of the scrappy antics of organizers, who, under the make-or-break urgency of factory strikes, stole
truck keys and threw them into sewage grates or funneled sugar into gas
tanks or smeared cement paste into the padlocks of factory gates in the
middle of the night. I remember thinking that I understood the function
of this all-night swapping of stories, that it was driven by the righteous
indignation and pride that sustained people through the insanity of the
job of union organizing—and at the same time worked to replenish it. It
was a way to take control of what our stories mean. And as I sat on the
motel bed listening, my own anger became more immediate and available, and it covered over the shame and sadness I had felt before. Looking
back, I wonder if the exercise worked on the others in this way as well, if
being able to center anger, to uncomplicate our relationship to the fight
or at least uncomplicate our responses to it, comes with practice, like
hope, and if practicing was what we were doing together in that room.

In the morning I picked you up, and we went to the office to make a leaflet. "The company broke the law, and we're filing charges," it read. Then
we drove around to the houses of the members of the comité so they
could sign it. Then we went to Kinko's to make copies. Then we went to
the factory to hand them out during the shift change. It was as if nothing
had changed. Our presence there on that day was an insistence that the
fight was not over, that you and your coworkers had, in fact, built a union
and that your union existed whether or not the company recognized it,
whether or not the government certified it. We wanted the consistency
of our presence to signify to your coworkers that the election loss was
just one part of the long process of forming a union—which is true more
often than not under current labor law, since there are no fines for anti-
union retaliation and no compensatory damages for workers whose
rights have been violated. Which is all to say that companies that wish

to remain nonunion can only ever be helped by breaking the law, and so they do.

It was 108 degrees that day. We squinted into the sun as we handed out our leaflets. We yelled at the drivers. We waved and smiled at El Mero Mero when he walked into the parking lot shaking his head, seemingly dismayed that we were back so soon or back at all.

Inside the factory that afternoon, the managers shut down production and held a pizza party. For the first time in the factory's twenty-plus-year history, all of the workers on each shift were allowed in the lunchroom at the same time. La Sandra had decorated with balloons and streamers and wall signs that read THANK YOU FOR VOTING NO! and NO TO UNIONS, and WE ARE UNITED (NOT UNITE). She stood in front of the workers and interpreted for El Mero Mero, who thanked the workers for their loyalty to the company and said that the company had acquired several new hospital contracts and that there would be increased production flowing through the factory, and that workers would have to work hard and cooperatively to achieve the level of production output that would be required, and that if anyone there didn't want to work hard or if anyone there was unsatisfied with how the vote had gone, they knew where the door was and they should leave right now.

El Mero Mero and La Sandra tossed some hats and visors that were embossed with the company's name into the audience of workers who were seated around the tables. Beatriz told us later that one hat landed near a table of union supporters. It fell to the ground at their feet, and no one bent to retrieve it.

That night, I was so tired my skin no longer seemed to form a barrier against the motel sheet; I sank into the fabric, and the outer wall of my cells broke open and interlaced with the polyester and cotton fiber. Still the TV was on, and I stared at it, glassy-eyed, until I could blink into sleep without having to decide that I wanted to. The moths were there, but there were many more of them. They piled on top of each other on top of my body. The ones underneath struggled to move.

On the way to the NLRB office the next day, the organizing director described Section 8 of the National Labor Relations Act, which outlines unfair labor practices in two separate parts. The first part, Section 8(a), she said, is a list of the things the boss is not supposed to do, and the second part, Section 8(b), is a list of things unions can't do, so our charges would all be 8(a)-something, depending on the category of each violation.

In the passenger seat, I scribbled into my notebook as we wound through the parking garage of the building that houses the labor board. I listed the hardest-hitting violations the company committed as we named them aloud: They fired you, the clear leader of the union organizing committee, during a work stoppage, which is "protected activity." They fired Santiago and Cecilia and Isabel, three outspoken pro-union activists, and the other soil sorter, Maria, who had taken part in the work stoppage but had since moved back to Mexico. They threatened to freeze and then cut wages and benefits. They threatened to drag out negotiations if the union won, to thwart any path to a decent contract. They interrogated and harassed union supporters. They spied on union meetings. They pressured workers into signing letters asking to revoke their union cards.

The director said that the labor board investigation into the charges would take many weeks. She said that, at the conclusion of the investigation, the board would decide whether or not to pursue charges against the company, and if they did, a board attorney would be assigned to try the charges in front of an administrative law judge. It will take months to even schedule the trial, she said. And in cases like these, where multiple charges will be under consideration, where the testimony of many witnesses will have to be parsed, it could take a judge another year or more to issue a decision after the trial adjourns.

If, after the entirety of this process, we managed to win, the director went on to explain, the court victory might—but also might not—include an order to reinstate you and Santiago and Cecilia and Isabel to your jobs. It might—but also might not—include an order for the company to pay your lost wages. If we won on the charge of harassment, the company might have to expunge the warnings from Antonia's record. For the rest—for all the threats and interrogation and surveillance—the most we could hope for is that the company be required to post a letter on a bulletin board inside the factory stating that they had been ordered to stop breaking the law.

The director said that the most we would likely win against a company like Sodexho—and our main goal, other than yours and the other fired workers' reinstatement and back pay—was the right to hold another election. If we did manage to get a hearing in front of a judge, and if that judge did find that the company had committed multiple violations in a serious enough manner, we might be lucky enough to repeat the election process, go through the same kind of gauntlet, the same kind of war. And if the company broke the law again the second time through—even if they made the same threats verbatim, fired exactly the same people—the only path forward through the legal system would be to again file charges and hope again for another hearing, another election, and so on. She told me these things in English, and as she spoke, I ran them through a kind of simultaneous translation in my mind—configuring the sentences I would use to describe this absurdity to you.

The unfairness of this process—that there would never be a real cost to the company or its managers for breaking the law, that companies almost always stand to gain by breaking the law—was not surprising, but it added to my astonishment that workers under this system ever actually win. But they *do*—only about half of the time if a company has more than two weeks to run its anti-union campaign, but over 80 percent of the time if the election occurs in less than two weeks from the day workers ask for one.

When I told all of this to you later, you scoffed at its cruelness, but you were calm. *Así es*, you said, which had become our refrain each time the campaign entered a new level of difficulty. *Así es*, I echoed back to you. That's how it is.

The same administrator who had collected our cards the month before told the director and me to wait while she figured out which lawyer was next in the rotation and would therefore be appointed to us. After a while, a middle-aged white man retrieved us from the lobby and led us several turns down a hallway to his small office. He sat behind a desk piled high with paper, smiling politely through the stacks—he in a rumpled but lawyerly suit and the two of us in our sweaty T-shirts and jeans and dirty sneakers—and told us that his name was Paul Irving. He replied variously to our descriptions of the company's legal violations with "Oh wow" or "Seriously?" But mostly he took notes, longhand on a yellow legal pad. Instead of looking down as he wrote, he watched our faces.

After filing our unfair labor practice charges, we told Paul that we had already confirmed a list of witnesses. You had been the first to volunteer, standing outside the factory after the vote count. You had handed the baby back to its mother and held one arm up to your forehead to shade your eyes from the sun. *Yo sí voy*, you said. I *am* going.

Santiago and Antonia and Cecilia said that they would also serve as witnesses. Then Raúl and Beatriz and Isabel and Pollo and Pollito and Analía—the whole little circle that had gathered at the edge of the parking lot.

In his office, I handed Paul a list of your names. *Wow*, he said again. And then, *Okay*, warmly emphasizing the second syllable in a way that seemed to signal that he wanted us to know he was impressed. It was a little patronizing, but not aggressive, not gross. I watched the director shift sternly in her seat, cross her arms and tighten but not exactly purse her lips, and I watched Paul read this language and immediately switch to a more formal demeanor. I sat marveling at this exchange, the way the director's small gesture shifted the physics of the room, the way it carved space for the serious tone and urgent pace of the work Paul and I would have to do together over the next six months.

Paul looked down at the list. *This is a good start, he said, but I'll need to talk to everyone eventually*, by which he meant anyone at all willing to talk to him about what had happened. Anyone who stopped work during the march to the office, anyone who signed a card and then signed a card revocation, anyone who was fired, disciplined, interrogated, threatened, or spied on. He couldn't start right away, he said. He had to finish another case, clear his schedule. Then there was the business of needing someone to interpret—Paul did not speak Spanish, and another attorney, Gael, was the only person in the regional office who did. Paul would have to arrange for him to be assigned to the case as well, so he could verbally interpret the interviews and then translate the affidavits that resulted from them.

I went back to Tucson later that week, to use up some days off as the board office sorted itself out. Under our own staff union contract (organizers had our own small union, called the Federation of Union Representatives, or FOUR, that bargained our salaries and other benefits and working conditions with the executive board and UNITE's international office, our employer), we were allowed three days off every two weeks, but no one on our team took that much time. We banked days during campaigns and then took time in between. I drove down the I-10 through another galaxy of moths. The infestation, which seemed to be peaking that week, intensified in the dark miles between the two cities. I stopped for gas at the Shell station on the Gila River reservation, and though it was a hot June night, ice scrapers had been stocked alongside the squeegees to help with the removal of moth remains, and I used the corner of one to chip away at the mess of their bodies.

The small house my girlfriend and I were renting in Barrio Santa Rosa shared a backyard with two other small rental houses. The woman who lived in one of the other houses kept chickens—their coop was nestled under a mesquite, just outside our bedroom wall. There was a bright moon during the nights I was home, which, according to the neighbor, was what caused the rooster to crow throughout the night, pulling me from a thin sleep even as my girlfriend slept on beside me.

One night, unable to sleep, I slipped through the back door and walked to an empty lot at the end of the block, which was elevated a few feet from the houses all around—it was a mound of dirt really, with a pocket of dark at the center where the light from the street did not reach. I sat in this dark space, on ground that was still hot from the day, and tried to feel the smallness of my humanness in contrast to the vastness of the sky, hoping to channel its diminutive magic toward the enormity of my anguish over the election loss. This anguish felt personal, though I knew it should not—the loss would affect *me* in no material way. As I looked at the field of stars, which seemed barely to hang in the sky with all their immense gravity and mass and heat and light, I did not feel small. I felt weighed down, compressed around some sort of heavy core. It was difficult to stand up under the sky and walk back to the house.

I returned to Phoenix after three days, though I wasn't due back for another two. I felt brittle around the core, and I had no way of explaining this to my girlfriend or to the friends we'd made in Tucson, who were really the friends she had made in Tucson. I remember that at the time I was glad for the brittleness. I mistook it for a growing toughness, the kind that gets painted into portrayals of strong women, the kind I admired in the director, the kind I admired in you.

The director left Phoenix the next week. The citywide campaign (our plan to organize all of the industrial laundries there) had been postponed—we would not get the go-ahead to start fights at any new laundries until we had resolved the long legal battle at yours—and so she agreed to take on a national campaign at one of Sodexho's competitors, a chain called Angelica. The rest of the team went with her—Dario and Ana and Manuel—to prepare the ground in cities where Angelica had nonunion factories. I stayed on alone. Or, I stayed on with you. I still thought we could win. And you wanted to train to be an organizer, so you could lead fights at the other laundries, and I wanted to work with you.

The director made the argument to higher-ups in UNITE that we needed someone to staff the court hearing and someone to build lists of workers and clients at the other laundries, to map the industry across the state so we could make strategic decisions about which fights to take on when, so I stayed on in that role. She also secured enough of a budget to hire you as a VO, a volunteer organizer, as we called the position worker leaders filled during "union leave," a benefit we wrote into contracts at unionized worksites, which enables members to take leave in order to help out on organizing drives at nonunion worksites. You were not on leave—you were fired—but we had to follow the rules of that position in any case, which meant we could pay you only your hourly rate at the factory, $8.20 and time and a half for overtime.

When Paul and Gael were ready to start their investigation, you gave your affidavit first, so we could demystify the process for the other witnesses, some of whom were getting cold feet. And since you had been

involved in every part of the campaign—from our bajo el agua prepa-
rations on through the election—your statement was likely to be the
longest, the most detailed. It would help Paul establish a baseline understanding of what had happened over the previous few months.

We arrived in the morning and shivered in the air-conditioned lobby
while we waited for an elevator to take us up to the labor board. The
administrator rang Paul to meet you, and you disappeared with him
behind the heavy door into the maze of hallways and offices. Since I
would also give an affidavit and testify in the trial, I could not go with
you, so I waited in the lobby for the first couple of hours, flipping through
the stack of old magazines and dozing on one of the chairs under the
official portrait of then president George W. Bush. I got up a thousand
times to drink from the fountain by the bathrooms on the other side of
the building, which caused the administrator to look up from her work
each time I exited and returned to the lobby through its wide double
doors. Finally, she sighed at me and, with a chiding exasperation, said, *I
just ordered some sandwiches for them—it's going to be a while.*

I don't remember if I asked her for something to read or if she offered
first, but I ended up with a binder of "advice memos" on my lap, the reading of which is not an ideal way to learn about labor law, or a good way
to feel at all optimistic about the chances workers have inside its parameters. I skimmed through hundreds of pages of memos from the board's
general counsel in DC, written to regional attorneys like Paul, advis-
ing them to dismiss charges against bosses for a litany of reasons: "We
conclude that the Region should dismiss the charge, absent withdrawal,
because the union has failed to meet its burden of proof," or "We conclude that the charge should be dismissed, absent withdrawal, because it
cannot be known if the intention of the Employer was discriminatory or
had a business purpose," or, simply, "We conclude that the charge should
be dismissed." The conclusions were followed by two or three pages

of "facts," describing the case and the alleged charges, many of which closely paralleled the charges we were hoping this very regional office would bring against Sodexho. The facts were followed by a page or two of citations—other board cases that supported the national office's conclusion: "See Litton Systems," "See South Carolina Baptist Ministries," "See Overnight Transportation," "See Coastal Electric Cooperative," and so on.

When you came through the heavy office door in the late afternoon, I could see that the interview had not been easy. Your shoulders were hunched, your arms crossed over your chest, and your gaze landed on the floor just in front of your feet. I came over to you and put my hand on your arm. Paul said, *She had a headache but wanted to keep going.*

Todo bien, you said. (All good.)

Paul told us that you'd have to come back to read through your affidavit after Gael had translated it to Spanish.

Claro, you said, after I interpreted this to you. *Nomás dime cuando.* (Of course. Just tell me when.) And then you linked your arm through mine and said, *Hermana, hija, amiga—vámonos* (Sister, daughter, friend—let's go), using the whole list of titles we had started calling each other.

In the elevator down, I asked if you were okay. You were just cold, you said. It had taken forever, you said. The fluorescent lights had bothered your astigmatism. They kept asking you the same questions and then asking whether something should be written with one word or another word. They asked you exactly what El Mero Mero had said when you were fired. They asked you to repeat what he said and then repeat it again. And what did La Sandra say in the meeting where she showed the anti-union video? And who else was there? And where in the room did they sit? And did you discuss the meeting with them after it was over? And do you have their phone numbers, and would they be willing to give a statement? On and on it went, you said.

In the car, you closed your eyes until we had crossed the Salt River and were making our way through the south-side neighborhoods. The shotgun bungalows and small aging ranch homes sat in stark juxtaposition to the high-rises dominating the central part of the city, where we had just been, and which we could still see towering in the distance. I said something about how we would have to prepare the others, and you sat up and opened your eyes and outlined a training, as if you'd already spent the day thinking it through: *First, I'll tell them what the office looks like, where they will sit. I'll tell them to keep it simple, to answer only what the lawyers ask, and to use the same words each time they answer a question. We have to tell them that the lawyers are not anti-union, that they are only trying to make a record of what happened.*

When we got to your house, I parked on the street with the passenger-side wheels up on the curb, as people tend to position their vehicles in that part of Phoenix. Your husband's truck was in the driveway. A rarity. I had met him only once or twice at that point. I went inside with you—to get the letter the company had mailed to your house a month or so after you had been fired. Paul needed it, but we had forgotten to bring it that morning, and I was going to run it back to the board before it closed.

Your house was dark, and the air in the living room was thick and sweet. You shushed me before my eyes had adjusted enough to the unlit room to see him—Julio, your husband—asleep on the olive couch, boots on, mouth agape, cowboy hat overturned on the floor next to his dangling hand. His hips were twisted in an unlikely position, so that his body hung on the edge of the couch, as if he could spring to standing at any moment, though it was clear he was out cold. You crept into the kitchen and silently opened the drawer you had called your "oficina" when we first met, where you had kept the small list of your coworkers and their phone numbers, and you riffled through it for the letter. Then you crept back through the living room and whispered, *Let's not wake him up*, as you pushed the paper into my hand:

> We write about the status of your position with Commercial Linen Exchange. On May 1, 2003, you left your job during your shift and refused to return to work despite requests that you do so and despite warnings that the Company would hire permanent replacements.
>
> As you know, by the time you offered to return to work, the Company had hired another individual to fill your former position. We are writing to you to be certain that you understand your rights. As a replaced employee, you are entitled to be considered for preferential rehire into opportunities that the Company desires to fill. Please contact me to verify that you are interested in re-employment opportunities and to be certain that the Company will know how to contact you in the event that jobs become available.

I had told Paul about this letter when we filed the charges. To me, it seemed good evidence that they knew it was illegal to fire you and Santiago and the others and that they were going to try to cover it up by claiming that you had not actually been fired but permanently replaced. But in order for the Mackay rule on permanent replacements to apply in this case, the company would have to claim that you had been replaced by new workers in the twenty or so minutes of the work stoppage. In that amount of time, a supervisor in the factory office would have to have noticed that exactly four soil sorters had left their workstations, then contacted four people who were looking for employment, called them into the factory, had them complete job applications, interviewed them for the positions, and begun the legal processing of W-2 and I-9 forms, all while you and dozens of your coworkers stood chanting in that same office, and La Sandra, who was the person in charge of all the interviewing and hiring and legal processing of new employees, was calling 911. It was plainly absurd.

When I returned to the board that evening, Paul was waiting in the lobby to receive the letter as the office was shutting down around him. He raised his eyebrows in disbelief as he read the text. *It's going to be interesting to see them make this argument in front of a judge*, he said. (And though this is precisely the argument the company's lawyers made during the trial, Sodexo later maintained that it has "never hired a permanent replacement worker in North America.")

We made a plan with the other members of the comité for them to go— one per day—to give their affidavits, but when Gael became unavailable for a time, the board suddenly had no one to interpret, and Paul had to postpone the interviews. The setback unsettled you. You chewed your lip as we called through the list of people who had to reschedule. *No, nothing is wrong with the case*, you said to them, and *Yes, we are still taking the company to court*, and *Yes, the agents from the government will want to talk to you*, but *No, we don't know when.*

Since Paul and I could speak without an interpreter, I gave my affidavit next. I told him about my job—that I was an organizer on the staff of UNITE's international union office, that I had been promoted to lead organizer, and the difference was that I would start making some of the smaller campaign decisions on my own—what messages to include on leaflets and during house visits, which workers to talk to and in what order, so that we could continue building the union at Sodexho as we awaited whatever would come of the charges we had filed. Another difference is that I would now be responsible for training the VOs and organizers the union brought in to work on campaigns in Phoenix. He asked me if that meant I was "in charge of" you. I said yes, because it was true, though I had not considered it before he asked the question.

I told him about our campaign. I had brought along a binder of materials—every leaflet and petition, agendas and attendance sheets from every shift meeting and committee meeting and general meeting, copies of our wall charts and the signed union cards and the photo book we had assembled at Kinko's, and a CD with a copy of our radio ad. I brought a box with the banner we'd painted and a file full of house-call sheets—the forms we completed after every contact we made with each worker. I brought copies of the card-revocation letters we received after the company launched that phase of its anti-union campaign. I brought my notebooks, which the administrator copied, page by page, during the hours that I talked with Paul. They contained my perhaps overly copious notes from every team meeting and nightly debrief, as well as my notes from house calls, which included dates and times and general impressions of workers and my numerical ratings of their level of support for the union and their capacity or lack thereof for leadership and my thoughts about whether or not someone had been home when a door was not opened.

The notebooks also included some personal notes that should not have been written in the same place: details on how I was feeling (lonely, tired, "pissed off"), what I was thinking (that we would win, that we would not win, that we "need more Almas" in order to win, that we "need more leaders like Alma if what we want is a workers' union and not a union run by paid staff"), what worried me most (that we would lose and the union would pull out of Phoenix and leave you "screwed over without a job"). I left these pages in when I handed the notebooks over to Paul because I was afraid that tearing them out would make him, and then eventually the company-side lawyers and the judge, suspicious of what was missing and why.

During a break to eat sandwiches, Paul said that most of the union reps who came into the Phoenix board office were older men. *You know, burly union guys*, he said. He wanted to know how I ended up in this job. I was short in my reply, doing my best to mimic the way the director drew her lines to maintain the spaces she carved out for herself. I said something simple, like: *If workers don't organize in this country, we're all fucked.* And then I lobbed the question back at him in a half accusation— *How did you get your job, Paul?*—and he, looking up from his lunch and across his disheveled desk, said: *Look, my job is to protect the NLRA, the only law that gives workers any protection while they organize, and I took this job because companies are always trying to undermine it to make sure workers can't organize, and I think that means we're fucked, too.* He said this with great earnestness.

Santiago was next to give his affidavit, and while we knew that he was not afraid, we were both nervous that the slow pace and the repetition of the interview and translation would frustrate or confuse him. We went to his house early—the sun was rising when I picked you up from your house on the way to his.

The three of us sat knee to knee on his small couch, and you told him that it would be a long day, that we had brought bottles of water and pan dulce to get him through until lunch. You told him that it would seem as though the lawyers were against us even though they are not. *This is what you'll have to do*, you said. *Promise to tell the truth, tell them your name and where you live and how long you have worked at the company, then answer their questions about when you decided to join the union, about becoming part of the comité, about the house visits you did during the blitz, and about the work stoppage and being fired.* You reminded him to bring his permanent-replacement letter so Paul could make a copy. We practiced with him for a while, asking him a few questions over and over, so that we could laugh together about how strange it was before he encountered it alone with the lawyers. And then you said, *If you don't remember something, it's okay. Just tell them you don't know. Don't make anything up.*

We sat in the lobby together that day while we waited for Santiago. You hummed a song I'd never heard, and I asked you about it. It's a cántico, you said, a children's song, called "Los Pollitos Dicen," which you had sung with your little niece over the weekend while you babysat her. I hadn't known that you had a niece, or that she lived in Phoenix, and so I asked about your other relatives, how many of them there were, how many of them lived close by. You listed the names of your eight brothers and sisters in descending order, and I repeated them back to you. Only one lived in Phoenix, you said, and you had been missing the others for a long time. Two brothers had been given land outside of Juárez, where they still live, and where and your family moved when you were a teenager. That's where you met Julio, where Julio Martín was born. Five years later, you moved to Nogales and started the job at the maquila. Before then, you lived in a small town in Etchojoa, where your family had moved from the ejido because there was a school nearby—at the ejido you had been walking more than two miles each way. You finished primary school, you were proud to say, en la escuela Benito Juárez.

You didn't have your papers for the first four years in the States, which meant you couldn't go home at all, and since you had started work at the factory, it was hard to get enough days off to make the trip across the border to your brothers' land and back—you missed most of the weddings and births, funerals and quinceañeras. You first lived in California, where Julio had a work permit and was doing farm labor, and you lived in a community with the other farmworkers and their families. You and two other women cared for the children while the parents with permits worked. People moved around a lot, you said, looking for more work or better work; just when someone started to feel like family, they moved away. Then in 1993, *you* moved away. You came to Phoenix.

I told you the names of my brothers, too, and you repeated them back to me. I told you that in Ohio, the pack of kids, of which my brothers and I were a part, roamed around wild in a swamp, avoiding the adults and, therefore, chores until after dark. I told you that there were migrant families who came to the village every summer, who lived in shacks just across the field from the small group of houses where we and the other white families lived. We played with the kids from these migrant families in the woods and in the river and in the fort we built together under the bridge, but we could speak with only one of them, Fernando, who was my age and spoke English and interpreted between the two groups. The farmer kept promising to put plumbing and electricity into the shacks, but every summer Fernando and his family and the other families would show up and find the shacks still the same.

At the start of talking about my relationship to these kids, I had imagined it would forge a connection between your story and mine, something about farming communities and solidarity, some alignment between the two packs of kids, the ones you cared for and the one I was part of—but just as with the stories we had traded about dry land and floods while slumped into our seat on the school bus, the more I went on, the more I was talking about disparity rather than common ground. *Sí, Daisy, así es*, you said. You so rarely used my first name.

Santiago finished giving his statement just after lunch—his was shorter, corroborating your story more than breaking new ground. On our way into the parking garage, there was a mess of dead moths in the open-air stairwell, the dry husks of their bodies mixed in with some leaves and trash. I pointed to the pile and asked if you thought it meant we were going to win or lose—you had told me you thought the moths that were all around that spring were messengers. Santiago said: *What, the dust?* And you said: *No, las polillas.* And then you teased: *Daisy is turning into one.* And then, maybe because you could see that this announcement had surprised me, you said: *I think I might be turning into one, too.*

Over the next weeks, Cecilia and Isabel and Antonia and Beatriz and Analía and Pollo gave their affidavits. After talking through the process with each of them, we gave them a ride to the board office in the rental car—not because they could not find their way on their own, but because parking was expensive, and the idea of navigating that part of downtown and the board office, where English reigned, was "terribly nerve-racking," as Antonia put it.

Instead of waiting in the board lobby for many hours on each of these days, we arranged with Paul to call us when he thought the interviews were nearing their end, and we spent the days organizing instead. We leafleted the plant with information about the board process. We circled the city, talking with your coworkers who we knew had witnessed some of the company's illegal actions, asking them to give statements. We made new wall charts, to try to stay on top of the heavy turnover since the election loss and since El Mero Mero's pointed message to union supporters about the location of the factory door. We added the names of new employees, found and mapped their addresses, and assessed whether or not they might support the union. (Most did not, and we wondered what, if anything was being said about the union during La Sandra's hiring process.)

We had a hard time finding Raul, who had stopped calling us back and stopped rolling down his car window to take stacks of leaflets into the factory. This didn't worry us at first—he always seemed to be flying through the entrance, late to work. But we needed him to talk to Paul. He had stood next to you during the work stoppage, translating what you said. His English was good enough to testify about the words El Mero Mero used when he fired you, specifically whether or not the word *replaced* was involved. We went to his house every day for a week, but he did not answer the door. One night we waited for him on the outer border of the parking lot, the two of us huddled under a floodlight so he could see who was calling to him from across the pavement when second shift let out. He walked over to us but was standoffish, wouldn't make eye contact. He said he was looking for a new job—that the night manager hated him now, and the pressure was too much. But he agreed to talk to Paul the next day.

I don't remember how many affidavits it took, but at some point during that summer of 2003, the board decided that there was enough evidence to charge the company and go to trial: The National Labor Relations Board versus Sodexho's Commercial Linen Exchange. Paul called us into the office and beamed while he gave us the news. He had never investigated such an egregious case, he said, had never gotten to proceed on charges against such a rabid company. He told us that some of the affidavits he took documented legal violations that went beyond the charges we had already filed, so the board was pursuing additional charges—twenty-seven unfair labor practices in all, plus nine election objections, which were special charges regarding the company's conduct just during the hours of the election, and which would weigh on the judge's decision on ordering a new election. It was unclear when the trial would occur or even when a date would be assigned. *Sometime in the fall if we're lucky*, said Paul.

In July, you received a second letter from the company, which had no opening salutation but was signed by La Sandra.

As of today I have one 2nd shift soil sort position available. The starting times for this shift are 4:00 p.m. on Thursday, Friday and 2:00 p.m. Saturday and Sunday. The scheduled days off are Monday, Tuesday, and Wednesday. Your wage would be $7.45/hour (the starting rate plus an adjustment for previous experience).

Please be advised that this position has been offered to all people on priority hire status, and will be given to the first person that contacts me.

This was *not* a reinstatement to your position, which had been on first shift with weekend days off and almost a dollar more in pay, and it did not "make you whole," which is what the language of our charge against the company demanded, which would require them to pay you for the work you had been denied during the months you were fired. It was a shit offer. You said something like: *I can't go back like this. It will send a signal that the company can fire you and bring you back in any position whenever they want to, and I can't afford a pay cut, and they are doing this now because they think I am more dangerous working from outside the factory than I am stuck working their soil-sort belt.* All of which was true.

We got on a conference call with one of the union's in-house lawyers in New York, who said you had to take the job even though it was a bad deal. That if you didn't, the company would offer it as proof that your firing couldn't have been as intimidating to your coworkers as we had claimed, or you would have been in more of a hurry to get back. We knew the company was playing out the argument they were going to make in court about your firing—that you were a permanently replaced striker, and they were doing what was legally required of them by extending you priority for rehiring when a position became available. The lawyer instructed us to get off the phone with him—*This minute*, he said, which I remember because as I was translating it, I knew you would cringe at the demand—and call La Sandra to tell her you would take the job. If you didn't call right away, he said, the company would offer the job to someone else and then shrug their shoulders in court, arguing that they had complied with the law.

We were in our little union office, so you dialed the company from the phone there, and when the line was transferred to La Sandra, I could hear you saying to her in Spanish, *It's Alma. I got your letter.* You said it a few times and then covered the receiver with your palm and whispered, *She won't speak Spanish. I don't know what she is saying.*

Even in the moment, it seemed an otherworldly cruelty, to require you to call her and then not allow you to communicate with her. La Sandra is fluent in Spanish—it's part of why she had the job she did. I don't remember if you handed me the phone or if I took it from you, but I gritted out the words that you'd said, saying that you would take the job. And La Sandra, with a throat full of gloat, said, *May I please ask who is speaking?* And then when I told her: *Oh, hello, Daisy, and what gives you the authority to speak on behalf of this employee?* and *I need to hear from her that you are authorized to speak on her behalf before I am legally allowed to speak to you.*

I told La Sandra that we were recording the phone call (though we were not) and so there was now a record of your acceptance of the offer, and that if the company did not recognize that and allow you to take the position, they would face additional legal charges. Though I was not at all sure that the law worked in this way and have since learned that (a) it would not, and (b) it would have been illegal to record the call in the state of Arizona without the permission of all parties, which would have rendered any recording—if one had existed—inadmissible in court. La Sandra got quiet for a moment, and we realized that we were likely on speaker, that other people, lawyers even, were in the office with her. Finally, she said that she would be happy to recognize your acceptance of the job offer, but she would not be ready for you until the start of the next pay period, which was the following week.

We planned a grandiose entrance, with you wearing a union T-shirt and union stickers and a union hat. You told me you wanted to walk into the factory with un tambor—a drum—which I misunderstood as a *tambourine*. And when I picked you up at your house to drive you to the factory, I presented you with an actual tambourine, and you broke into a deep laugh that was both a real response to my mistake and also a welling up of nerves over having to go back to work as the face of the still-active tension in the factory.

Later, you admitted that you were sad, too. Sad because you were getting used to organizing full-time, and you were getting used to me and my strange music, which had branched off from 106.3 to CD mixes of Aterciopelados and Caifanes, and you were getting used to drinking bad gas-station coffee and bottles of vitamin water and navigating our circular patterns around the city with street maps and greeting each other in the mornings as you opened the passenger door of the car with "Polilllllla!" instead of "Mija" or "Amiga" or "Hermana" or "Compa," which were the many titles we'd had for each other before. Your laugh that day was on the verge of maniacal because it held all of this. I laughed, too, and howled and cried, and we gasped for air and calmed down for a few beats, and then you tapped the tambourine against your leg, and we started laughing all over again.

Though we had planned for you to arrive a few minutes early so that you could walk through the front office and hallway and down onto the production floor, all in your union garb, by the time we got to the factory, you were almost late for your shift. I drove the rental car into the parking lot, right up to the front door of the office, and though technically this was trespassing and we would not hear the end of it later during the trial,

I lay on the car horn as you got out and blasted it continuously as you walked up the stairs that led to the office. You shook the tambourine the whole way.

And then we were back on our old campaign schedule: working together every waking moment when you were not on the clock at the factory. I'd pick you up in the morning, and you would have dinner and your uniform packed in a big purse so as not to lose time going home between house calls and work. With this schedule, you and Julio rarely saw each other awake. I did not ask how this affected you. You did not seem to mind.

The union could not continue to pay you as a VO—it would have been illegal, not to mention fodder for division among the other union supporters—and it was hard that you were now back to sorting dirty hospital linen in a sweltering factory plus spending all your free time with me for less money than you had made before the campaign began. Of course this was the point the company was trying to make: look at Alma, worse off than before.

While you worked or slept, the other committee members took shifts riding along with me, too, visiting all of the union supporters who still worked in the factory to walk them through the charges the board had validated and was bringing against the company—and, as always, assessing and rating and mapping the remaining strength of the union.

Inside the factory, most of your new second-shift coworkers, even the ones we knew had voted for the union, even the ones who would still warmly answer the door for us at their homes, would not speak to you. A rumor was circulating that the company would fire anyone seen talking to you or sitting near you or going to the bathroom at the same time as you. The company had installed new security cameras in the lunchroom, where the holes in the ceiling had appeared during the election, but they had also installed cameras throughout the factory and in the front office and in the hallway, and outside the factory, too, pointing in various angles at the parking lot. So the supporters who still worked at the factory, who had not taken La Sandra's advice to quit, avoided you. The faction of coworkers who were vocally against the union were emboldened to make your life hell, hurling "groserías," as you called their taunts, refusing to use your name and calling you La Sindicalista (the Unionist) instead, making fun of your tattooed eyeliner and your shoes and your bangle bracelets and your posture and whatever you had brought for lunch. *I don't know what they are hoping for,* you would say. *Another giant seven-cent raise, maybe a whole ten cents this time? A few extra minutes to pee during break?* I remember you joking, *Felicidades. Ya son libres.* Congratulations. Now you're free.

Our work together was more targeted than the swath of home visits I was doing with the other committee members—we needed to fill gaps in the record Paul was assembling. We had Antonia's statement about her warning, but needed to talk to Reina, who was working near Antonia on that day, so she could testify about what Antonia told her when she got back to her iron machine. We had Pollo's statement about La Sandra saying that the factory would close if the workers unionized, but we needed Alberto, who was in the same meeting, to corroborate Pollo's story. According to Paul, the trial would hinge on this kind of corroborative testimony. But Reina and Alberto and others who had seen and heard the company break the law—Guillermo and Lupe and Santos—were afraid, and so the conversations we were having with them were longer and more difficult than any we'd had before. At first, the visits ended with *I don't know,* or *Let me think about it,* or *I still support the union, but my family needs this money,* to which you would say, *Your family deserves more money than we are making, and so does mine.*

We returned to these houses, some of them many times, talking through what it would be like to give a statement, what it would be like to testify, to speak through a courtroom interpreter, in front of lawyers and a judge and the bosses, who they would have to see and talk to and work under the very next day after testifying. We practiced "Raise your right hand," we practiced "Say and spell your name," and we practiced speaking into a microphone and waiting for the interpreter to finish a sentence before continuing on. I told them where I would be in the courtroom: *Right there, to your left,* I said. *You don't have to look at the company people. Just look at me if you are afraid.* Eventually, they agreed to testify. Every one of them. Thirty-two workers gave statements to Paul and were prepared to testify, which was 15 percent of the workforce at the factory, the largest percentage Paul or anyone at the labor board had ever seen, by many multiples.

That summer, we learned where each of these people was born, and what brought them to the States, and how they arrived in Arizona, and why. We learned who liked to cook, and who liked to drink, and who liked to dance. We learned who went to church with whom, and who watched which TV shows, and where everyone was getting their bulk beans and oranges and on-sale jeans and sandals. We sometimes couriered between houses—tomatoes from Antonia's garden to Reina's house, clothes that Cecilia had mended to Santiago. We spent time with husbands and wives and boyfriends and parents and aunts and uncles and cousins.

Reina's youngest son always wanted to wear your bracelets and would run into the backyard to avoid having to return them to you when it was time for us to leave. Lupe's daughter liked to sit on my lap while she went in to stir whatever was on the stove for dinner. Analía's son let me help him with his third-grade homework, which was in English, which he was just beginning to speak. We made stops that were natural extensions of these relationships, but which, at the time, seemed unrelated to the union fight: We went to a neighbor's house to translate notes that had come home with kids from school. We went to a grandparent's house to call immigration lawyers. We went to a cousin's house to help complete unemployment forms or file for workers' compensation for an injury at another workplace in a different industry.

One evening, we ate dinner at Antonia's house with her family and then listened to music and danced in the living room. You stood next to me, moving slowly and off-rhythm in order to demonstrate a proper salsa technique. I shuffled gracelessly and only sometimes in the right pattern, and you and Antonia alternated between clapping for me and shaking your heads. I remember that Antonia closed her eyes for a while and moved in fluid, floating circles through the space between us.

I drove you home late that night, and Julio's truck was parked half in the driveway, half in the yard, and I knew right away from the way you shifted in your seat that something was wrong. You reached over and turned up the volume on the song that was playing, loud enough that we couldn't talk. We sat together until it had just about ended, and then you got out without saying anything and closed the car door and went into the house. The next day, I waited for you to bring up what had happened, but you did not. I did not ask about it. I did not want to cross what I was reading as a boundary you were wordlessly inscribing. I told myself this was out of respect. It would be a violation, I thought, of our friendship, our comradeship, to impose the nature of our roles in the union (I was paid to organize you, after all, a job predicated on coercion, even if well-intentioned) onto your private life.

One night, Beatriz came with us to talk to Alberto, and afterward we sat at her house drinking lemonade while she sewed a dress for her daughter and tried to teach me how to use the machine. The jeans I was wearing were rolled at the cuffs, too long on my short legs, as pants tend to be. She had me take them off, and I sat wrapped in a bedsheet as she showed me how to make a hem. You had her baby grandson draped over your forearm, with his head at the crook of your elbow, and you bounced around the room telling the story of crossing the border in Tijuana to join Julio, who had already crossed and was working fields in California. Border Patrol caught you and Julio Martín, who was still a small child, and drove you back across the border. The two of you crossed again a few days later and took a bus to Fresno. Beatriz mentioned that she hadn't met Julio yet, and you said, *He mostly sleeps when he's not at work,* which was the first time I heard you say something that I knew was not the truth.

At the time, I was still going to the union office each night, filling my campaign notebooks with summaries of the conversations we had with your coworkers, tallying the number of visits we had completed and the number we'd attempted but did not complete, noting whether or not we had gone to the factory and with whom we spoke, describing the leaflets we distributed and the dates on which we distributed them, and how many workers accepted them and which workers refused them. I updated the wall charts, tried to keep the lists clean. There were no other organizers with whom to debrief any of this information, but this was the system I had learned, and I followed it every day in the belief that this detailed record of information would help us win. And besides, we were talking to a lot of people. What they told us about their lives was important. And I didn't want to forget.

But I had long since stopped taking notes on the things you said. We were together so constantly, and I did not feel that I was organizing you any longer. I did not consider a future in which I would not be able to recall something about you.

That summer, we heard a lot about violent boyfriends and husbands. We sat with a new coworker, who told us through split and swollen lips that domestic violence shelters called Immigration on people without papers, so she had nowhere to go. We had heard from another worker about a church that would sometimes let undocumented women stay for a night or two, but she did not want to go. You put together a list of the women who had this kind of trouble plus some of the members of our organizing committee—the ones who could drive and the ones who lived near the houses with the violent men. We made copies of the list, and you passed them around during our visits, telling people to call through the list— day or night—if they were afraid. One night, Analía did call, and three women showed up at her house with baseball bats. You called me that night, and I rushed from the motel to pick you up at your house, but by the time we arrived at Analía's, her boyfriend was gone.

I have read that the relative newness of the word *solidarity* is demonstrated by the fact that it has yet to sprout adjectival or adverbial wings. Things are not yet solidaire or solidatious. We do not yet do things solidariously. But on the way back to your house that night, you were wired, your eyes burnished with the adrenaline of the missed confrontation. You said: *The company can do what they want with their recognition. We already have our union.*

By the end of that September, the miller moths had mostly died off, but one night we stood at Raúl's door, certain someone was in the apartment, though no one responded to our knocking. He had quit the laundry after giving his affidavit, as he'd said he would, but now that we were preparing for the hearing, we needed to talk to him again, needed him to go again to the labor board to prepare with Paul for his testimony. You pointed to a small, drab moth that clung to the stucco wall near the doorframe. I reached out to nudge it, worried that if someone were to come through the door, it would be smashed. I must have startled it—it fluttered frantically, flashing crimson at us from under the brown and gray.

In the car, you asked if I was still dreaming about moths, and I said yes, and you asked what the dream was like. I told you: *There are so many of them they cover my body. They move their* . . . And I could not remember the word for *wings*, so I flapped my hands at the sides of my body, and you said, *Las alas.*

We spent most of August and September preparing for the trial. We drove the city in an orbit between the houses of your coworkers who were set to be witnesses, the labor board office, the union office, and your house. Everyone had to practice their testimony with Paul, so that he could be sure he had all of the pieces of the story he needed to tell in court, and so that he could determine the order in which to call each person to the stand to ensure the most coherent narrative. During these practice sessions, we sat in comically oversize office chairs in a conference room down the hall from Paul's office, arranging into three-ring binders photocopies of the many hundreds of documents that would be entered into evidence.

In October, the trial began. Its opening consisted of two days of arguments about the trial schedule and how many people the company could have in the courtroom from the not one but two law firms they had hired to defend them (four lawyers, administrative law judge Lana Parke decided) and how many representatives they could have from the management of the factory (two, but La Sandra was the only one who stayed for the duration) and how many tables (one) and chairs (six) they would be allowed use and whether or not the interns from the law firms who carted around the boxes of evidence with their industrial hand trucks would be allowed to sit in the back of the courtroom to observe the trial (they were) and whether or not workers who would not be called to testify by either side would be allowed to sit in the back of the courtroom to observe the trial (they were not).

The courtroom was windowless, a secure space at the center of the NLRB offices with two key-access doors, one of which opened to the lobby and the other of which opened to the series of hallways that led to the board agents' offices. It was a conference room, really, with furniture configured in such a way that it resembled a courtroom. It was cold and fluorescent. I shivered through the first afternoon as the lawyers bickered and stipulated their way through the basic facts of the case: the address of the factory, that it is a laundry factory, that it is specifically a healthcare laundry factory, that it is owned by a company that is in fact a company under the standard legal definition of *company*, that the workers worked for the company at the company's address, and so on.

We spent over an hour debating the relevance of the company's proposed stipulation that the factory is in "a rough part of town," a phrase the company wanted to enter into the record. We (by which I mean Paul and I, since, as a witness, you were not allowed into the courtroom) concluded that the company wanted this language in order to justify calling the police those many times as a reasonable response to seeing people who didn't work in the factory in the parking lot in the middle of the night—so they could argue that it wasn't anti-union harassment. We spent another hour amending the wording of certain documents because La Sandra, who sat, politely smiling, just fifteen feet to my left, had gotten married over the summer, and so the company's lawyers argued that we had identified her incorrectly in some places, since her last name had legally changed.

The judge liked a cold courtroom, she said, it keeps everyone awake. She could see me shivering and advised that I bring a warm sweater.

On the second day, we had to provide the company with a list of the witnesses we planned to call, which was difficult to compile because a rumor was going around that the company had hired private investigators to follow anyone who was thinking of testifying against them and that the investigators were reporting to immigration authorities. In preparation, we had made rounds of visits to confirm and reconfirm our witnesses, and we parked the rental car several streets away from their houses and apartments to allay their fears that the investigators were following us. *Who cares if they are following us?* you would say. *It's our right to tell the judge what they did. And you don't have to look at anyone in the courtroom but Daisy. And I will be right there in the lobby waiting for you when your turn is over.* Almost all of the people who had given affidavits ended up testifying.

By the end of the first week, our table in the courtroom was crowded. Paul sat to my left, and because the trial was to be the biggest in terms of number of witnesses and amount of evidence, and likely the longest, in the regional office's history, another lawyer had been tapped to assist Paul. This other lawyer, Bill Mabry, sat to my right. The director had returned to help with the start of the trial, but after testifying for a full day in order to frame our case with UNITE's organizing methodology and detail about the early phases of the campaign, she left again, and so the fourth chair was stacked high with files of evidence, and I became the union's representative during the trial. I helped Bill label and organize evidence and fed it to Paul while he questioned witnesses. I took notes on witness testimony and wrote lists of questions, follow-up questions, and questions for cross-examination, and edited lists of questions Paul was planning to ask future witnesses based on testimony entered into the record. I had a stack of pink and orange sticky notes that I was to use if something urgent came to mind during Paul's interrogations. I passed notes to him saying things like: *Ask if Sandra said she would be corrida (run off) instead of despedida (fired)—the word the interpreter is using is not the word Sandra used, that's why she's saying no.*

I took the stand for a day and a half, most of which was a tedious cross-examination in which the company lawyer tried to get me to say either that I had told workers the union "would make them rich," or that

if they signed a union card they would "get free health insurance," or that
once the union had won "any worker who had not signed a card would be
fired." I had not said these things, so my responses were short and repetitive, and after a while they combined with Paul's repeated objection of
"Asked and answered" to create a strange rhythm.

You were next to testify. You were nervous but trying hard not to
appear nervous. You raised your hand to promise to tell the truth, but
you were looking at me while you did it, and the judge made you do it
again after instructing you to turn in your seat to look at her. You stated
and spelled your name, and the court recorder instructed you not to lean
in to the microphone when you spoke, that it would muddle the recording he was making. He told you this in English, and the interpreter, who
sat next to him and in front of you, interpreted it, but in doing so some
problem with her microphone was discovered and needed to be fixed,
and you sat silently in the witness chair and sipped water from a foam
cup and tried not to look over at La Sandra, who was sitting with the
company's army of lawyers just twenty feet away, and your body closed
in on itself against the cold of the room.

You wore your sunglasses—the overhead fluorescents were hard on
your eyes. The company lawyer objected to the sunglasses, but after a
stilted interpreted discussion with the judge about your astigmatism,
she allowed you to keep them on. You had a screaming headache, you
told me in the bathroom during the first break hours later. We were not
allowed to speak to each other while you were under oath, but I followed
you there and whisper-asked how you were doing from the stall next
door after checking under the partition for other people's feet. You still
had given almost no testimony, because after the fixing of the microphone and its cords and dealing with the sunglasses, the company lawyers kept raising objections about a hand-drawn map of the factory that
you had made months before, and whether or not it should be admitted

into evidence, and how it should be labeled if it was indeed to be entered into evidence. Paul argued against their objections, they objected again, and on and on.

The interpreter was ordered not to interpret any of the objections or arguments in Spanish and only to interpret questions directed to you, so for most of the several hours, you looked bored and bewildered. If you looked at me too often, the company lawyers objected that we were in some way communicating, so you did not look at me (this despite that I had told you and other witnesses to look at me if you were afraid). You sipped water from the foam cup. You rubbed your temples. You asked for a sweater. You fidgeted. You closed your eyes.

Paul planned to ask each worker who took the stand why they had signed their union card. This was to combat two arguments that the company had laid out in its opening: (1) that some workers who had purportedly signed cards had not actually signed cards, that instead some of the signatures had been faked, and (2) that the workers who had signed had been duped, that they had signed cards not knowing what a union was and that they were later surprised and dismayed to find out what they had joined after the company—in its great benevolence—revealed the truth to them. After the bathroom break, Paul asked you: "Did you sign a union card, and if so, why did you sign it?" And you said that, yes, you signed the card, and you did it because you do not think people should have to risk their lives to make a living, that you wanted to fight for—*luchar* is the word you used—safer working conditions and better pay.

The interpreter knew that *luchar* is the word for "to struggle" or the word for "to fight for," but she allowed for the slippages between the two languages to construct a kind of aggression that did not exist in what you were saying. "I wanted to fight," she kept saying in English, and "I wanted to fight the company," and "I wanted to fight with my coworkers." The judge turned toward you, looked at you over the rims of her glasses, and studied your face. I passed sticky notes to Paul: *She is mischaracterizing the word Alma is using!* And Paul whispered that he could not object to the court's official interpreter.

After an hour of this, Paul got to the line of questions about the day of the work stoppage. He asked you why you had participated in the march to the office, and you responded, "Yo quería luchar por mejoras en la compañía," and the interpreter said: "She wanted to fight. She wanted to fight the company," which was such a bald misinterpretation that I yelled out into the courtroom, "That is *not* what she said." And the judge, angry at the disruption, instructed me to leave, despite the fact that I was the union's only representative in the courtroom. I tried to explain to you what was happening as I got up and gathered my things, but the head company lawyer objected to my speaking to you, and the judge sustained his objection, and you started chanting into the witness microphone: "Union, union, union" in your best American English accent. You were still chanting as the courtroom door closed behind me. After that, the judge adjourned the trial for the rest of day, and we found each other in the parking lot and went to get milkshakes at Burger King.

You were allowed to finish your testimony when the trial resumed in the morning, and I was allowed to return to the table to sit between Paul and Bill as we continued to present our case. On the nights you were not at work, you spent hours with me in a small conference room down the hall from the courtroom, preparing evidence and questions for the next day. Some nights, we drove down the street to Hamburger Mary's, a gay diner, where I would drink beer and eat a veggie burger and you would eat a version of a quesadilla, the gargantuan size of which made you laugh each time it arrived at the table. My girlfriend in Tucson admitted at some point during the haze of the trial that she had started sleeping with the woman she worked with, and on one of these nights, after I had finished a second beer, I told you about this, that I was sad, and you insisted we stay at Hamburger Mary's until late that night in the hope we would find someone new for me to date, "someone nicer," you said.

That night, you told me you thought the moth dream meant that I was afraid we were going to lose. You said this matter-of-factly, but you were watching me, too, to see how I would react. And I said that, yes, I was afraid we were going to lose. And you told me you were afraid, too.

In fact, I was growing more afraid by the day, because on the nights you were working, I stayed in the labor board conference room until very late, researching the cases I had scrawled into my notebook during the day, the names of which the company lawyers and Paul invoked and argued over as precedent to the facts in the trial. In this way, I learned what Paul meant when he said that the right to organize in this country had been "eroded," or that it had suffered a "death by a thousand cuts." I read about the 1938 Mackay Radio Supreme Court decision, which gave companies the right to hire permanent replacements. I read about the 1953 Livingston Shirt Corporation decision, which set a precedent for companies to hold anti-union captive-audience meetings. I read about the 1964 Fibreboard decision, which set a legal precedent for companies to threaten factory closure. I read about the 2002 Hoffman Plastic SCOTUS decision, which ruled that, while undocumented workers are afforded some protection under the NLRA, employers that fire undocumented workers during organizing campaigns, even if it was clear that they were firing them for being union leaders, could not be compelled to give them their jobs back.

So being afraid that we were going to lose was no surprise. And there was no relief in saying it out loud, except that there was someone to whom to say it. You tipped your chin up slowly and nodded once, a gesture I had seen many times during house visits when the person we were talking with shared a story or a detail more intimate than what you had expected. An acknowledgment that a rare and precious thing had been released, and that you were watching it travel the distance between the people who were present and then fill the space of the room or yard or wherever we were.

Before resting our case, we had to call to the stand every worker who had given affidavits in order to enter into the record every detail of every legal violation with which the company had been charged, and then to corroborate those details with secondary testimony. Santiago testified. And then Cecilia and Antonia and Analía and Lupe and Isabel and Reina and Beatriz, and over a dozen others of your coworkers.

Though he had quit the factory and stopped responding to us, Raúl testified as well. We had subpoenaed all of the witnesses, so they would have a record of their need to be excused from work in the factory, but Raúl didn't respond to his at first, and Paul had to follow up by phone and impress the seriousness of not showing up when he was called. So he did show up, but he waited outside the building under a tree for his turn, instead of sitting in the union-side waiting room. Under cross-examination, the company lawyer discredited his testimony by forcing him to reveal that he had offered to sell a list of union supporters to El Mero Mero and to other laundry companies in Phoenix.

Every one of the organizers who had taken part in the blitz had to be flown back to Phoenix from wherever in the world they were, in order to testify about the card-signing process and about which workers had signed cards with them and where and when they had signed. This was the process we had to undergo to enter the cards into evidence, to prove that a majority of workers had wanted to unionize before the company launched its attacks and successfully flipped fifteen workers to an anti-union vote.

On the night the organizers arrived, I walked into the motel bar as some of them were placing bets, but when I asked what they were betting on (this was a hearing, not an election), no one wanted to say. Finally, Dario told me they were betting on how long it would be before I was promoted to organizing coordinator, a step above lead organizer and a position that would move me out of the staff union bargaining unit and into management. *You're white, and you went to college*, he said. *That's just how it works.* The adamance of my response surprised even me. I would never move to management, I said. I wanted to stay close to the fight, on the ground, with the workers, I said. *We'll see*, he said gently. No one meant any offense.

The next day, the company began its defense. La Sandra and El Mero Mero testified, as well as most of the department leads and some of the workers who were against the union, whom we had started calling Las Viejas (the Old Ladies), a disparaging title we used in part to make light of the outsize influence they held in the factory. They testified that the company had made no anti-union threats, that the company did not surveil them, that the company did not interrogate them, that Cecilia had indeed pushed La Sandra during the work stoppage, and that they had signed union cards during the blitz because organizers had lied to them.

One of them, Luz, testified that she had signed her union card only because I had told her she would lose her job if she did not sign it, and the company lawyer asked her if the person who threatened her in this way was in the courtroom, and she said yes. He asked her if she would point to the person who said this to her, and she pointed to me, though she turned her head down and away as she did it. This exchange was not as dramatic as it may sound, to the possible disappointment of the lawyer. When she finished testifying, she had to leave the witness stand by passing through the narrow space between the interpreter's station and the table where Paul and I were sitting, which she did in a hurried scramble, as if she were afraid that I would lunge at her. This was hard to see. I did not want her to be afraid of me; it ran counter to my intention, and it troubled my idea of the position I was inhabiting, which was to be on the side of you and your coworkers—no matter which way they had voted— against the company, which had violated their rights, simply because it wanted to be able to keep paying shit wages for dangerous work. And so, without thinking, I said out loud, *Está bien, Luz.*

When I told you that evening what had happened, you rolled your eyes. *She chose to lie*, you snapped.

Your coworker Julia, who hid from us after signing her card and then opened her door and could only say *I'm sorry, I'm sorry*, was subpoenaed to testify by the company. She was so frightened that she would not or could not raise her head enough to look at anyone or to make her voice heard by the court interpreter. The lawyer for the company—a large man with a loud bellow of a voice—got very close to her and demanded that she look at him. When she did not, he objected repeatedly to the judge, who, in turn, tried to force Julia to look at him. Instead, Julia shook in her seat until the judge dismissed her. The government lawyers had to help her walk from the witness booth to the door.

The most important legal violation with which the NLRB had charged the company was firing you and Santiago and your two soil-sort coworkers, Isabel and Maria. This was the charge that, if proven, was most likely to cause the judge to order a second union election. The heart of the company's defense was its claim that you had not actually been fired but permanently replaced. El Mero Mero and La Sandra both testified that the moment you left your workstations, a former worker happened to call the factory, and that she also happened to have, right there in her living room, three friends who were looking for work. La Sandra told them to come right down to the plant, that it appeared several soil-sort positions had just become available. They testified that the three people showed up, and then interviewed for and accepted the positions, all while the work stoppage raged on.

During this testimony, the judge kept stopping the lawyers to ask La Sandra and El Mero Mero to reiterate what they were saying. More than once, she asked them, "Are you sure?" and, "Is this your testimony?" And once, to El Mero Mero: "I will remind you that you are under oath."

When the trial adjourned after eighteen days spread out over October and November of 2003, and La Sandra and the company lawyers and their team had left the courtroom, you came in from the witness waiting room, where you had spent many days, because there was some notion that you might have to take the stand again to clarify the record after this crazy testimony about your firing. We stood together, leaning exhausted against our table, which was still piled high with evidence. Paul thanked us for our hard work, and we thanked him for his hard work. We high-fived each other. I told him that I could not imagine what shape the trial might have taken if we had been appointed to any of the other lawyers in the office, of whom, I had gleaned during the weeks of the trial, only a few were at all pro-union and none as staunchly as Paul. And he said something about feeling inspired by us, that there were still people out there organizing in the way that we were, the sincere sentiment of which inflected his voice as he said it. We had spent hundreds of hours together that summer and fall, preparing for the trial, putting on our case, and we would likely not see him again for a long time.

There was something unsettling, too, in knowing that the campaign was no longer in our hands, that there was no longer a single thing you or any of your coworkers or I or any organizer could do to win recognition for the union in your factory. We could only wait for a ruling. Paul told us there was no way to know how long the judge would take to make her decision, but it would be many months, and maybe as long as a year.

8: Fires

NINETY-TWO YEARS BEFORE the final adjournment of our labor board trial in Phoenix, People of the State of New York v. Isaac Harris and Max Blanck (the two owners of the Triangle Waist Company) got underway. It had been eight months since the fire. The city had still not quieted in its marching and mourning. Outside the courthouse, Clara Lemlich stood among a group of women—some factory workers, some mothers and sisters and friends of the dead—chanting, "Murderers, murderers, give us back our children."

Inside the courthouse, Harris and Blanck were not being tried for murdering 146 of the 500 or so humans who were working in their factory at the time of the fire, because that is not how the law works. They were being tried for first- and second-degree manslaughter—or, the crime of killing a human without malice—for the death of one single human: Margaret Schwartz, who was twenty-four when she burned alive on the ninth floor of the building that housed the Triangle company in Greenwich Village. They were being tried for the manslaughter of Margaret Schwartz because the district attorney's office figured that she—her body, her death and its circumstances—represented the best chance of gaining a conviction against Harris and Blanck, a conviction that would have to stand in as justice for the other 145 humans—122 women and girls and 23 men—who had died in the fire.

Margaret Schwartz represented the best chance for conviction because (1) unlike some of the other victims of the fire, her body had been identified, and (2) unlike most of the victims, her body was autopsied, and the doctor who conducted the autopsy would state, in the shortest testimony of all 155 witnesses in the trial, that she died of "asphyxia by smoke" and that her body "was almost completely charred," and so it would be hard for the company not to concede that she had in fact died in the fire, and (3) her body was found among a pile of bodies in front of an exit door that should not have been locked but was, in fact, locked, and (4) Isaac Harris and Max Blanck knew that the door was locked, had, in fact, locked the door on purpose (thus establishing the grounds for the manslaughter charge), because they suspected that the workers were eating into their profits by stealing bits of cloth and ribbon and thread, and so they made the workers leave through another door, where their dresses were patted down and where they turned out the contents of their pockets for a security guard, and (5) a survivor of the fire, Kate Alterman, was going to testify that she was standing at the locked exit door with Margaret Schwartz, that she "pulled the handle in and out, all ways," but could not open it, and that Margaret "got hold of the handle, and then she tried," and then "a big smoke came" and Kate couldn't see, but she called to Margaret "and she didn't reply," and then she "noticed the trail of her dress and the ends of her hair begin to burn."

In his opening statement, Assistant District Attorney Charles Bostwick, who was the lead prosecutor at the trial, asks the jury to imagine the courtroom as the factory. He wants them to imagine it so much that he nearly paints the not-yet-burned-out walls of the factory onto the insides of the courtroom. "I think I should stop here for a moment and try and fix in our minds what are the different parts of the building, so that you can have, beside the mere words 'Greene Street' and

'Washington Place' some definite and fixed notion as to the location and so that we may understand each other," he says. "I am going to assume that that portion of the wall"—he gestures toward the east wall of the courtroom—"is Washington Place; I am going to ask you to assume for the moment that that portion of the wall"—he indicates the north wall of the courtroom—"is Greene Street. There were windows on the Washington Place side, and there were windows on the Greene Street side." He then draws the jury's attention to the northeast corner of the room. "That is the corner of Washington Place and Greene Street." In this establishment of the scene, he asks the jurors to create a room inside of a room, to live, for the many long hours the trial would span, inside the factory. He was asking them to let their bodies inhabit the space where other bodies had burned.

He goes on in this way for several minutes, constructing the factory as he walks around the courtroom, gesturing to empty space: here were the cutting tables, and here were the troughs in the tables, where too much scrap material had accumulated, and here were the stairs, and here were the elevators, and the windows, and the bathrooms, and the dressing rooms, and so on.

Toward the end of this spatial exercise, still walking around and pointing to the details of the now-conjured factory, Bostwick transposes his address into the second person: "So, you see, in that corner"—he indicates the southeast corner of the courtroom—"if you took the passenger elevators of the stairway, you would find yourself in Washington Place. If you went down the elevators here"—he gestures to the northwest corner of the courtroom—"or went down the Greene Street stairway, you would go out into Greene Street."

And then he recounts how the factory begins to burn: "At the cry of 'Fire,' those on the ninth floor ran in every direction. Some ran to the Greene Street door, some got out the Greene Street door and went to the street, some went to the roof, some got on the freight elevators. It was natural for them to go to the Greene Street door, because I will show you that that was the everyday and only method of exit at night. So that many rushed to the Greene Street entrance, knowing that that was the usual place of exit. Some ran to the fire escape on the north side of the building, others ran to the Washington Place elevator, which made two or three trips, and some escaped that way. Others ran to the Washington Place door. One of these was Margaret Schwartz, now dead. And it is for her death that these defendants are now on trial." And then Bostwick gets to the core of the situation: "Gentlemen of the jury, that door was locked. Those who ran to that door cried out 'That door is locked. My God, we are lost.' They were lost. That locked door barred their escape."

His first witnesses are engineers, who he asks to describe the factory to the jury in still more detail. How many inches tall were the tables, and how many inches apart were the tables, and how far were they from the walls, and what did the doors look like, and the stairwells, and how many inches across were the stairwell landings, and how high were the windowsills, and in which direction did the doors open? And on and on. With each new witness, he reviews his projection of the factory onto the courtroom—"That there is Washington place," and "the Green Street door is here," retracing the ghostly setting nearly one hundred times during the three-week course of the trial.

Bostwick calls firefighters and police officers who had responded to the fire. They testify to receiving the first alarm of fire at 4:46 p.m. and the second alarm of fire at 4:48 and the third at 4:55 and the fourth at 5:10. They testify about the intricacies of the fire alarm system. They give testimony about seeing fire and are cross-examined by the company's lawyers about whether or not they had actually seen fire, and some of the firefighters recanted their testimony to say that they had only seen smoke.

They testify about the direction the smoke was traveling: up. They are asked to theorize about why smoke tends to travel upward: they do not know. They testify that the overhang between the eighth and ninth floors was "full of people," and the term *overhang* is misheard and then misunderstood and then finally clarified as the cornice of the building outside and below the windows on the ninth floor. It was nine stories above the street. It was "possibly two feet six inches wide, or thereabouts." It was full of people.

The firefighters testify to driving water from a hose at 125 pounds of pressure against the side of the building a few feet below the cornice in order to cool it enough to make it possible for the people who filled it to continue being alive there, clinging to the side of the building, to prevent them from jumping. But a man did jump. A firefighter testifies to seeing him jump, saying: "When he jumped, it appeared to encourage everybody else." He testifies that a life net was moved onto the sidewalk below the jumping people, and that with it, the firefighters, "caught one girl" and "she was tipped out onto the sidewalk," and "that girl was alive."

He insists on this because there is some back-and-forth in the courtroom about whether the life net had worked at all, if it was able to "resist even a single individual," implying that perhaps the presence of the net had encouraged the people on the cornice to jump. "Wasn't it found," Bostwick says to the firefighter, "I don't know whether you know this or not—wasn't it found that by reason of the great distance from the floor—that is, the street level, to the height from which these individuals jumped—that the weight increases in such tremendous ratio while they are going through the air, that the net could not resist even a single individual?"

But that firefighter says: "I lifted her up when they tipped it, and I said, 'Now go right across the street,'" and "She walked ten feet, but it was like an automatic motion . . . probably six feet and dropped," and "I took it for granted that that net would fill the service that it was intended to fill," and "if they had come one at a time, we could have helped," but "when they came entwined with one another, it was impossible."

The firefighters testify that the fire spread "with great violence," and the fire spread "with great speed," and the fire spread "almost with lightning rapidity." One firefighter states that when they fought their way up the stairs inside the building and when they arrived on the eighth floor, it was "in entire possession of the fire," which causes some confusion about whether he means that the fire had consumed the floor or whether they were saying that the fire had not spread beyond that floor. It was the former, which is settled when another firefighter clarifies the phrase by confirming that "the whole floor was one conflagration."

At the end of the first week, Bostwick calls a rag trader to the stand, a man who bought scrap fabric from the factory for papermaking. He testifies that he was the only rag trader to do business with the Triangle factory, meaning he was the only person to collect the fabric scraps there, and that in between his collections, the scrap piles grew. He testifies that his last collection had been on January 15, and that on that day, he pulled 2,252 pounds of fabric from the scrap gutters under the cutting tables, mostly from the eighth floor. He testifies that it had been sixty-nine days between the last collection and March 25, when the fire started in one of these scrap gutters. He estimates that the scraps in the gutters at the time of the fire weighed one ton or one ton and a quarter. Similar scraps are introduced into evidence, so that Bostwick can later, during his concluding argument, refer back to them as a tinderbox. Court adjourns for the weekend.

On Monday, Bostwick begins calling workers to the stand. Many of them speak only Yiddish or Italian or spoke mainly Yiddish or Italian or preferred to speak in Yiddish or Italian in the courtroom and did so with the help of the court's official interpreters. It is impossible to know from the court transcript what happened in the space of this interpretation, but long sections of this testimony are difficult to follow. The workers appear at times to be confused by the court's instructions on how to answer questions. They are told many times to respond only to what is asked. They are told to respond only with what they have seen and not what may have happened. They are told to describe only what happened and not their idea of what happened. Sometimes they sit in silence and do not respond at all, as if, whatever came through in translation did not take the form of a question. They are told to respond. They are told to respond again. *No answer* appears as an answer to a question forty-two times in the transcript. They are told to make marks on diagrams of the factory. When they say that they do not know where to make a mark, they are told again to make a mark on the diagram. They make marks on diagrams.

Adding to the muddle of translation is the fact that the lawyers on both sides, as well as the judge, seem to have little knowledge of the kind of work that went on in the factory, what the workers were doing with their hands and bodies for all those many hours each week, and so the questions they ask at times have little foundation in the reality of the factory or what happened there when it caught fire.

The judge intervenes during Charles Bostwick's questioning of worker Isidore Abramowitz to clarify the size and layout of the cutting department and the witness's proximity to the first flames:

Q. What was the first thing you did when you saw the fire?
A. *I spilled a pail of water on it.*
Q. And where did you find the pail?
A. *Right near the table there was a small partition with three pails of water on the top.*

Q. Those pails stood on the partition?

A. *Yes, sir.*

Q. Did they stand on a shelf?

A. *On a shelf.*

Q. There was a shelf?

A. *Yes, sir.*

Q. And was that shelf fastened to the partition that was opposite the freight elevators?

A. *No, sir; it was fastened to the wall.*

Q. There was a shelf fastened to the wall; what wall, Greene street wall?

A. *Yes, sir.*

Q. And on that shelf were how many pails?

A. *Three pails.*

Q. Did you get to the place where there was a pail?

A. *I stood right there; the shelf and the pails was near the table.*

Q. How far did you have to go from where you were at the moment when you first noticed the fire to the place where the pail was?

A. *I didn't have to go any place, it was right there. . . .*

Q. You just turned around, is that all?

A. *That's all.*

Q. From where you were standing could you reach a pail?

A. *Yes, sir.*

Q. Did you reach a pail?

A. *Yes, sir.*

Q. When you reached it was there anything in it?

A. *Yes.*

Q. What was in it?

A. *I suppose water.*

Many of the workers speak quietly on the stand. They are told to speak up. The judge says, "Would you kindly talk a little louder," and, "talk out loud," and "talk louder now," and, "If you will only answer a little louder, you will make it lots easier for everybody," and "I want you to answer in a tone that is loud enough for the Juryman who sits the furthest away from you to hear you easily; do you understand that?" and "You say to this witness, Mr. Interpreter, that he is talking so low that I can't hear him, and that he must answer every question in a tone that is loud enough for every one of the Jury to hear him. Tell him that I won't tell him that again," and the company lawyer said, "I want you to speak over here," and "I want you to talk over this way and louder," and "talk louder," and "speak louder," and "louder," and "louder."

The judge orders some workers to testify in English when he deems their English to be good enough, even if they state that they would prefer to testify through the interpreter. Sometimes the lawyers crack jokes during their questioning, and sometimes these jokes are at the expense of the witnesses, perhaps to ingratiate the lawyers to the jury, which appears to confuse and worry some of the witnesses. "I could not understand what you meant by talking because I don't think I am so excellent in the English language to understand it all," one worker says. "Therefore, you have to excuse me if I made a mistake." None of the banter or business of the court is interpreted to witnesses.

Bostwick asks each worker witness to get up from the stand and walk over to the courtroom door and to use its handle to demonstrate for the jury how they tried to open the locked factory exit door. Mary Bucelli and Joseph Brenman and Ida Nelson and Yetta Lubitz and Ethel Monick and Becky Rothstein and Sophie Zimmerman and Lillian Weiner and Katie Weiner tear at the courtroom door, rip at its handle. They reenact their screaming and kicking and pounding. They weep. The door does not open. It is locked.

When the blackened lock from the factory door is brought into the courtroom as evidence, it sits, cold and sooty, encased in glass, on a table next to the witness stand.

When the "female workers," which is how these subsections of the official transcript are labeled, take the stand, the defense attorney raises questions about their ability to remember anything clearly from the mess of the fire, which is perhaps why Bostwick waits until the end of his case to call them, waits until after the engineers and firefighters and police officers and just plain "workers" had finished testifying.

The company's defense attorney Max Steuer, one of the most famous trial lawyers of the day, questions sixteen-year-old Ethel Monick:

Q. And there was a great deal of excitement there, of confusion, wasn't there?

A. *I don't understand what you mean by excitement.*

Q. You really don't know what I mean by excitement?

A. *No, sir.*

Q. Were you just as quiet and calm at that time as you are now?

A. *Just as I am now, because I was never in such a fire, and I didn't know it was a fire, so I ran looking for an escape, I didn't know about being excited.*

Q. You do know what excitement is, do you, if you were not excited.

MR. BOSTWICK: There is a difference between excited and excitement.

THE COURT: Very slight.

MR. STEUER: Only in Mr. Bostwick's own imagination.

Q. Now, I first asked you do you know what it is to be excited?

A. *In what case?*

Q. Well, did you see anybody that was excited while you were in that quiet and calm condition, just the same as you are now, did you see anybody that was not calm?

A. *The other girls, I don't know whether they were excited or not. I didn't ask them.*

Q. You didn't ask them whether they were excited, so you don't know; is that it?

A. *Yes, sir.*

Q. When the girls were over at the door you called out to them "Here is the door," you didn't know then that there was any excitement, that they were excited?

A. *They all rushed to the door that is all I know.*

But if the prosecution had a star witness, it was one of the women workers: Kate Alterman, who spoke English well enough not to need an interpreter in court, and who saw Margaret Schwartz die. During his questioning of Alterman, defense lawyer Max Steuer breaks a cardinal rule of cross-examination, which is never to allow a witness to repeat testimony that can harm your client. When Steuer asks Alterman what she did when she heard the cry of fire, she responds at length, though her response now lives on in the "Library Notes" section of the digital transcript, which is a researchers' manual re-creation from the damaged original document:

Was Margaret S[ch]wartz with you at this time? Yes, sir. Then I went to the toilet room. Margaret disappeared from me, and I wanted to go out the Greene Street side but the whole door was in flames, so I went and hide myself in the toilet rooms, and then I went outside away from the toilet rooms and bent my face over the sink, and then I ran to the Washington Place side elevator, but there was a big crowd and I couldn't pass through there. Then I noticed someone, a whole crowd, around the door, and I saw Bernstein, the manager's brother, trying to open the door, and there was Margaret near him. Bernstein tried the door; he couldn't open it, and then Margaret began to open that door. I take her on one side, I pushed her on the side and I said wait, I will open that door. I tried, pulled the handle in and out, all ways, and I couldn't open it. She pushed me on the other side, got hold of the handle, and then she tried, and then I saw her bending down on her knees, and her hair was loose and the trail of her dress was a little far from her, and then a big smoke came and I couldn't see. I just knew it was Margaret, and I said Margaret, and she didn't reply. I left Margaret, and I turned my head on the side and I noticed the trail of her dress and the ends of her hair begin to burn. Then I ran in, in the small dressing room that was on the Washington side. There was a big crowd and I went out from there and stood in the center of the room between the machines and between the examining tables, I noticed afterwards on the other side near the Washington side windows Bernstein, the manager's brother, going around like a wild cat on the windows, and he was chasing his head out of the window and pulled himself back. He wanted to jump, I suppose, but he was afraid. And then I saw the flames covering him. I noticed on the Greene Street side someone else fall down on the floor and the flames covered him, and then I stood in the center of the room and I just turned my coat on the left side with the fur to my face, the lining on the outside, got hold of a bunch of dresses that was lying on the examining tables and not burned yet, covered up my head and tried to run through the flames on the Greene Street side. The whole door was a red curtain of fire, but a young lady came and she began to pull me in the back of my dress and she wouldn't let me. I kicked her with my foot and I don't know what became of her, and I ran out through the Greene Street side door, right through the flames, onto the roof. My pocketbook began to burn already but I pressed it to my heart to extinguish the fire.

When she finishes, Steuer asks her to repeat the story, and she does. She repeats it almost exactly, deviating in only a few minor details: omitting the fact that the brother was going around "like a wild cat," for example. Steuer lectures her about this. And she says, "Well, I don't imagine whether a wild cat or a wild dog. I just speak to imagine just exactly."

He has her repeat the story a third time. And she does, again nearly verbatim. It is clear that she has practiced her testimony. And why would she not practice what she would have to say about a deadly industrial fire, which she survived but which killed many of her coworkers and friends, some of whom she watched burn, in a language in which she was not fluent, in a courtroom in front of her former bosses and their lawyers and a federal judge? Why would she not practice?

But Steuer argues that the evidence of practice amounts to memorization, and memorization implies that the story had been constructed by someone other than Kate Alterman, by some force other than her memory recording the fire itself. And did she receive a letter from the union? And did she go to the union office? And did she meet with a union representative? And did she speak to the union lawyer?

Once feared lost, but then located by the writer Leon Stein, who was also a longtime editor of *Justice*, the newspaper of the ILGWU, this transcript tells its story without illuminating much about the witnesses themselves. It is a trial transcript after all, not a text that is meant to contain anything other than the facts of what transpired, not a container for grief or fear or rage—and so these things, which must certainly have resided in the imagined factory of a courtroom, are difficult to discern.

In reading through it, I get distracted from its lessons about the mechanics of storytelling in courtrooms, and I begin to notice instead the internal echoes in the language of the proceeding. What the witnesses say—the words they use to describe their own experiences—build patterns that, in my reading of the transcript, begin to speak loudly over the arc of the narrative the lawyers on each side are working very hard to construct and control. Two witnesses refer to groups of bodies as lying in *heaps*. Five witnesses use the word *piles* instead. There are also the two witnesses who mistook bodies for something else. One firefighter: "When I got over there to extinguish this fire in this trim and windows that I spoke of I stepped on something that was soft, in my hurry and anxiety to finish up my work, and I looked down and my attention was called to a body by that means. . . . When I looked at the one I stepped on I saw three or four that I had not noticed previous." And another: "I didn't see any bodies when I first looked around the floor. I seen a pile of rubbage, which turned out to be bodies afterwards, but I didn't see no bodies."

For a trial that at its purest distillation is about a fire and a locked door, it is no surprise that the word *door* appears 3,620 times in the trial transcript. The word *fire* appears 1,686 times in the transcript. The word *lock* appears 745 times. *Locked*, 367. *That door is locked*, 16. *That door was locked*, 6.

The word *jump* appears 130 times. *Jumped*, 57. *Jumping*, 22.

Fell, 41. *Fall*, 25.

The word *flew* appears just once, in Ida Nelson's description of doing what some of the workers did to survive, wrap bolts of cloth around their bodies to protect themselves from the flames:

Q. You had goods on you and the goods didn't catch fire and nothing happened except that your hands were scorched?

A. *Yes, the goods were burned.*

Q. What goods?

A. *Plain white goods.*

Q. You mean you grabbed goods from the table and put goods
   around you?

A. *I grabbed it from the bookkeeper's desk, I found there a piece of goods, and I covered myself with it.*

Q. While you were running from the Washington place door to the fire escape, did you pick up any goods then?

A. *When I ran towards the fire escape I thought I would be able to get out from the fire escape without doing anything else.*

Q. So up to that time you had not taken any goods and had not covered yourself?

A. *No.*

Q. But after you saw these big flames at the fire escape and you were going towards the Greene street door, then you took time to pick up a piece of goods and put it around you and go out of the Greene street door, is that right?

A. *I grabbed it and I flew through to Greene street.*

Q. You grabbed these white goods out of which they made waists?

A. *Yes.*

Q. That very thin goods?

A. *Yes.*

Q. And with that around you you ran through the Greene street door, is that right?

A. *Yes.*

At the end of the trial, the judge read Article 6, Section 80, of New York's Labor Law: "All doors leading in or to any such factory shall be so constructed as to open outwardly where practicable, and shall not be locked, bolted, or fastened during working hours." He instructed the jury that in order to find Harris and Blanck guilty, they must find that the door was locked during the fire, that the defendants knew or should have known it was locked, and that the locked door, beyond a reasonable doubt, caused Margaret Schwartz to die.

The jury deliberated for less than two hours and returned a verdict of not guilty. After the verdict, one juror, Victor Steinman, summed up the reasoning behind the group's decision: "I believed that the door was locked at the time of the fire, but we couldn't find them guilty unless we believed they knew the door was locked." Nestled in a scrum of police officers, Harris and Blanck left the court through the judge's private exit and made it to the subway under the pursuit of protesters.

One month after their exoneration, Harris and Blanck relaunched the Triangle company in a new location, on Fifth Avenue and Sixteenth Street. They had collected an insurance payout of $60,000, which amounted to about $410 per dead worker. It wasn't until 1913, nearly two years later, that the owners reached a settlement with the victims' families to resolve pending civil suits. They paid $75 per lost life—a bargain netting Harris and Blanck $335 per worker. That year, they moved the factory again, this time to a bigger space on West Twenty-Third Street, just blocks from the building that would become UNITE's international headquarters in New York. There, Blanck was fined twenty dollars by a building inspector for locking a door during work hours. The inspector warned him that the factory was rife with fire hazards and refused to issue the company's products with the MADE UNDER SAFE CONDITIONS label—a sort of precursor to a fair-trade seal—which had been implemented industry-wide as the result of the public outcry that followed the fire. The next year, Harris and Blanck were fined again, after they were caught sewing fraudulent safe-conditions labels into their shirtwaists.

Another theory about moths' attraction to light is that it is a survival mechanism—they know instinctively that they have a better chance of escaping whatever nocturnal predator if they fly upward, toward moonlight, than if they fly down, into the darkness of earth at nighttime. Human-made light, like fires and porch lights, like the light in the parking lot we gathered around for our meetings, are traps for this mechanism. The moths are wired to fly *toward* light, but they aren't built to fly *into* it.

Perhaps a more interesting question lepidopterists ask: Once a moth arrives at a light source, what makes it stay, either petrified on the fixture or flapping erratically in the beam? One theory is that a moth's eyes are not designed for the arrival—it never expects to get to the moon—and the glare of a streetlight up close overwhelms its light receptors, disorienting it. What's more, once a moth's eyes have adjusted to light, it takes even longer to adjust again to darkness. In fact, dark adaptation takes them so long, the theory goes, that even if a moth escapes from light, by the time it can see in the dark, it will forget the problem and fly right back to the fire.

Another theory is that when light overwhelms its visual receptors, a moth's eyes conjure illusions of dark pockets—Mach bands—which appear to float amidst the illuminated air. It flies toward the safety of these dark spaces, hoping to hide, then finds that the darkness disappears on arrival, forcing the moth to fly on and on toward the next one.

If you Google "moth trails at night," you will find ghostly, long exposure shots of moths spiraling around in floodlights—perhaps chasing a series of vanishing illusions of safety, perhaps trapped in a cycle of dark blindness and forgetting.

9: Las Polillas

AFTER OUR TRIAL adjourned, we met with the comité in the shade of the chinaberry tree in Santiago's yard, as we had done every Wednesday since the election. We had a system for these meetings: I would pick up a bag of ice and a case of water in small plastic bottles and then pick you up from your house. You and I would go to the office and load the rental-car trunk with metal folding chairs and the blue cooler, in which we put the ice and water. Then we'd pick up Cecilia and then Antonia and then Analía, who all sat in the back seat together while you rode shotgun until we got to Pollo's apartment, and then he would ride shotgun, and you would pile in the back with the other women. At Santiago's house, we'd arrange the metal chairs into a circle under the tree, their legs pressing down into the layer of dust that coats the hard-packed desert ground. We'd pass out the water bottles—both to the people who had come in the car with us and to the others who had gotten there on their own—and then we'd begin. Through that summer and fall, the agenda for these meetings remained the same. We gave four kinds of reports: on what happened at the labor board, on what happened in the factory, on conversations with union supporters, on conversations with new coworkers.

By that fall, you were running the meetings, facilitating the group through this agenda. I would give the labor board report and then sit on the cooler at the edge of the circle and take notes while you called on the other members of the comité to give their reports in rounds. You knew what information we needed, what to dig for with follow-up questions as each person spoke: Who did you hear that from? Did they hear it directly from El Mero Mero or secondhand? How many new people started in your department this week? And what are their names, and who are they stationed next to, and where do they sit at lunch? How many of them did you talk to? Did you ask if La Sandra talked about the union during their job interview? We were tracking the company's messaging and tactics, anticipating its strategy. We were probing for new legal violations, and, as always, we were mapping and remapping the factory.

At the end of this post-trial meeting, the group decided not to meet again for two weeks, and then to lessen the frequency of our meetings to once per month unless there was pressing news. We would stay in contact by phone, but we all needed a breather, and we knew it would be a long time before any new information came from the labor board, before we knew whether or not we would have another election. The comité members said goodbye to each other in a series of handshakes and shoulder slaps, and then we dropped off the carload of people in reverse order from the pickup: Pollo then Analía then Antonia then Cecilia, and then you.

At your house, Julio's truck was in the driveway, so I did not go inside, a practice we had silently adopted the summer before. We said goodbye in the car—*It'll only be a week*, we said—I was supposed to catch up on time off, which I had not taken during the trial, but the goodbye felt strange. It would be the longest we had been apart in the ten months we had known each other.

I told you I was going back to Tucson, but I did not go. Instead, I stayed in the motel. I watched telenovelas and slept in short fits and opened the window a small crack to smoke. I kept the room dark and ate granola bars and ordered pizza and drank Jameson from a flimsy plastic cup and water from the bathroom tap that could not get cold even though it was November. There was a violent fight in the room next door one night—not the first time that had happened in that motel—and an ambulance came to take a woman away. I watched the police pull into the parking lot, but I didn't open the door to their pounding. In my journal I wrote, "I'm so tired, I don't know why I don't sleep."

The next week would be the three-day training, with you and the shop stewards from Mission Linen (where your husband's cousin had once been steward), still the only Phoenix laundry under union contract, and Mariana Rivera from the Lake Havasu laundry, and workplace leaders from other industries and unions that were organizing immigrant workers. I introduced UNITE with the story of the Triangle shirtwaist factory fire, trying and mostly failing to repress an upwelling of emotion the story was meant to give rise to in others, consumed by the details of the accounts I had read the night before. Each night the moth dream was a mess of soot and smoke and tiny scales. And at the end of the three days, you raised your hand and asked why it is that some people are driven to fight while other people fall down in their fear.

We took part in the training because we needed to launch campaigns at other laundries if we were going to make a go of the citywide market campaign. And we couldn't pull that off with fly-in organizers alone. We wanted laundry workers to take charge of organizing the nonunion laundries, and so you and the others were there to be trained on the method and discipline of organizing conversations, of having them with people who are not your own coworkers.

The training was timely, since we had recently learned that the union had won a "card check"—meaning that workers could win a union without having to go through an NLRB election if a majority of them signed cards—at a hospitality laundry called Top Shelf on the other side of

Phoenix. Though companies today like to force workers to demonstrate their support for the union twice over—once by signing union cards, and again by voting for the union in an election held weeks or months later— and pretend that this is the way unions have always been formed, card check is an old process outlined and supported by the NLRA. In fact, in the early years of the NLRA, most unions were formed through this process, called voluntary recognition, in which employers forgo the election process and recognize the union based on evidence, such as signed cards, that a majority of their employees want to unionize.

The story of the Top Shelf card-check agreement, like a lot of union stories, was inordinate in its own special way, though likely mostly true: Workers at a Top Shelf factory in the Northeast—the first of the company's handful of factories to organize—went on strike to demand better pay and safer conditions. They did this in the only way workers can strike for better pay and safer conditions without being permanently replaced by their bosses—by filing ULP charges at the labor board after the company made some threats and fired one of their coworkers. Calling the strike a "ULP strike" in protest of the company's illegal behavior affords workers the right to strike without being fired or permanently replaced.

They struck for months through a particularly frigid winter, and finally, after gaining some local news coverage, the owner of the company, who had been suspiciously difficult to locate, called the union for a meeting. The UNITE president flew in from New York to meet the laundry boss in the location he had requested—the private back room of an Italian restaurant. The boss, the story goes, was the portrait of a mobster: gelled hair, gold chain, fat cigar, bomber jacket—the works. The union didn't know how many other laundry factories he owned or where they were, and later, it added to the mob mystique that his other plants seemed oddly located, in locations far-flung from the site of the strike. The UNITE president was prepared for a hard bargaining session, but the meeting lasted just minutes. The boss asked him what it would take to get the union to quiet down, and he immediately conceded to all of the president's requests. The strikers won a Cadillac contract, and it was agreed that, in its other factories, the company would allow organizers into the lunchrooms to talk with workers and that they would voluntarily recognize the union if a majority of workers signed cards. Also under the agreement, the union promised to end the strike and not to strike any other Top Shelf factories—a promise of "labor peace" in exchange for the company's agreement not to campaign against the union, and to "remain neutral" during the organizing drive.

When I explained this deal to you, you widened your eyes in incredulity. You could not believe the good fortune of these workers—all they had to do was sign cards, and they'd have their union.

On the first day of the execution of the agreement, we gave a five-minute presentation in the Top Shelf lunchroom, which was really a short description of the union that we read from a script that had been approved by the company as part of the deal. Then we asked the workers to sign union cards. Only a handful of them would take the cards from us as we walked around the room. A few of them did sign right then, but most of them would not. Most of the workers would not speak to us or make eye contact with us—we could tell that the company had not remained neutral, as the agreement required. In fact, over the next few days, we learned that Luis, the plant manager, had threatened workers that the laundry would close if the union won. He called undocumented workers into his office and told them he would be forced to fire them if the union won. He instructed department leads to follow workers into the bathrooms to make sure they weren't talking union.

As we moved from table to table and realized that the company had stonewalled the process, we backed off from any talk about the union and instead tried to engage workers with basic questions about themselves and the factory: Which department do you work in? How long have you worked here? Where in Mexico are you from? Anything to garner even a modicum of engagement. But in order to avoid talking to us in front of anyone who might report back to management, many of the workers scattered from the lunchroom and headed early to their workstations, though there was nowhere to sit there and lunch was the only time during an eight- or ten-hour shift when they could rest.

You sat down next to a woman with a bandaged hand—blood from a wound was welling through white gauze. I could hear you asking if she worked in soil sort, like you did. You had heard about wounds like this before. Without looking up from the table, the woman nodded so slightly it was nearly imperceptible. Your voice softened and you asked if the injury happened at work, but she sat frozen and did not respond. You clenched your jaw but otherwise hid your frustration well.

Days later, we learned from another worker that Luis had removed a safety guard from the soil-sort conveyor, enabling it to move linen down the line faster. The woman's hand had been pulled under the belt, and it tore at her skin until someone pushed the emergency stop. We went to her house to see if she wanted to talk to a lawyer or file an OSHA complaint or to see if she just needed help doing the dishes. She peeked through the front door, which she had opened only wide enough for us to see a sliver of her face. You greeted her warmly and asked if we could come inside, but she shook her head no. We heard her voice for the first time: *I'm sorry, but I need my job.*

When we got back to the car, you were undone with outrage, slamming your palm on the dash with every other word. *Her boss ripped the skin off her hand, and she won't open the fucking door,* you said. Bearing witness to this woman's fear made you angry. *We aren't dogs,* you said. *I am not a mule,* you said. *Do they like being treated like mules? How are they not more fucking angry?*

We won the card check at Top Shelf by a slim margin on the last day of our timeline when we convinced three wash department workers to sign. We discovered that Luis was not cutting power to the washers before sending workers in to clear jams, just as Pollo had described happens in your laundry. We talked to the washers in the parking lot after work for a long time until finally their anger over being put into that kind of danger outweighed the fear of losing their jobs. Though we'd been talking with them in the parking lot on the windowless side of the factory, in the cover of one of the laundry trucks, you got them to follow us around the building, to hold their cards up against the glass of Luis's office windows to sign.

In Tucson, I had moved out of the house my girlfriend and I were renting and moved in with a friend who was also breaking up with her girlfriend. I remember convincing this friend that it would be a good deal to live with me because I would so rarely be in the house, maybe one weekend a month, since the rest of the time I would be staying at the motel in Phoenix. But when I went home for the weekend after turning over the Top Shelf cards to be counted, I learned that this new housemate had started inviting my ex-girlfriend over to watch movies with her on our couch—her own ex had found them together, spooning in the dark. So I put most of my things into the trunk of the rental car, drove back to Phoenix, and did not check out of the motel again for many months. I did not feel angry about this. I was relieved—happy, even. I had started to suspect that I had been manufacturing, or at least ginning up, personal turmoil to simulate an intensity I suppose I craved. But that intensity now existed, with great urgency, in our organizing.

On the heels of the card-check win for the union there, the Top Shelf contract negotiations were the first in which either you or I had participated.

We were mostly there to observe and to take notes and to build strategy and messaging from what happened at the table to help the union grow and strengthen in the factory. The union sent a negotiator from the New York office—the same person who had hashed out the details of the card-check agreement after the president and the company's owner agreed in principle to the deal. The company's lead negotiator was its in-house attorney, who had overseen the card-check agreement for its side. This made for an odd dynamic in the factory's office conference room, where the bargaining took place: two highly educated white men who knew each other from this previous dealmaking did almost all of the talking. They did it in English because neither of them spoke Spanish, which meant that they could not speak to any of the workers in the room. The only other white person in the room was me, and I also did a lot of talking, in the form of translating, as best I could, what the two negotiators were saying to each other. Luis, who was Latino and spoke both Spanish and English, sat next to the company lawyer on the company's side of the table and almost never spoke at all. He spent the days looking glum and doodling on a legal notepad. The union negotiator from New York sat at our side of the table, and you and I huddled in the corner with three Top Shelf workers so that I could interpret quietly and not distract from the business of bargaining. These three workers were the only ones who volunteered to attend the negotiation of their contract, though we managed to rally small groups of their coworkers to listen in for a few minutes at a time during their breaks.

As the negotiations unfolded, it became clear that the card-check deal, beyond addressing how the two sides were meant to behave during the drive for union cards, also included some stiff parameters with regard to the contract. Which is to say, much of the contract had already been decided by the time we sat down to negotiate, making what happened in that conference room all the stranger, at least to you and me.

For instance, because of the prefabricated agreement, some of the issues we had campaigned on—stuff that really pissed off the workers in the factory, like a supervisor who timed bathroom breaks at three minutes, and a leaky swamp cooler that dripped down onto one of the dryers, and missing safety latches on the rail hooks—were not items we could bring to the table, and we had to handle them through sidebar with Luis, getting him to verbally agree to make fixes, which were then hard to sell as bargaining victories to the workers who would have to vote to ratify the contract. The workers had good reason not to trust the things Luis said, which was part of why a majority of them had signed cards in the first place.

What did you expect? the union negotiator from New York said when I questioned the fairness of this situation. *It's not going to be the best contract, but we didn't have to fight for three years to get it.*

Who is "we"? I launched back accusingly. My intention in asking this was to impress upon him that *he* would not have had a role in any fight in Phoenix anyway, that he would have swooped in only after the grueling years it took to win the fight in order to bargain a contract.

And he volleyed the accusation back straightaway: *These workers*, he said, waving his arm at the office window that overlooked the factory floor, *they didn't have to fight for three years and come to work every day in a war zone, even if you think that's what's best for them.*

Later he said, *Are we going to organize the industry or not? Are we going to make it less deadly or not? We can't bring one hundred thousand laundry workers into the union if every group of two hundred has to have a three-year fight.*

And, of course, this was true.

Still the bargaining was hard to watch, hard to know that it would result in only the second union contract at a Phoenix laundry, after Mission. In the ratification meeting with the factory's workers, the New

York negotiator pushed the agreement with a hard message: you aren't prepared for a real fight, you aren't prepared to strike, so this deal is the best we can do. And the workers voted right there in the company lunchroom—74 percent yes, 5 percent no, 21 percent abstained—to ratify. Through this contract, they won important safety protections about heat exposure and access to drinking water. They won some job protections in the form of clauses about seniority and just cause and a grievance procedure. But the economic package was weak—some workers got fifteen- and twenty-cent raises, but some got just five-cent raises, and a handful of workers in one department got no raises at all for the first year of the contract.

We both knew La Sandra and El Mero Mero could use these meager wage increases to their advantage, and just two days later, when we met with the comité in Santiago's yard, we learned that there was a rumor going around on first shift saying that the union had frozen wages at Top Shelf (which wasn't true), and how lucky your coworkers were that La Sandra (crowned the heroine of the company's story) had stopped the union at Sodexho. In our circle of chairs, we talked about how to respond to this message from the company. You explained that it was not true that wages had been frozen, that some workers had actually gotten more than three years' worth of your factory's raises, and also that the situation at Top Shelf was different—they had won their union without having to fight, which meant both that they were not in a position to leverage a better contract and also that they had traded away some things they might have won in exchange for not having to fight for them (you left out the fact that the workers had not been part of making this trade, and so did I). And contract bargaining would be different at your factory, we all agreed, where, when we finally win, it will be the result of a fierce and sustained fight. The company will know that you could shut down the factory if that's what it takes—you had done it once already.

The Top Shelf factory and the asphalt island on which it stood abutted patches of desert. This is how southwest Phoenix was at the time—industrial spaces popping out of newly bulldozed swaths of the Sonoran Desert. On another of these asphalt islands, which we sometimes passed on the way to Top Shelf, was an ongoing construction project, from which a warehouse slowly emerged during the time we executed the card check and bargained the contract.

One morning, the director called to tell me that this warehouse would soon be an Angelica laundry, the newest of thirty-five plants owned by the company she had left Phoenix to organize. They were going to start hiring in the next few weeks, the union's corporate researchers had told her, and we needed to get union supporters to apply for jobs there, to "salt" the factory, which is how we described seeding a workplace with activists inclined to help us organize from the inside. We made a list of people, some laundry workers, some family members of laundry workers—cousins and sisters and nieces and roommates—people we thought would be good at making friends quickly. We called the workers from other industries who had participated in the three-day training, too, and made lists of their pro-union family members who were looking for work. We started rounds of visits that same afternoon, and by the end of the month, two of the people we recruited had made it through the hiring process and were working in the new factory. They fed us information, and bit by bit, we built our lists and maps and quietly made more contacts in preparation for a blitz.

On that same phone call about the new Angelica factory, the director told me that UNITE's president had announced that the union would be merging with HERE, the Hotel Employees and Restaurant Employees Union, which I had heard of but knew little about. It seemed strange to me that a merger would be announced in this way—by edict from on high. I knew UNITE to be careful about its framing, good at cultivating the image that decisions, especially major ones, happened democratically among the rank and file. I asked the director about this, if this is how mergers typically happen, and she said that she didn't know how mergers typically happen—this was her first one as well—but, yes, that they were likely ironed out by executives on both sides before union members weighed in. The process seemed not to bother her, and so, at the time, it did not bother me. She was surprised by the news, though—it had been a tightly held secret. *But don't worry*, I remember her saying. *Nothing in Phoenix will change.*

The union was growing in Phoenix, and to build momentum and instill solidarity among the laundry members, we started holding monthly cenas in the same hall where we held the first meeting of the organizing drive at your factory. The dinners were open to all workers at the plants we had organized (Mission, CleanCo, Top Shelf), those in the process of publicly organizing (yours), and the few members of the growing comité of the bajo el agua campaign at the new Angelica facility. You and I would spend the afternoon preparing the hall—putting out the folding tables and chairs, draping the tables with colorful dollar-store covers, and labeling sections of the room so that workers from each factory would sit together. Then we went to El Pollo Loco to pick up trays of chicken and beans and rice and corn and tortillas and pico de gallo. Then the workers arrived with their families, and from one side of a bank of tables, we spooned the food onto their plates as they filed by in a line. Someone's cousin's mariachi band played on the small stage in the front of the hall, and the kids, who were dressed up for the occasion, ran around in small, giggly groups. After everyone finished eating, the elected shop stewards at each of the three union factories stood to give reports from their shops: membership numbers as an overall percentage of the workforce (constantly and carefully tracked in right-to-work Arizona), and grievances, both those they had filed and those they had won—small but important victories, which energized the room and demonstrated for the not-yet-union workers how the union can operate inside their factories once they have collectively bargained contracts of their own.

At the first of these cenas, we chartered Local 2732, the union of Arizona laundry workers, with the minor fanfare of a "si se puede" chant. (This *we* being one of the slippery, divergent ones. You belonged to this local, and I, of course, did not.) We had framed the charter certificate ahead of the cena, and it rested on a tabletop easel near the potluck desserts. It meant that Local 2732 was officially constituted, its own democratic entity, with its own budget and bylaws. It was formed as an affiliate of UNITE's Western States Regional Joint Board, which was headquartered in Los Angeles. This is the way the union was structured: locals, which were made up of the union's members in a shop or city or state, each with their own set of locally elected leaders, were affiliated with regional joint boards, which had their own regional conferences and conventions and regionally elected leaders, and which, in turn, were affiliated with and comprised the international union UNITE, which had its own international conferences and conventions and elected leaders and an executive board made up of the leaders of the joint boards.

You did not want to hold an elected office in the local—you weren't interested in the local or regional politics of the union, and you weren't as compelled by the internal programs and services the union provided to workers who were already members: classes and trainings and the bargaining of second and third contracts after the first contracts expired. You wanted to be an organizer, you said. You liked the hard work of bringing nonunion workers into the union. So the shop stewards from Mission, Rigoberto and Maria, were formally nominated and then voted into office at the local as the president and secretary-treasurer. A few weeks later, a business agent from the regional office in Los Angeles came to Phoenix for a weekend to train them for these roles, and we attended the training to learn how to help them administer the local. You took careful notes during this training in your loopy, floral handwriting: *Robert's Rules*, quorums, record keeping, and so on. Over those two days, I felt as though I were watching the union morph in your mind from the solid shape of a righteous idea into something more practical and malleable, a set of processes that you could maneuver, that you could drive. You interrupted often to ask questions, to the growing irritation of the person who was training us. You noticed his irritation but did not seem to care—you did not quiet yourself.

On the way to your house after the training had ended, I asked if you regretted not running for office, because you had seemed so interested in the training. And you said, *Let Rigo and Maria run the local now. I'll run it when they retire and it's triple the size.* Then you started listing our next organizing targets—the remaining nonunion laundries in Phoenix—in the order we had positioned them in our strategic plan while slapping the back of one hand against the palm of the other, humorously reminding me to keep my eye on the ball: Angelica, Milum, G&K, Prudential, UniFirst, ACE.

In March 2004, four months after the end of the trial, Paul called my cell phone. It was late evening, an odd time for him to call—the labor board office had already closed for the day.

I'll give you the good news first, he said, because he did not know if he could hold it back. We had won something called a "Gissel," a bargaining order, which meant that the judge found that the company violated the law so egregiously that there could never again be a fair election in the factory. She ordered Sodexho to recognize the union outright and to begin contract negotiations. Her forty-page decision included a pointed description of the lie La Sandra and El Mero Mero had told about permanently replacing you. It was what had pushed the judge to consider such an extraordinary remedy, Paul was sure. The decision also included an order that you be made whole—brought back to your original positions on your original shifts at your original pay rates plus back pay for the time you were fired. Antonia's disciplinary record would be expunged. And the company would have to do what is typically required of companies prosecuted in board cases: post a list of the illegal actions they had been ordered to stop committing on a bulletin board in the factory.

We won on every charge except Cecilia's firing. In her decision, the judge wrote that she believed Cecilia had pushed La Sandra during the work stoppage. *If the judge found that La Sandra was lying about firing Alma*, I seethed to Paul, *why would she believe her about Cecilia? And what am I supposed to tell Cecilia? And how do we appeal?*

Paul interrupted. This was the first Gissel in Arizona history. *Just take the win*, he said.

Losing the charge on Cecilia's firing was not the bad news, though. The bad news was that, in the time it had taken Paul to read the decision that afternoon, the company had already established its intent to "file exceptions," which Paul explained was functionally an appeal. When I asked how long the appeal would take, he first said that he had no idea. And then he said, *Years. It's going to take years.* And in the meantime, the company could continue not to recognize the union.

In May, UNITE's international union office collaborated with the Service Employees International Union (SEIU), one of the largest and fastest growing unions in the country, to launch a public-pressure campaign targeting what they were calling the Big 3 multiservice corporations: Sodexho, Compass, and Aramark, all three of which make their money by providing services to other corporations and government agencies and schools. The services they provide range from laundry, as in the case of your factory, to food service, security, groundskeeping, waste management, and so on. The campaign was built on the theory that, working together, the unions could apply enough pressure on the three companies to win card-check neutrality agreements, like the one we had executed at Top Shelf, but on a mass scale—agreements that could cover tens of thousands of workers across the country. The campaign would be an enormous undertaking, including marches and rallies and protests and class-action lawsuits, all happening in concert across the United States and Canada, as well as in France and the United Kingdom, where two of the companies were headquartered.

The fight at your factory was to serve as the key case study for the rationale behind this immense campaign: that these companies were bad actors who broke the law egregiously in order to keep workers from unionizing, and they had to be forced to accept a neutral stance with regard to the union in order to give workers a fair shot at organizing. Your laundry was also an illustration of the dangerous conditions and unlivable wages that were foundational to the way the Big 3 did business. Our organizing, now in its second year, with no end in sight, was a powerful argument for the necessity of card check, proof that the only way to organize without having to launch thousands of fights like the one you and your coworkers were enduring was to win an agreement for a process free of intimidation from bosses and local managers.

In June, we flew to San Francisco to launch this campaign at an SEIU convention. It was your first time on a plane. You looked through the window during takeoff, craning your neck to watch as the ground dropped away. Having you there as "the voice of Big 3 workers," as it was described to me, was crucial to the choreography of both the campaign and the convention, which, as all union conventions are, was tightly organized around the virtuous ideal of rank-and-file leadership.

You were slated to speak on two separate stages—once at a lunch for student supporters of the union, and again the next day from the main convention floor—so we wrote two speeches, and on the plane we rehearsed them over and over, until you had memorized not just the words, but also the rhythm of my translation, so that we were fluid, synchronized, even down to our hand gestures and voice inflections and tonal shifts. We practiced until the plane began to descend, and then you stopped talking and white-knuckled the armrests.

Both speeches would begin with a description of the work that happens in an industrial laundry: *I work in soil sort*, you would say, *the first department in the plant, where bags of dirty laundry are brought in from hospitals. We sort thousands of pounds of contaminated linen, often without proper protective equipment. I have been stabbed by needles. I have seen parts of bodies and bodily fluids and surgical tools come down the line in the tangle of linens.* Then you would describe the wash department, then the dry department, then iron and fold and packing, and each of their respective dangers.

You would describe the campaign at your laundry: that a movement of workers rose up and declared that they wanted to form a union, that the company attacked the union, viciously and illegally, that a federal judge had found its actions so egregious that she ordered it to recognize the union outright and bargain a contract, a decision the company was appealing through a process that would likely take many years.

The hotel ballroom would be filled with thousands of SEIU members—workers who navigated their own workplace dangers, who had led fights of their own—so we decided we would focus the second speech more on the campaign itself. You would give the name of the video the company played two hundred times—*Little Card, Big Trouble*—and the thousands of people would hiss. You would tell them you had been fired for leading a work stoppage and a march on the boss, and everyone in the huge room would boo. You would say that you and your coworkers were now waiting on the labor board appeals process, and the audience would know what this meant; they would hiss again. You would say, *That is why we are launching this national campaign. That is why we are asking you to join us. The only way to win in Phoenix is to beat this company and its competitors everywhere, all at once.* To this, the room would roar alive, filled with the collective will to fight.

SEIU booked us adjoining rooms in the fancy conference hotel. After checking in, you knocked on the door in your room that opened to a door that opened into my room, and after I opened the door on my side, you said, *Oh, hello*, in English and feigned surprise to see me, and then you laughed in delight at the joke. We had planned to go out to find food, but you looked tired. You had worked second shift the night before and lost sleep to make the flight. We ordered room-service sandwiches and sat in my room, practicing the speeches for the next day. You paced as you spoke and kept stumbling over the words, though you'd had them down on the plane. With each mistake, I suggested we stop for the night, that we get up early in the morning instead to practice some more. But each time, you started again at the beginning. You did this until we got it right.

That spring, I had started going back to Tucson some weekends and had started dating someone I met at a bar after he performed a song by Postal Service in drag, which to twenty-six-year-old me was the epitome of sexiness. While you and I were flying to San Francisco, he was driving there from Tucson—a wild twelve-hour gesture to surprise me—and he was there the next morning, when you knocked on the door, catching me in the process of attempting to smuggle him out.

You and I were closer to each other than I was with anyone else at the time, closer in some ways than I had ever been with anyone. But it was a specific shade of closeness. I had met Julio in a few brief encounters, and I had met one of your sisters and your niece and two of your nephews and three of your cousins, but you had not met anyone from the slim portion of my life that happened outside the union. This was, in a way, by design, part of the deliberate culture of organizing within UNITE. None of the workers in Phoenix had ever met anyone from any of the organizers' lives outside the union, because that is not how the role of organizer was meant to function. We were not really supposed to be friends.

And though we had not abided this rule (we *were* friends, among the other ways we related to and relied on each other; compañeras, hermanas, polillas), it was still something of a violation that this person was there, inside the space of our organizing, that you were meeting him, that you stood in the hotel room door and shook his hand while being acutely aware that I was trying to sneak him out to prevent such a meeting. I was awash with shame—my face burned with it. And judging by the quick shift in the angle of your gaze, you did not want to bear witness to this shame. It embarrassed you to see it.

You delivered the speeches powerfully that afternoon and evening. In the room with the students, you asked them to stand. You asked them to stay standing if they promised to support the dining hall workers on their campuses, who worked either for the same company you did or for one of two other multiservice giants just like it, and who were going to be fighting for the right to organize. You asked them to raise their fists into the air if they promised to keep fighting until the workers won the changes they demanded. The students stood. They raised their fists.

We had less time on the big stage, in front of the full SEIU general assembly, so you described only your department in the factory before detailing our ongoing campaign. *It is called soil sort*, you said, *because in this country, laundry workers have to handle thousands of pounds of dirty hospital linen—by hand—before it is sanitized.*

Before it is cleaned rather than *after*, as is the practice in industrial laundries in other parts of the world—because "clean sort," as the other practice is called, is harder on the machines, causes them to wear down faster, so companies have to replace them more frequently. In this country, it is the bodies of workers that take on the risk and wear, physically buffering the machines from damage and shielding the company from added expense.

The exhilaration of being onstage helped fill what was otherwise a day of negative space as you withdrew from me. You would not make eye contact. You called me by my first name. You wanted me to know you were angry about what you saw that morning.

Our flight home was early the next day. When our taxi got stuck in traffic on the way to the airport, we managed to stress together about our lateness without saying a word. Only after running through the terminal, boarding the plane, finding and settling in to our tiny seats, taking off, and ordering our Coca-Colas did you say: *I don't understand. I thought you were a lesbian.* I was confused by this at first, and it took me a few beats to register that you were not angry that this fling of mine had shown up and intruded on the sober space of our work, but that you were not expecting to meet a lover—not then, not ever—who was a he. You were angry because this seemed to violate a confidence between us, because it undermined a piece of information about who I am that was entrusted to you, that had become part of our *solidatious* bond.

I am, more or less, I said, because I did not know how to say the word *queer* in Spanish. And you said: *Well, he is a man, isn't he?* And I said: *Yes, he is a man, but he was born with a woman's body* (though those were also not the words I would have used if I had been speaking with fluency), and you said, *Transgénero,* and I nodded, and then we sat there for a long time before you said: *I just didn't know you were dating anyone. Why didn't you tell me, polillita?*

You would ask me, periodically, about this fling in the months that followed, just checking in on how it was going. I did not have much to report. I wasn't home enough in Tucson to sustain it, and I'm not sure I would have wanted to anyway. After the weekend it finally ended, in a fight fueled by too much alcohol, I came back to Phoenix and told you about it, though I remember thinking that I should not. I knew alcohol was a source of some level of strife in your house, and I didn't want you to think less of me after knowing I'd been so drunk. When I told you, I tried to raise this issue, to ask if you and Julio ever fought like that. *Not like that*, you scoffed. And then you said, *It's better not to fight with drunk people.* And that was all we said about it.

The firewall on fraternization in UNITE extended beyond how organizers were meant to relate to workers. For the most part, the organizers (at least the ones on our team) applied it almost as stringently with each other. I had never met anyone from any of the other organizers' lives outside the union (unless they were dating another organizer, which happened from time to time), and they had not met anyone from mine. I knew that Ana had a boyfriend that she flew to see on her weekends off, but I did not learn his name until I had known her for nearly a year, and I never knew anything about him beyond that. Dario had twin two-year-olds at home during the time he was in Phoenix, though I didn't learn about them until years later, when they were four or five. We did not ask each about these things. The aperture of our relationships was tightly focused on the task at hand.

Just three weeks later, in July 2004, UNITE officially merged with HERE at a special joint convention in Chicago. This was five months after the two unions' presidents announced that a merger would occur, and the

UNITE organizing director reported the announcement to me over the phone, and the *American Prospect* published a story describing the preordained structure of the merged organization, in which the UNITE president would serve as general president and the HERE president would serve as president of hospitality and other details.

The rationale for the merger, at least as it trickled down on the UNITE side from organizing directors to coordinators to lead organizers to organizers, was simple: the big hotel chains where HERE had won some hard-fought leverage were major customers of some of the laundries we were organizing, so it made strategic sense for the laundry workers to join with the hotel workers. Also: HERE had big organizing aspirations, but they were nearly broke, and UNITE had money, due, in part, to the dedication of its early garment-worker members to building their strike funds and being smart and forward thinking enough to establish a bank. What I did not know at the time is that the president of UNITE had long wanted to lead a bigger union, and since it was unlikely, if not flat-out mathematically impossible, to win enough ground fights during his tenure at UNITE to satisfy that desire, a merger was the easiest way to expand. His ambition was partly personal, but, as I understand it now, it was also political. As much as he wanted to be the leader of a larger organization, he also wanted to build a more powerful labor movement, one capable of making bigger gains for more workers. As the story went, the UNITE-HERE merger originated during a conversation between the two union presidents on a picket line, over the sounds of marching feet.

You and I flew together to the special convention in Chicago, where, as had been reported by union spokespeople months earlier, the merger was "expected to be ratified" by the members. On the plane, we laughed quietly over the guy sitting in the aisle seat, who would sink against me each time he fell asleep and then jolt awake when his cheek touched my shoulder. You didn't want anything from the drink cart and then cupped the sides of your neck with your hands and kept your eyes closed the rest of the way.

The convention was slick, managed, scripted. On the second day, UNITE members marched from one side of the city while HERE members marched from the other. They met in a park for their first joint rally as a single union and then later, in the convention hotel, ratified the merger by yelling "Aye" and "Sí" at a stage lit like a rock concert. Both presidents spoke, decrying the state of the labor movement, calling for a rebirth, a doubling down on organizing, a true movement of working people. This was the first time either of us had heard either of them speak. At first, we did not know which president was which: both white men, both in nice suits. Their speeches were rousing and not at all meant ironically.

We wore UNITE shirts and jeans that day, and you wore new sandals that you kept bending down to brush clean with your hands. After the vote, we helped circulate boxes of newly screened UNITE HERE shirts through the crowd. We ended up with the last two from one of the boxes, both XXL, and even over top of the old union shirts, they hung on us, loose and long. You said we should buy belts and cut off the sleeves and wear them as sundresses. You are taller than I am, so the shirt landed on your legs just above your knees and my shirt hung down to my shins. You covered your mouth with one hand as you sometimes did when smiling and said that I should come to your house when we got back to Phoenix so you could hem my dress-shirt—that it would be a real shame if I tripped and fell in front of some boss while walking a strike line.

By the time of this convention, you were something of a rock star, though neither of us knew it before landing in Chicago. For over a year, since the blitz at your factory, we'd been sending dispatches, signed by you, accompanied by your photo, through the union's international office to staff and organizers and locals across the country. Since the launch of the Big 3 campaign, the union had bumped up the circulation of these dispatches to inspire union members to support Big 3 fights in their own cities, and to serve as a reminder to local and regional elected leaders across the merging UNITE HERE, which was also focused on hashing out agreements at national hotel chains, that laundry organizing was crucial, and winnable, and teaching us how to fight and win in a place like Phoenix.

People you didn't know greeted you, many of them English speakers, trying out an "Hola" and shaking a fist in the air to signify their solidarity. Your face flushed with the attention, but by then I knew you well enough to know that you were proud, too. You shook your fist back every time, bracelets jangling, "Hola, compañero," you would call back, or simply "Ándale," a phrase that can hold many meanings, but which you were using as a kind of affirmation.

On our second night in Chicago, the organizing director, who had also flown in for the convention, told us that HERE planned to send a team of organizers to Phoenix later in the year in order to execute cardcheck agreements at two hotels. We took this as good news. In theory, UNITE HERE could bargain with union hotels to contract their linen service with union laundries, which, by our calculus, was good leverage at nonunion laundries. Plus it fit sweetly into our organizing plan, which was to war with Sodexho as part of the new national campaign, to win at Angelica as part of that company-wide campaign, and then to go after the next-biggest hotel and restaurant laundry, Milum Textile Services, which happened to be adjacent to one of the hotels where HERE had a card check.

You were to give a short speech on the big convention stage about our organizing in Arizona, and when the time came, the vice president from the Western States Regional Joint Board, with which Local 2732 was affiliated, introduced you as if she were calling a sporting event: "Maria.

Alma. Gomez. García!" The crowd exploded in a raucous standing ova-
tion. You high-fived your way down the aisle and climbed the stage
stairs. The organizing director followed behind to interpret. You began
as we had practiced in my hotel room the night before, with a statement
you said was "the plain fucking truth": "En Phoenix, sí se puede!" The
chanting that followed was floor-shaking.

In the weeks following the convention, I heard rumblings of merger trouble in other cities, mainly consisting of UNITE organizers complaining
about a toxicity in the organizing culture of HERE, about the way HERE
organizers were treating each other and the way they were treating workers who were leading organizing fights in their hotels.

But in Phoenix, those early days of the merger were convenient and
smooth. You helped me pack our office into a few boxes and haul the
grungy couch back to Goodwill. We moved the boxes to the HERE office
at the local Odd Fellows building, which was staffed by two people—the
Local 631 manager, Jorge, and the office administrator, Lisa, who were
married to each other. They were not an organizing local—they had not
organized nonunion workers in many years—but they were both kind
people, and Jorge was a diligent business agent, who processed and
tracked grievances at the workplaces where HERE members had collective bargaining agreements. They cleared a desk for us. They started bak-
ing double batches of banana bread and springing for extra doughnuts to
ensure that there was enough to share with us. Jorge agreed to train the
shop stewards in any laundries we organized, and Lisa agreed to process
the Local 2732 dues, so that we could stay focused on organizing. They let
us use the office copy machine to make our lists and leaflets and petitions
and union cards, so that we no longer had to go to Kinko's. In compari-
son to our old setup, it was a bonanza of ease and efficiency. It was lovely
on all fronts.

On the wall over our new desk, we hung the printed photo of strikers from the Uprising of the 20,000, their black coats draped around them like great wings, and we dug into our organizing. We were still bajo el agua at Angelica, still building our lists there. We followed Milum trucks to map their clients. And as part of the Big 3 campaign, we launched a new front, at the cafeterias of Arizona State University, where the food-service workers across campus were also employed by Sodexho.

One afternoon, we met with one of these workers at her home, in a trailer park just a block away from the university. She had a shift schedule, complete with worker names and phone numbers, from a bulletin board at the deli where she worked at one of the campus dining halls, just as you had eighteen months earlier. We were meeting with her to collect it. Inside her living room, she told us that the anti-fatigue mat at her workstation had been removed, or stolen maybe by another worker for use at their own station, which is something that happened often with too few mats to go around. Her feet and hips ached, she said, from standing on the hard floor, and she shifted her weight from one foot to the other as we talked. She told us that her weekly schedule had changed again, for the third time in a month, making it impossible to arrange steady care for her one-year-old daughter, who slept on a chair in the corner while we talked.

Some of her neighbors in the trailer park worked for Sodexho, too, though not in her deli. They were scattered across the dining halls and retail spaces on campus. She stepped out onto her small landing to point out the trailers where these other workers lived, and one of them happened to see her and came over to say hello. While they talked, another coworker arrived. This campaign was not secret, there would be no bajo el agua phase—the company knew we were coming for them; the unions had already announced Phoenix as one of ten cities where they would open ground. So we walked around the park with them, knocking on trailer doors, until nine workers had gathered together, and we held a union meeting.

Four days later, the woman who had given us the list called—the company was pulling workers into captive-audience meetings, saying something about cards being like blank checks to the union, which was confusing because, while workers were openly talking with each other about forming a union, no one had signed or even seen a union card. It wasn't that kind of campaign, though apparently the company didn't know it.

This was a corporate campaign, in the vein of the one our union's predecessor, ACTWU, had developed against J. P. Stevens in the late 1970s, also called a pressure campaign. Our goal—the point of making contacts among the food-service workers—was not to quietly build the structure of a union that could withstand the company's anti-union campaign, as had been our goal at your laundry. The goal was to set off a flash point that would be one of dozens at Sodexho and Compass and Aramark worksites in the ten designated "open ground" cities across the country. The point was for the companies to think that we had live campaigns everywhere, to overwhelm their ability to fight back, and to bring them quickly to the table and into an accord on card-check neutrality, as had happened at Top Shelf, but this time on a national scale.

We had also drummed up some support among local student activist groups, and when Sodexho launched this anti-union campaign, we formed a delegation; our comité at the laundry—you and Santiago and Cecilia and Antonia and Analía and Pollo and the others—along with these student supporters and a handful of the food-service workers with whom we had made contact. We went to the university president's office with a letter, asking him to instruct the company to remain neutral and to allow workers to form a union through card check—asking him to threaten, essentially, that the university would cut its contract with the company if it didn't. The president would not meet with us, to the surprise of no one, but you were indignant about it anyway, and you slapped the letter down on the receptionist's desk and spelled your name out for her through gritted teeth.

Also to the surprise of no one, the captive-audience meetings decimated the delicate early network of union supporters. After a few weeks of this intimidation, almost no one, including the woman who had given us the shift schedule, would talk to us again.

I don't know if the architects of the Big 3 campaign imagined that when the unions ultimately won card-check agreements, the worksites where they had chosen to set off these flash points would be among those to get card checks. That is not what happened, which may have been for the best, as any chance we might have had at winning a union among these workers, even through card check, was completely scorched.

During all of this, the status of your union was still on appeal, and you were still working full-time on second shift in the laundry, making $7.45 an hour. But we had hope that this national campaign would force Sodexho to withdraw its appeal of the bargaining order we had won, that we would at long last negotiate a contract, and that then you would be free from having to hold the embattled union together from inside the factory and could take leave from the plant to focus on training as an organizer. One problem with this plan was that being licensed to drive and to rent cars is a prerequisite for a job as an organizer. The union was unlikely to pay for you to be on an extended organizing leave from work, much less put you on staff, if you could not work independently, so we decided that I would teach you to drive.

On the first day of our lessons, we sat in the car in the parking lot of the UNITE HERE office, and you revved the engine while it was in park to get used to the gas pedal. The next day, you inched the car forward and screeched the brakes a few times before saying that you'd had enough. And the next day, I goaded you into practicing again, though you had not wanted to, and you drove the rental car into a tree. We hit hard, and even after the car had stopped advancing, your foot held the accelerator to the floor for what felt like a long time. The tires spun and spun, digging themselves down into the dirt. I could not remember the work for *brake*, and so I yelled "Stop!" in English, over and over until you did. I had never seen you so afraid. I put my arm around your shoulders. You shuddered. *Polilla, we're okay*, I said.

You went home on the bus that day, and the next day, you did not answer your phone. The day after that, you called me and told me that you would not learn to drive, that I had to promise never to ask you to again. *You have to have a license to be an organizer*, I said. *Yes, I know*, you said.

When the new HERE organizers arrived, they were surprised to find us and our maps and charts and strategic plans covering the office walls. Their boss, the head of organizing on the HERE side, had told them there was no organizing happening in Arizona, that their mission was to move to Phoenix to revive the little HERE local there, which he described to them as "an outpost of the union." They were sent to build an organizing program and culture from scratch, to find and train a team of organizers. They were sent to take charge, said the male organizer of the pair, on their first afternoon in the office. And this despite the fact that organizers employed by the international union (as we all were) were not meant to take charge of locals (unless they are doing so hostilely), especially where local elected leadership is in place, as Jorge was for Local 631 and as the Mission shop stewards were for Local 2732, a local they had not known existed.

Yet here they were, said the two organizers, who were also a married couple, and they had moved all the way from the Northeast, where they had been graduate students at a prestigious university and then leaders among a group of graduate students who were fighting to form a union with HERE. They had left their lives and friends behind and had already purchased a house in Phoenix, because the union told them they were needed here.

In fact, the husband of the couple had arrived with the understanding that he, specifically, had been sent to lead the local out of its defunct state and backwater ways, and he was visibly taken aback to hear that not only were there organizing campaigns actively underway, but that I was also a lead organizer, a title that put me at equal rank to him.

This information was exchanged fairly quickly, in the span of about twenty minutes. The conversation happened in English, so you did not understand most of it, but you could read the tension between this new organizer and his wife, who had barely spoken, and Jorge, who seemed as offended as I was, and me. When we got to the car, you raised your eyebrows and drew out the word *pendejo* (asshole) in a comical singsong. And then, more seriously, you said, *Don't let him push you around.*

When the HERE organizer first asked to meet with me, I thought it was to learn about our campaigns—to learn about what we had already organized, what we were currently organizing, what our next targets were—so that the two of us could identify opportunities for helping each other, which, after all, was the promise of the merged union. Instead, we spent most of the meeting arguing ideologically about why workers fight to form unions. At the meeting's outset, he asked, *Why do you think workers fight to form unions?*—his voice, even at the start, a mix of defensiveness and aggression, as if he were performing an argument he'd been trained to have but did not really want to have, or was not totally sure he knew how to have. I was not expecting the question or his demeanor, and he relaxed a little in his chair as I stumbled to come up with a coherent response on the spot.

By this point, I had been holding the question you asked at the end of the three-day training in mind for half a year—*What gives some people a will to fight even while others fall down in their fear?*—and so I answered his question in the way I would have answered yours at the time (though I was certain, even then, that what he had put forth was a test and not a question). I said something about people being tired of living and working in the conditions they do, and being both angry and hopeful enough to risk their jobs to change those conditions.

That's not it at all, the organizer said in a tone that indicated he was pleased. *It is because they trust us as their leaders.* An odd and combative exchange followed, at the end of which he insisted we meet again the next day, and because I did not want him to think he had intimidated me (and did not want you to think I had let him push me around), I agreed.

The next day, he came to the office with a list of questions—typed and printed out—that rested on his knee as he spoke. The questions were intrusive; some even sought to excavate my personal past. They were the kind of thing you might ask in conversation with a close friend, and I did not want to answer them—or I did not want to answer them to him—and so I didn't. I suggested we talk about work instead, about organizing in Arizona, about what we were going to do and how we were going to do it. He was an organizer. A coworker. Why did he feel entitled to ask about my life outside of the union? Why were his questions printed out?

A few minutes into this meeting, I started taking notes, because it was clear that the encounter was more ambush than exchange, and I wanted to have a record of what was happening. I wrote out the phrases he used: *We will not be able to work together if you don't trust us*, and *It is clear that we can't trust you*, and *This does not bode well for you*. I wrote, *This is basic, entry-level organizer stuff*, and *How did you get this far without learning to tell your story?* and *Telling your story* (which he defined alternately as "what made you want to organize" and "what keeps you in the fight" and "what turned you into someone worth following") *gets workers to tell you theirs*, and *We don't build unions without getting workers to follow us*, and *You can't push workers if you don't know their story*, and *You wouldn't have made it through one month of training in our union.*

Looking now at this series of phrases scrawled in my old notebook, I'm not as disoriented by them as I was at the time. Instead, I see that slipperiness of union-building pronouns, starting with the *we* that I had long struggled to decipher even in the language of UNITE. Now these other pronouns—*you, they, us, our*—which he used in reference to organizing in ways with which I was unfamiliar or unacculturated, were also difficult to grasp. The organizer was building a union with these words that did not look much like the one I thought you and I were trying to build.

I told him that I did not think trust could be manufactured via questionnaire. I told him that I thought it was gross, not to mention dangerous, to require people to bond with you via the sharing of personal stories. He shook his head at me and glared. I don't remember how I weaseled away, but Jorge had overheard this exchange from the other room, and he rolled his eyes to signal his sympathy as I passed his desk on my way to the parking lot.

The next day, the organizer asked to schedule yet another meeting, and when I told him I'd rather not, he stormed out of the office and slammed the door.

I was, of course, angry about this. When you asked how the meetings had gone, I told you that you were right, that he was an asshole. But asshole or not, I understood even then how mystifying these confrontations must have been for him (and his wife, too, though she almost never spoke to me). They had moved across the country under the promise that they'd get to build a union of the kind they had been trained to build and of which he would get to be in charge. Instead, they encountered an already-growing union that was not structured at all around the kind of leadership to which he saw himself ascending.

Both the organizer and I spent the better part of the next few days calling our directors and other organizers and lead organizers and friends from our respective sides of the merged union, trying to figure out what had happened and how we were supposed to work together. I know he made these calls because he told me that his director had instructed him to meet with me again (which I would not do), to keep pushing me to answer the questions on his sheet (which I would not do) and tell him my "story" (which, if I am being honest, I did not know). I emailed our director the notes I had taken during the meeting. She called and empathized but cautioned me against letting it interfere with my work. *There are a lot of jerks in the union*, she said. *Don't waste your time with them. Focus on the campaigns.*

You were not invited to these meetings with the organizer. He had not even asked your name, as you pointed out in the car after calling him "pendejo." And I did not insist on your attending—having to interpret for him would only double the meeting time, I reasoned. Besides, the argument he wanted to make seemed reserved for staff organizers. He wasn't meeting with Jorge or Lisa or the laundry local leaders. His argument about leadership—which was mainly, it seemed, about *his* leadership—focused on the idea that union power consists of workers' trust in their leaders, in their willingness to do what their leaders tell them to do.

This was not the substance of the power we were building, at least not as I had come to think of it. His notion of union power was top-down, a vector rather than a container, more interested in determining the position of the people who made up the union with respect to each other. This clashed with what I had come to imagine as a kind of cup—a *solidatious* cup—with room enough to encompass both the small, repetitive tasks that comprise organizing (the loading of the copy machine to print the house-call sheets, the unloading of the folding chairs to set up the committee meetings) and the moments of new power manifested (the thunder of voices as they bounced off the factory wall and back onto the bodies of the people who stood in the parking lot shouting, transmuting the air and space between them into a new energy).

I started going to the office early in the morning or late at night, when no one else was there, to sort house-call sheets or make copies or pick up supplies. In between these odd-hours bookends to the day, I would pick you up at your house and we would drive our circles and knock doors and talk to workers, and then I'd drop you off again. Over the course of several weeks, I moved our files and records out of their cabinets and into boxes that slid around in the rental-car trunk. We listened in on conference calls about the Big 3 and Angelica campaigns from a picnic table at the park down the street from your factory. I hung our organizing charts on the wall in my motel room and updated them there at night. We ate lunch at La Salsita or at Eliana's or at your house, when Julio was not at home. I was avoiding confrontation with the organizer, but I was also protecting you (I told myself) from his bad behavior and from the disappointment of the merger not working out as we had hoped. I did not want you to have to wonder about what kind of union you had spent those years fighting to join or to know that the organizer believed you had done it in order to follow his leadership, to follow him.

It did not strike me at the time that this paternalism—my decision that you should not be involved or even aware of this internal strife—was also a vector, a top-down decision that outlined a hierarchy (one I had long ignored).

This conflict with the organizer raised in me an acute awareness and a mounting anxiety over my own organizing practices, a need to justify the ways in which the organizing conversation I'd been trained to have—the one I'd trained you and other workers and staff organizers to have—was different from this other method, which seemed a minefield of manipulation. We were trained to root out workers' "issues," the things they'd most like to change about their jobs, in order to agitate around them, to use them in order to stoke anger, which we are trained to understand as the key emotion to overcoming fear. And I had been trained, mostly by way of observing the practices of the organizers around me, to firewall my personal life and not to dig into the personal lives of workers for fodder to push them through the fear of a fight. We agitated on issues at work, not issues at home, and the difference marked the line, in my mind, between good organizing and the creation of a coercive system that would, at best, do nothing more than replace the coercive system in which workers were already engaged with their bosses at work.

In house calls, I found myself continually working through this reasoning, obsessing over these differences, examining every word exchanged for signs that I might be causing harm. I did this as we sat talking on people's front porches or in their living rooms, zoning out from the conversation to pick apart whatever I had just heard myself say instead of listening. More than once, you had to nudge me with your knee or the back of your hand to let me know it was my turn to speak.

During this time, I started to lose a lot of weight. The trouble was not that I had decided to stop eating, or that I spent any time thinking about eating or not eating—it was just that I could not seem to remember to do it. One afternoon, when I picked you up in the parking lot after your shift, you looked at me from the passenger seat, your concern spilling over into real annoyance. You looked at me with an expression I recognized as one my mother would sometimes put on when I was small and having some kind of tantrum, as if she wished she could inject me with a strength I did not have. *What is happening to you, Polillita?* you asked, and then dug into your bag and handed me an orange wedge left over from your lunch.

Some mornings, I could not will myself to leave the motel. I would call you to tell you I didn't feel well, which was only partly true—really it was that I could not, or perhaps just did not want to, talk to anyone, not during house calls, not at all—and then I would sit in the motel room and watch reruns of *Dawson's Creek* and smoke cigarettes through the open window. I would then close the window and try to seal the curtains shut by pushing chairs and pillows up against their seams to stave off any Phoenix sunlight that tried to stray around them. Most mornings, I recorded the moth dream in my notebook: *Polillas*, it says, again and again.

In December of 2004, almost two years from the first time I sat on the olive couch in your living room and you told us you knew what it is to fight, Sodexho gave in to the mounting pressure of the national campaign and agreed to let UNITE HERE and SEIU organize twenty thousand of its workers by card check, without interfering in the process. The other two of the Big 3 would also likely settle soon, we were told.

The point on which Sodexho would not relent, as the deal was explained to me, had been the demand that the company withdraw its appeal of the bargaining order at your factory. The corporation's international office insisted that the local management in Phoenix simply would not agree to drop the appeal because they did not believe that a majority of the workers currently in the factory wanted to form a union. And so, despite the judge's legal decision that there was no fair, untainted process by which to establish whether or not you and your coworkers wanted a union, we were going to have to go through a process anyway. After the company's two-year anti-union campaign, we had to see if we could build majority support for unionization among your coworkers all over again.

10: Fires

YOU ONCE TOLD me that moths are messengers, that I needed to listen to what they were telling me. I tried hard to do this but could not discern any message. The moths weren't *telling* me anything.

The internet, unsurprisingly, has a lot to say about how one might interpret dreams about moths. One site reports that moths "connect to the nocturnal, feminine, psychic, and shadow—uncharted parts of the psyche of the dreamer," and that they might "indicate a tendency toward self-destructive behaviors." I tend to enjoy these pseudo-soothsayings, even though I don't understand or put much stock in them. Another site: "To dream of a moth represents a person or situation that is imposing itself upon you." According to a third site, "Seeing a moth following the light may indicate that you have a strong desire for something that you may be hiding in your waking life. Being flocked by moths can indicate being overwhelmed by the desires of everyone else." A fourth site concludes, "Moths are curious creatures, flying in a cloak of darkness, yet are attracted to bright light. Their presence can give mixed feelings of wonder and unease, as it is hard to know what their intention is."

Even under the auspices of dream, the moth's power, its agency or the meaning behind its agency or lack thereof, is unclear: desirer or desired, determined pursuer or faithful servant or mere sufferer of impositions.

In dreams as in language and biology, we have little idea what the moth is doing or why.

I once told a friend about the dream. That, in it, I was covered with moths except for my eyes, that I watched them shiver their wings in preparation for flight. She said, *Maybe you were afraid there was something you weren't seeing*, which was perplexing until she explained that a lot of people associate moths with blindness. I had not yet read about their slow-adapting eyes.

The ancient Greeks depicted the human soul as a figure with wings: a moth, or possibly a butterfly. *Soul* for them was not an immortal entity or spirit. It was something closer to a living being, a conscious, breathing body. They named the moth figure *psyche*, making the word a homonym meaning both "the invisible, animating principle that directs a physical body" or a person's "driving force" and any one of the scaly-winged insects of the world. *Soul* and *moth* were the same word.

Psyche is also a goddess, characterized alternately as a princess loved by Eros (or Cupid, to the Romans) and a princess who fell in love with Eros. In a myth recorded in the fifth book of Lucius Apuleius's *The Golden Ass*—the only ancient Roman novel in Latin to survive in its entirety—Psyche is a too-beautiful mortal, who is envied by Venus, and who has a hard time not looking at things she has been told not to see.

In a quest to humiliate Psyche, Venus commands Cupid to pierce her with a poison arrow that will cause her to fall in love with a hideous man, but Cupid bungles the errand, pricks himself, and falls in love with Psyche. To save her from Venus, Cupid brings Psyche to a hidden palace, where she communes with disembodied voices and, in the dark of night, with Cupid, whom she cannot see. At first, Psyche agrees not to inquire about his identity, but then one night, she lights a lamp. Cupid is asleep on the bed. He is delicate and ethereal; his great feathered wings are folded softly at his back. Psyche leans in closer. Her hand trembles, and hot oil spills from the lamp. Cupid wakes up, livid at her defiance. He levitates from the bed and flies away.

Psyche wanders the world until she finds Venus and commits to serve her in the hope of being allowed to see Cupid again. Venus designs a gauntlet of impossible tasks, the last of which is to enter the underworld to obtain a box of beauty from Proserpina. Psyche doesn't know how to get to the underworld except by dying, so she climbs a tower, intending to jump, but a voice, which seems to arise from the tower itself, tells her how to complete the task alive. As a final directive, it warns her to restrain her curiosity about the contents of the box, not to open it.

Psyche navigates the lures and traps of the underworld and reemerges "ravished with a great desire," as one translation has it, to see what's in the box. She opens it and falls down in the middle of the road, "a sleepy corpse without sense or motion." Cupid finds and revives her, and just as she regains consciousness, he chides her for looking. "Again," he says, "you have almost perished by the same curiosity."

Apuleius's version of the myth makes no mention of Psyche transforming, but some accounts have it that, as Cupid scolds her, she transforms. Small, iridescent wings, far different from the bird wings of Cupid, unfurl from her back, and she ascends skyward.

The Greeks knew that moths flew into fire. They were probably picking wings out of wax more nights than not. And though Psyche, the goddess depicted as a moth, is not alone in the mythos of women who want to have or see or know or be more than they are supposed to, this story— about a woman who was told not to look but who had a sort of death drive to see—seems a convoluted way to think about what drives us, to think about our souls. What does it mean to raise the idea of self-sabotage and the question of what drives us to it, then call it *soul* and then call it *moth*? Does the moth know what it desires? Does it know if it's driven *to* the flame or driven *by* it? Does the moth know that it is, by definition, *drive*? (Is the moth simply a way around an either/or?)

Most ancient images of Psyche depict her as winged and in a state of unlooking. She is blindfolded. She closes her eyes. She shields her eyes with her arm or hand. She looks away from whatever is in front of her. Cupid holds her head at such an angle that she cannot see him.

But in my favorite representation of the myth, Giuseppe Crespi's painting *Amore e Psiche*, she is neither blind nor winged. She is pre-goddess, just a woman, in the act of looking. She lives to look—you can see it in the angle of her neck, the curve of her body. She leans in with the lamp. Cupid is awake but remains on the bed. He hides himself in his hand's shadow as the lamplight pours over Psyche. It is her body that is illuminated.

I do sometimes try to let go of the moths—mainly for fear that my fascination or obsession has oversymbolized them, has taken the shape of a hammer that I'm banging around childishly, pounding a bunch of soft bits of information into the space of grief, the space of missing you and what we built together in Phoenix over those years.

And that may be, but then something happens and connects them to the fight, connects them back to you. Something like this: I see the name Sol Stetin—who was president of the Textile Workers Union of America (one of several unions that, through a series of mergers, eventually formed UNITE) and architect of the J. P. Stevens campaign—in an email about the beginnings of this very book, from an editor, who happens to be Stetin's granddaughter. He is a figure from the union's history whom I have generally admired for his willingness to let go of his own institutional power for the good of J. P. Stevens workers and their campaign. The email prompts me to read more about him, and I discover that he was also the cofounder of the American Labor Museum at the Botto House in Haledon, New Jersey. The Botto House had been the home of Pietro and Maria Botto and their four daughters, who worked in silk mills and were leaders of the Paterson Silk Strike in 1913.

When twenty-four thousand silk workers walked out, Paterson's anti-union mayor passed an emergency ordinance, making it illegal for the strikers to gather on public property, hoping, I suppose, that the move would disorganize the strike and force workers back into the mills. In response, the Bottos turned their house into a headquarters for the strike, and for five months, workers rotated in and out, holding meetings, trading food and supplies, and listening to speeches delivered from the second-floor balcony by labor figures like Elizabeth Gurley Flynn, Carlo Tresca, and Upton Sinclair. This strike was one of the last in a wave of garment strikes that were inspired by the Uprising of the 20,000 and were intensified by the shock and rage people felt as a result of the Triangle fire.

Paterson had branded itself the Silk City of the United States, because a majority of the country's silk textiles were produced in its mills. Raw silk in the form of moth cocoons was shipped there from sericulture farms farther north, where the silkworm and the white mulberry tree had been imported by the British over two hundred years earlier in hopes that both the moths and the trees would fare better here than in their own boggy soil. By the 1830s, as the Canuts were revolting in the streets of Lyon, seizing the heart of the European silk industry, sericulture had taken enough of a hold in Massachusetts and Connecticut to fill the growing demand for silk, and the industry in this country became wholly independent.

By the mid-1860s, the eggs being laid by the two hundredth or so generation of US silk moths were hardy enough to be exported to Italy after a crop of moths there was wiped out by disease. Still, an artist and amateur entomologist living in Medford, Massachusetts, Étienne Léopold Trouvelot, hoped to make the US moths even more productive. In 1869, he imported egg masses from Europe to crossbreed with local silk moths. The egg masses came from the *Lymantria dispar* moth, which, until July 2021, was commonly known as the "gypsy moth," a name finally recognized as the slur it was and discarded by entomologists, though the moth has yet to be assigned a new common name. Trouvelot conducted his experiment in the forest behind his house, intermingling the larvae from both species as they hatched and fed and molted. He did not safeguard against their spread into the surrounding woods, and one spring, twenty years later, the trees over many acres bloomed grandly, then defoliated and died. When inspected, they were teeming with caterpillars. By then, Trouvelot had lost interest in moths, had turned instead to astronomy, and was well into a successful career that involved painting the stars.

The first instar of the *Lymantria dispar* caterpillar is small and lightweight. They tend to hatch on warm days and then spin down on a silken thread from whatever leaf they were on and are borne aloft by the breeze. They glide along—ballooning, it's called—sometimes for miles, before landing. They have the ability to digest the foliage from just about any tree, and in this way over the next fifty years, they dispersed and ate clean tens of millions of acres of hardwood forest.

In 1923, the federal government attempted to contain the moths. Workers were sent aloft to scrape egg masses off the branches of oaks and aspens and apples and sweetgums to form a barrier zone—thirty miles wide, from Long Island to the Canadian border. They burned every stone wall within the zone to incinerate the egg masses. They inspected shipments of lumber and flour and cranberries and sweet corn. They draped burlap over millions of trees to prevent the moths from depositing their eggs under the bark. The workers sprayed an arsenic-and-copper compound, called Paris green, from horse-drawn wagons, saturating the landscape but also their clothes and hands and arms. It burned them, ulcerated their skin. The exposure gave them nerve damage. And even then the barrier zone failed.

So you see how it goes. I'm not just grasping at threads. I was looking up Sol Stetin only because I had learned from the email that he was the grandfather of the person who became this book's editor. I learned, subsequently, that she was also Julia Alvarez's editor at Algonquin Books, which had published her book *In the Time of the Butterflies*, the novel about the Mirabal sisters that I was reading in the motel in 2003 before we started calling ourselves Las Polillas.

During these same years of the bursting forth of *Lymantria dispar* and the failing barrier zone, an internal war was raging at the ILGWU. Fannia Cohn, who had worked closely with Rose Schneiderman and Clara Lemlich in 1909 to build strike committees at the garment factories that were struck after the Cooper Union meeting, organized her own ILGWU local in Brooklyn that same year—Local 41. There she organized garment workers to fight alongside Clara's Local 25 in the strike wave that continued on, through the Paterson Silk Strike in 1913. The following year, she traveled to Chicago to organize garment workers and form a local there before returning to New York in 1916 to become the first woman elected to the union's executive board. Back in New York, she discovered that, though the Triangle fire had brought about real change—from forcing the passage of workplace-safety and child-labor laws to seeding movements around minimum wage and workers compensation—the ILGWU itself had not evolved. The union, whose vast majority of members were women, was still led by men, who remained, for the most part, flatly opposed to letting the women lead.

Refusing to allow her new position as the first woman on the union's executive board to be a mere token of representation, Fannia convinced the other members of the board to fund an education department, modeled after the one in Local 25, which had been developed by strikers during the Uprising. She hoped that education, through a wide-ranging curriculum, could eventually give rank-and-file women greater control over the direction of their union. Through this department, Fannia brought thousands of garment workers into courses on economics, literature, history, and current events, all organized around the belief that workers—and especially women workers—should not settle for small change, should not be placated by a few-cent raise and slightly cleaner bathrooms, but should seek empowerment in the broadest sense, should demand that their union be an engine of transformation for their lives and communities. And that is what they did.

In 1917, emboldened by this education, the women of the ILGWU began to demand representation in the leadership of their union. Their rebellion budded on the shop floors among the membership of Local 25 and then spread to Local 41 and then to locals in Chicago and Philadelphia and Boston, places where women made up a large majority of the membership. They organized what they called a "shop delegates league" to campaign for a more democratic union and to oust the male leadership of the locals and elect their own leaders. The women petitioned and marched and rallied. They stormed union meetings. They occupied local offices, barricading doors and locking out the men. In 1919, as their push gained momentum, the leadership of the national union conducted a hostile takeover of Local 25. They broke into the office, changed the locks, split the local into three separate entities, and placed male trustees in charge of each.

The union's record of this period is chaotic, partly because factions among the male leadership co-opted the women's rebellion as an opening to expand their own fight over internal democracy. As a result, much of the union's official history focuses on the story of that fight—left versus right and communists battling socialists—instead of the story of the women, who, agitated in Fannia's classes, sparked the bigger war.

In her book *Common Sense and a Little Fire*, which serves as a crystalline portrait of Clara Lemlich and Fannia Cohn, as well as Rose Schneiderman and Pauline Newman, another worker leader from the time, historian Annelise Orleck writes that the union's own historian, Louis Levine, credited the women's rebellion as the instigation for the broader fight, though he fails to get at the heart of their rebellion or its co-optation. Levine writes: "The desire of this group of 'girls' to impart a 'soul' to their union . . . gave rise to an organized and persistent effort to 'rejuvenate' the local by getting rid of 'old' leaders and officers who were regarded as 'too practical' and 'conservative.'" Orleck responds: "What Levine neglected to say is that all of those 'old,' 'practical,' leaders were male in a local that was more than 75 percent female." Levine was right that the "old" leaders were too conservative for their membership, who together had grown a will to fight for a more radical union, but he missed that these rebel members were mainly women, who didn't want to simply belong to this radical union once they'd built it; they wanted to lead it, too.

Despite its overshadowing, the women's insurgency continued under Fannia's encouragement for five years, through 1923, when the union's executive board launched a rash of tribunals to quash it. They hauled in the rebels who had still not left of their own accord and expelled them. That year, twenty thousand men joined the ranks of the ILGWU and forty-five thousand women left—over half the total number of women in the union.

Fannia did not leave. She refused, and her position on the executive board made her unexpellable. But the internal fight dispirited her. Orleck writes that she "was driven to the brink of breakdown several times . . . and to actual physical collapse twice." Fannia stayed because, according to Orleck, while she did not trust the union to work in the interests of its women members, she trusted women's organizations, led by the wealthy but built on the idea of a cross-class solidarity, even less. So she lived and worked in isolation in the union for another forty years, condemned by both sides—by the militants, for not leaving with them, and by the union's leadership, for her refusal to condemn the rebellion. Of the breakdowns, she said, "It is not the work that broke me down, but rather the atmosphere that surrounded me."

Finally, when Fannia Cohn was seventy-seven, still apparently a thorn in the side of the union's male leadership, the ILGWU's then president, David Dubinsky, who, when speaking to other powerful men, referred to her as his "cross to bear," as they all had pushy women among their ranks whom they considered to be theirs, forced her to retire. The union held a nice luncheon where everyone stood in turn to praise her long, historic career. "Cohn accepted the tribute with her characteristic close-lipped smile, shook hands with her colleagues, and came back to work the next day—and every day after that," Orleck writes in an essay about Fannia. "An exasperated David Dubinsky ordered her personal effects packed and her office space cleared out to make room for her replacement. He changed the locks on her office door. Resolutely, Cohn continued to come in. She would sit for hours, with her coat and hat on, upright and silent in the hallway outside of her old office at union headquarters. The standoff lasted for a full four months, until on December 23, 1962, she failed to appear. Friends searched her apartment and found her body. The tiny, unswerving activist had died of a stroke."

Rose Pesotta, one of the young garment workers who found her voice in Fannia's classes, stuck around in the union, too. She went on to lead strikes from New York to Los Angeles and later succeeded Fannia as the ILGWU's vice president and its only woman executive, a role that she, like Fannia, fought to make more than a token.

Rose later wrote two memoirs about union organizing. In the first, *Bread Upon the Waters*, she recalls joining Local 25 in 1913, after her older sister helped her find a job in a New York shirtwaist factory. "At its meetings I learn about the 'Uprising of the 20,000' women and girls in 1909, my sister Esther among them, who walked out of the waist factories in protest against intolerable sweatshop conditions . . . imbued with their spirit, others now carry on . . . ," she writes in regard to the same stories I would hear and learn to tell over ninety years later.

The book documents a campaign among immigrant workers, whom Rose calls "the Mexican girls," in Los Angeles, where a group of mainly women workers grew a fierce network of grassroots solidarity, and where their fight, the Los Angeles garment workers' strike of 1933, was largely settled by a union leader from New York in a meeting they were not invited to attend. Later, Rose sought permission from Dubinsky to run for a leadership position in the Los Angeles local this movement had formed, but he turned her down. In 1938, she resigned from the ILGWU with a letter to Dubinsky that included a scathing critique of institutionalized sexism in the union. In one part, she writes, "Although you mention the fact that the 200,000 women members are really the backbone of our organization (November 6th installment-Journal-American) this fact is consistently pussy-footed by our leadership, who because of this formidable backbone are comfortable in the saddle today."

In another part of the letter, Rose writes of Fannia "Fannia Cohn's service to our organization is only recognized by those on the outside who can dispassionately evaluate such unselfish efforts on the part of one person, for the cause of worker's education. But most of the credit is now the heritage of the director who has entered the field after the thorns were weeded out, the marshes dried and all other obstacles removed."

In reading about Fannia Cohn and the rebellion she inspired, I encountered similar sentiments from other early woman leaders of the union. In 1917, Pauline Newman wrote: "We learned that there is a mysterious bond between working sisters . . . and we only wished that devotion and sisterhood would have more opportunity to lift its head."

As I read this passage, my first response is *Amen*, or even *Amen, sister*, as women in unions tend to call each other. Rose writes of a bond here to which I certainly aspired but on which I mainly trespassed. I was not a "working sister," and locating myself in this *we*, in this long history of women in the union, is a complex exercise—I manage to end up on both sides of at least a few locked doors. (And if this writing is a practice of longing for an uncomplicated *we*, or for a *we* that is not in need of ongoing examination, let it resist any telling that pretends one could exist.)

11: Las Polillas

IT WAS THE organizing director, again, who called to give me the news. This time, that there would be a card check at your factory. She framed this, at first, as good news: we would no longer have to wait the undefined number of months or years to hear back on the status of the company's appeal, and it would be better than having to go through another election, and the company had promised that the managers and supervisors would remain neutral.

The fact that Sodexho's corporate office had been unable to force the local managers to agree to withdraw its appeal as part of an international settlement with the unions did not bode well for its capacity to police their behavior during the card-check process, she admitted. *But, look*, she said, *it's just one final push to prove to everyone that a majority of the workers want to have a union.* No, she said, the old cards, now over two years old, would not count—the people who were still working at the factory after signing the first time would have to sign again. And, *yes*, she knew that the labor board judge had made a legal decision stating that it was unreasonable to ask the workers to do this, to have to decide all over again, after the company had totally scorched the ground in the factory, which is why the judge had issued the Gissel remedy, the order for the company to recognize the union immediately and outright instead of holding a second election. *But*, said the director, *if we want to win a union, this agreement is now the fastest way to do it.* At this, I thought, childishly, *No—the fastest way would be for the company to drop its fucking appeal and recognize the fucking union*, which had been the demand on which we had been very publicly campaigning in three countries on two continents for half a year.

I did not say this out loud to her because I understood that this demand had already been traded away, and that it was my job now to shape a new story about the way forward for you and the comité and the rest of the workers in the factory, just as the director was shaping this story for me. Plus I had gotten better by this time at controlling my affect, better at straitjacketing my emotional responses. It had been nearly a year since my upwelling at the three-day training. So it surprised me that my anger at the unfairness of this situation, at least the unfairness of it to you and your coworkers in Phoenix, was still so twinned with despair that I had to unseize, one by one, the muscles in my throat in order to say *I really don't think we can do it.* I did not believe that a majority of the workers in the factory would sign new cards, after being so thoroughly beaten down by the company's actions and the forever timeline of the board process. And she, her voice and demeanor moving from the sugar-coating she was not very good at back to the bald frankness I admired in her, said, *Well, we really fucking have to.*

So after two years of a rabid fight in the laundry, your factory was to be the centerpiece of the new national agreement between Sodexho and the conjoined UNITE HERE and its partner in the campaign, SEIU. It would be the first card check of many hundreds across the county. The negotiator from New York, the same person who had been in charge of the Top Shelf deal, had settled this massive agreement as well, and he referred to what was to happen at your factory as a "test drive" of the process that was designed to bring twenty thousand new members into the union. Any broken cogs we discovered in the machinery of the agreement—in the scripts we were to read, in the schedule governing when and how long we were permitted to be in the lunchroom, or with regard to the quickness and severity of the penalties put in place to encourage both sides to follow the rules—could be fixed, and fine-tuned, he said, before the card-check engine rolled on to other worksites. This meant that all parties—both unions and the company and their competitors in the industry—would be watching. *So no pressure*, joked the director. At least with so many eyes on them, she said, La Sandra and El Mero Mero would be more likely to behave.

We had to win—not just for you and your coworkers and other people who worked for the company, but also for workers at the other two Big 3 multiservice corporations, which had not yet settled with the unions, and which were waiting to see how the card check went at your factory. If it happened painlessly for all involved, if it was clear that the process was efficient and inexpensive, then those companies would realize it was easier and cheaper than fighting to keep the company union-free.

As the director spoke on the other end of the phone, I imagined La Sandra and El Mero Mero, who were likely on a similar call at that same moment with whomever was in charge of breaking the news to them on their end, learning that union organizers would be allowed into the factory, that they would have to remain "neutral" during this process. I imagined them feeling as though the pressure was on to prove what they had been claiming for years, what they must certainly have believed at that point— that a majority of the workers in the factory did *not* want to have a union.

In fact, the union negotiator from New York who had settled the deal told me, as he walked me through the precise details of the agreement over the course of the following week, that La Sandra and El Mero Mero had been told by the corporate lawyer on the company's side to expect that the union would win. To this, La Sandra reportedly replied, *No way in hell.*

But don't worry, the union negotiator said. *The company's lawyer had reprimanded her and instructed her to project to workers the expectation that the union would win.* After all, what the company had won was very valuable to them: In exchange for allowing the union access to one-fifth of its US workforce, the company would have "labor peace," meaning that the unions would halt the national campaign and retract their many tentacles, which included multiple lawsuits and on-the-ground flash points, like the one on the campus of ASU. It meant that workers would not strike. It meant that the unions had agreed not to organize workers at sites not put forth by the company. It meant that the contracts bargained through the process would not be aligned by date, minimizing the ability of workers across worksites to act collectively at the point of bargaining or in the future.

I was in the motel when the director called to give me this news—that a card check would have to happen, and that we had to win it—and after we hung up, I vomited into one of those flimsy plastic cups wrapped in its plastic sleeve. Then I called you and explained it to you as she had explained it to me: We would have to sign cards again. It was the fastest way to win. It was a sacrifice on the local level, for you and your coworkers, but a lot of good would come of it. Twenty thousand workers would not have to fight as you have had to fight.

When I was done talking, you were quiet for a long moment and then, dryly, you said, *Bueno*, and hung up the phone.

I drove to your house right away. We sat on the olive couch, both of us on the verge of crying. We nodded to each other, as if giving permission to cry, but then did not. You threw some mail that was piled on the cushion next to you across the room. You shook your head. *We won't get enough people to sign*, you said.

Aside from the members of our comité, which had grown smaller in the time since the election, your coworkers were exhausted and

exasperated and afraid. The turnover in the factory had been manipu-
lated and controlled by the company—La Sandra had handpicked dozens
of new employees, and most of them would not speak to you or to any of
the comité at the factory, nor would they open their doors for us at their
homes. The agreement was set to go into effect in two weeks, and from
that point we would have only six weeks to get to a majority.

We did not need any added challenges, but there was still another:
The cards that you and your coworkers would have to sign would not
state that you wanted to join UNITE, the union you had been fighting
to join for years, or even UNITE HERE, the new union, which we had
announced after the merger via a leaflet drop at the factory. The cards
would state that you wanted to join Service Workers United (SWU), a
new union, an entity jointly affiliated with UNITE HERE and SEIU,
which had been created when Sodexho acquiesced to the corporate campaign so that the project of running so many card checks and bargaining
so many contracts could be handled efficiently. No one had ever heard of
SWU, so we would have to add educating people on what it was and why
it existed to the already long list of things to explain to your coworkers
about this process.

The next day, we held an emergency meeting in Santiago's yard, and
you calmly explained the deal to the comité in the way I had explained it
to you, which was the way it had been explained to me. We had prepared
flip charts in the morning, and we held them up a page at a time as we
talked through the agreement. Page one: *We won! The company gave in.
20,000 Sodexho workers will have the opportunity to join the union.* Page
two: *Fired soil sort workers will move back to first shift at old pay rates
and get back pay! Antonia's warnings will be expunged!* Page three: *In
exchange for winning these things now, we will sign cards again. We have
six weeks to get to majority. When (not if) we do this, we will finally head
to the bargaining table!*

The people in our little circle were stone-quiet except for Santiago, who gave a low whistle through his teeth. Antonia folded her arms across her chest and kicked her feet, which did not quite touch the ground, back and forth, raising a small cloud of dust. Whatever optimism we had tried, probably too hard, to convey was not well received.

Two weeks later, we blitzed again. The organizers who had flown to Phoenix for the first blitz and again for the court hearing were back. And the new union, SWU, sent its own group of organizers, who would be in charge of executing the card checks at other worksites as the national agreement unfolded, for training. Plus we had recruited volunteers from Mission, Top Shelf, CleanCo, and Angelica, and some of the roofers, ironworkers, and painters who we had befriended during the three-day training. On the Thursday before the six-week card check launched, we ran a briefing for this massive team. We made handouts: "Sodexho Phoenix Laundry: A Brief History," and "Major Issues in the Factory," and "Worker Demographics and Turnover," and "Details of the Labor Peace Agreement," and "Our Message on the Doors," and "Company and Union Scripts to Be Read Aloud in the Lunchroom." The session took all day.

On Friday, we went into the factory at the start of the first-shift lunch cycle, wherein each department takes its turn having a lunch break. You had requested the day off from work so that you could be present all day as we launched the card check through these cycles on each of the three shifts. Your request for the day off was denied at first, and so I called the organizing director, who called the negotiator in New York, who called whomever he had been working with at the company's headquarters in Maryland, and two days later, El Mero Mero told you that you could have the day, but without pay.

So you and I were there together. The organizing director was there. The negotiator from New York had flown in to observe. A group of lawyers from the company was there, and so were all of the factory's managers and supervisors and administrators. As per the agreement, La Sandra spoke first. She stood in the front of the room, in between the line of microwaves, half of which were broken, and the soda machine, and she read the company-side script, first in Spanish and then in English, to a group of forty or so first-shift production workers, who sat at the tables in the middle of the room as the horde of company and union representatives stood around its edges.

She was nervous. She kept positioning the document from which she read in front of her face in such a way that it muffled her voice as she announced that the company would recognize the union if a majority of workers signed cards. One of the company lawyers kept interrupting her, telling her to move the paper down so that her voice could be heard. "Sandra, Sandra," he kept yelling, as if barking at a dog. She moved the document away from her face and read that workers had the right to sign a card or not sign a card, that they had the right to speak to union representatives at the factory or in their homes or not to speak to union representatives. Her hands shook, and so the document shook as she spoke.

I looked over at you as this was happening, and you smirked a little and then folded your arms firmly and glared down at the floor as if hyperconcentrated on the words she was speaking. We both knew that seeing La Sandra in this way—bullied and nervous, as someone deserving of sympathy—would cause a mixed reaction among the people in the room, and by our calculus, the card check was already so tainted, so nearly unwinnable, that any hint of Sad Boss would not help us.

When she had finished her script, you read the union-side one in Spanish, and then I read it in English, which was some brief and neutered version of telling workers that forming a union would mean that the company would negotiate with them, that the union was an organization that represented laundry workers across the country to help them improve wages and working conditions. Then La Sandra and the lawyers and managers and supervisors and the union negotiator left the lunchroom. You moved to the front of the room, where La Sandra had stood, and signed your new SWU authorization card, and then each of the members of the comité signed their cards, and then we enacted the plan we had designed and practiced in Santiago's yard when we mapped the lunchroom and its tables, assigning ourselves in teams to different parts of the room and to the people who typically sat there. A few workers signed cards there that day. The vast majority would not.

The director insisted that we include the husband-and-wife HERE organizers—our theoretical comrades—in the blitz. Since they didn't speak much Spanish and didn't know much about industrial laundries or the work that happens there, or the particular sets of issues that arise from that work (just as I did not two years earlier), it made sense to pair them with our strongest worker leaders. The organizer who was sent to take charge asked to be teamed with you, and though neither of us liked the idea, you said, *My God, let's not put him with anyone else*, and that is how you spent your first two days in a car with him.

On the first day, after we had run the morning meeting with the massive team of house callers and handed out the packets of addresses and cards and leaflets, I pulled you aside and told you to call me if he started being an asshole, if he started asking you questions that made you feel uncomfortable. You raised your eyebrows dramatically and said, *Like what, is he going to ask what color my underwear is?* You said this to make me laugh, I know—we were under impossible pressure—but also to remind me that you are who you are and that you would not be bothered by this arrangement.

That night, before the ten o'clock debrief of the twenty or so teams that had gone out that day, I pulled you aside to check in. *It's fine. He barely talks*, you said, and then brandished a small stack of signed cards with a smile.

We were allowed to be in the lunchroom for the first five days of the agreement, but after two days, no one was signing there, and the house-call teams had already knocked on every door, most of them two or three times. By the end of that first weekend, we were just barely over 30 percent on cards. The organizing director and the union negotiator and the organizers who had flown in returned home. Our friends from the other unions went back to their campaigns. We went to the office that Monday, after everyone had gone, and sat down in the small room adjacent to the bigger room where Jorge and Lisa and the HERE-side organizers had their desks, where we had papered the wall with our charts and maps. We swiveled in our chairs in the quiet. *It's better that they're gone*, you said, as if we had just cleared a chessboard to better envision where next to move. And then we spent the morning mapping; if Emilia signs, then Maria O will sign, if Roberto signs, then his two friends on second-shift wash will sign, and so on.

You went back to work on first-shift soil sort. During the day, I did house calls alone or with Cecilia, who would remain fired from the factory, but who still held enough sway with some of your coworkers for them to open their doors when they saw her. During your breaks at the factory, you did what you could by talking with the few coworkers in your department who had not signed. It was difficult to make contact with the people you most needed to talk to, those who worked in other departments and had different break times. The supervisors were monitoring your trips to the bathroom, allowing you to leave your station to go only when they knew no one else was in there. This limited reach was frustrating. At night, you paced the office as we sat among our charts and strategized. We counted the number of cards we would need to get signed in the remaining five weeks of the agreement in order to win, and then we added five to that number, because we knew that the person who would authenticate the card signatures by comparing them to company hiring files (a local church official deemed neutral, or neutral enough, by both sides) was sure to throw out at least a few—the card of someone whose English-fluent child had filled out their W-2, the card of someone who had signed their forms with an X. We combed our lists with that number in mind, highlighting the names of workers we had even the slimmest hope of convincing to sign. And though we attempted this exercise every night for weeks, we could not find a way to get to the number we needed.

The HERE organizer often lurked in the other room of the office during these sessions. Sometimes, he would wait until we were done and then come into the room to tell me that he wanted to meet with me again, to tell me that was he sent to Arizona to be my lead, my supervisor, my mentor, and that even if I didn't know it, I was required to meet with him. But I would not agree.

In the fourth week of the card check, we were still hovering at 40 percent or so and had not collected a new card in many days. I went to the office in the morning to gather house-call sheets and lists for the day, and he was there, looking at our maps and numbers and plans. *You aren't going to make it*, he said.

He could see that our comité had limited reach, that other than your soil-sort department and Pollo's wash department and Antonia and Analía's iron department, which were all on first shift, most people had not signed. He knew, as all staff in organizing unions are trained to know, that this meant that the organic worker leaders in other departments and on other shifts—the people who had the standing with their coworkers to move them one way or the other—were not with us. And he pointed out to me, in a tone of voice that oozed condescension, that losing would permanently fuck up these workers' chance to have a union, and would fuck up our plan to organize the laundry industry in Arizona, and would fuck up the launch of the national labor-peace agreement with Sodexho. And he pointed out that the card check should not have been launched if we were not certain we would win. And he pointed out that he would not have agreed to take it on knowing that it would hurt workers, that organizers should *not*, he emphasized, be in the business of harming workers' chances of forming a union. And he said, *Imagine what it will be like for Alma when you lose, how quickly the company will find a way to fire her again.*

With a week to go in the agreement, we needed five more cards to arrive at a simple majority, meaning that even if we got those, we wouldn't have a buffer for the authentication process. At least half a dozen times, we had been to the house of every worker who had not signed. We went by ourselves. We brought other people from the departments where they worked. We brought the shop stewards from Mission. And when none of that made a difference, we reached beyond the small circle of our local: To one house, we brought a neighbor who was friends with a coworker's husband who was a member of the ironworkers' union (she signed). One afternoon, we made a rash of visits with a priest who was a friend of a friend of a friend of mine in Tucson. His collar helped us get in the door at a few houses, and two more workers signed cards.

What the HERE organizer did not know about the factory from looking at our charts is that the strongest "leader" among the workers who would not sign cards was La Sandra, who, in her position as human resources manager, had spent the years since the election growing the group of workers who were loyal to her. Her "comadres," as she called them—Las Viejas, as we called them—spent a lot of time in the factory away from their workstations, roaming the factory floor, talking to people about why they should not sign union cards. In doing this, they seemed to have locked down all of the remaining workers and set up a hard barrier between us and them.

We arrived at the house of Luz, one of Las Viejas, who had meekly pointed me out to the judge in court a year earlier, as she was unloading groceries from the back of a pickup. This was a lucky break we would remind each other of often in the months that followed, because there is no chance she or any of the other Viejas would have opened their doors for us, though that had not stopped us from knocking. You sent me to talk to her while you waited in the car. *She's very proud that she can speak English*, you said.

I got out of the rental car that afternoon in the final week of the card check, and she yelled from across the lawn that she did not want to talk to me, but she stayed where she was standing as I approached. I put my hands up, as if in surrender, and told her that we only wanted to ask her about negotiating the contract, to get her opinion, because she was an important person in the factory, that a lot of people respected her, listened to her—which was true. I said that the card check would end that week—which was true. I told her that the next step was bargaining—which was partially true (we would get to bargain only if we won)—and that, like it or not, the contract would dictate working conditions and wages for everyone in the factory, whether they were a member of the union or not. I told her that it didn't make sense for us to bargain with the input of only half the factory, that we needed to know what she and the women in her department wanted to prioritize, what they wanted most to change.

She responded tersely, so I panned out, as I was trained to do, and started asking her about the roses in her yard, about the chilis growing in the pot on the porch, about her family. We talked for a long time. A teenager came out to get the rest of the groceries and then kept opening the front door and poking his head out to ask her questions—*Where are the chips?* and *Is so-and-so coming by later?*—as a way, I imagined, of checking in on her. *That's my godson*, she said. *He worries about me.*

The idea that we would bargain the contract without her input must have festered, because finally she started asking me about the negotiations, about the process and who would get to be there and when they would begin. She signed her card against the window of the truck, and then you got out of the car and came over to where we were talking. The two of you did not speak to each other. I could tell from your posture, the way you locked your knees and held your hand to your hip, that you were not ready to let slide the lie she told in court. And though I tried a few times to move the conversation into Spanish so you would know what we were saying, she would not make the switch. She took two empty cards into the factory the next day, then gave them, signed by two of the other Viejas, to Antonia, along with a warning for Antonia to "keep her ugly mouth shut" and not tell anyone they had signed.

It took a couple of weeks for the signature verifier to announce that we had won the card check. You were at work when it happened. You found out because La Sandra started calling groups of Viejas into the office, apparently to give them the news.

Months later, after the contract was ratified and had gone into effect, the union furnished a list of dues-paying members to the company as is required for administration, and La Sandra, stunned to see their names on the list, called the three Viejas back into her office, where they flatly denied signing the cards. La Sandra tried to get the corporate lawyers involved, to investigate or to overturn the results of the card check, which we had won by two cards, but they declined to take up her cause.

There was a lot of crying in the lunchroom on the day of the announcement. It was as if someone had died, you told me when I came to meet you in the parking lot after your shift. We stood among a small group of first-shift supporters and hugged. Santiago and I honked the horns on our cars a few times. We didn't want to push the celebration too far— we'd still have to try to grow the membership in the weeks and months to come. We celebrated more at the next of our monthly cenas, which we made special by adding a jumping castle and some other games for the kids and by buying meat and vegetables, which Jorge grilled in the parking lot.

I almost do not remember the contract negotiations, though getting to them had been a goal of the work we did together over those years. I remember the small conference room at the airport hotel. I remember that we used simultaneous translation headsets that squealed deafen-ingly when we got too close to the radio unit, which was hard to keep our distance from because the room was small and we were crowded into it. This was my first time doing simultaneous translation, and the bizarre-ness and difficulty of listening while speaking scrambled my brain. And since I was translating, I did not take notes on the bargaining, which took place between the corporate lawyer who had barked at La Sandra during the launch of the agreement and the union negotiator who had secured the national labor-peace deal. Even if I had taken notes, there would not be many of them, because the negotiations, which for a new contract typically take many weeks, lasted about six hours spread across two afternoons.

We learned in the days after winning the card count that the national agreement between the union and your company had included a pre-fabricated contract, one that left only small pockets of space for what the negotiator called "local nuance." Those were the last two words I wrote in one of my notebooks, though there were many pages left to fill, and though I do not remember why I put that notebook aside, I imagine now that it was difficult to look at those words, to know that they were what remained after years of promising workers that *you* would bargain the contract, that *you* would decide what changes to prioritize, what to fight for.

It was not a terrible contract—over thirty pages of protections and improvements that included raises and just cause and a grievance procedure. We could not bargain for specific safety improvements, because they would add to the price of the contract for the company, which had been costed out and deemed a fair exchange for labor peace, but there would be a health-and-safety committee, elected by the members in the factory, which would be trained by the union and could work to enforce federal safety standards.

You and I led the comité through the motions of real bargaining anyway: We conducted a survey among your coworkers with questions about what they would most like to focus on improving in the contract, and then we relayed the results to the union negotiator. This communication about the bargaining process was still important, we told ourselves, though we knew that nothing the surveys illuminated would manifest in the contract unless it happened to be included already. We elected a bargaining team to be at the table with the negotiator, and a contract action team to supposedly coordinate messaging and actions in the factory while the bargaining was ongoing, which at that point was purely for show—though thinking back on it now, I am not sure for whom this show was being performed, other than maybe the two of us. The hollowness of the performance seemed to take a toll on you that the years of fighting for a union had not, and afterward you were more tired than I had ever seen you.

The contract was ratified after a fifteen-minute lunchroom presentation by a vote with secret ballots that were left blank by most workers.

We decided that you would not take union leave right away, though this benefit—the ability to take a leave of absence from the factory in order to organize other laundries without losing your job—had been included in the contract. More accurately, *I* decided. You wanted out. You wanted to help prep the campaign at a laundry in Flagstaff and to blitz at Angelica and build lists at Milum. You needed a break from the tension among your still deeply divided coworkers. But I convinced you to stay, arguing that it would all have been for nothing if no one was there to make management follow the contract and to launch the health-and-safety committee and to build the membership among the half of the factory who had not signed cards.

So you stayed, and I started spending a few days a week in Flagstaff, running a campaign there and living at a Best Western. Some weeks, Dario would fly in to help, and Mariana Rivera, the worker leader from Lake Havasu City, took union leave from her factory instead. On weekends when there was work to do in Flagstaff, I would drive down from the edge of northern Arizona's San Francisco Peaks to pick you up, and we would drive back up together to do house visits. The factory there was small, just one shift, and we won the campaign after just two months.

On the day that I cleaned out my Flagstaff motel room of the wall charts and house-call sheets and leaflets and union cards, I packed them into a box and started the drive to Phoenix. There was a heavy rainstorm. A motorcycle cut me off on the highway, and I hydroplaned off the side of a steep bank. The rental car rolled and rolled and then landed on its hood under a tree. I climbed through the shattered back window and back up to the highway to call for an ambulance, but I dialed your number, reflexively, instead, and then was surprised to hear your voice at the other end of the line.

After checking to see if I was okay—Was anything broken? Was I bleeding?—you asked if the union cards were still in the car. They were, so we hung up and I climbed back down the embankment to retrieve the box of documents, which I then carried down the highway to the next exit, where I waited at a diner for a taxi to come from Phoenix and drive me to my motel there.

The next day, I stayed in bed. My phone had died, but I didn't charge it, because I did not want to talk to anyone. In the afternoon, you took three buses to bring me caldo made with veggie stock and you wrapped my neck in towels that you made hot with water from the tub faucet. You picked glass out of my hair while I sipped the soup.

Jorge had gotten permission from the regional joint board of the union to move the locals to a new building, with space enough for the HERE-side organizers and Jorge and our team to each have separate offices. Mariana and Dario helped me hang our Angelica and Milum charts there and make a filing system for our campaigns, new and old, in a set of metal cabinets that were affixed to the walls. Instead of hanging our xeroxed photo of the Uprising of the 20,000, which had hung in our old office, I bought a poster of the same image and another one with a photograph of the union protest that happened after the Triangle fire and hung them in frames on these new walls.

This happened after the director had negotiated a kind of cease-fire with the HERE-side higher-ups, whereby they informed the organizer who was sent to be in charge that he was no longer to be in charge, or that he could still be in charge of hotel organizing but not laundry organizing and not of anyone on the laundry-organizing team, which he was instructed to leave alone. She pushed for this deal after discovering through our nightly phone debriefs that I was avoiding the office and working mainly from the car, though she made it clear she had little patience for this "rift," as she called it, and told me that, for the good of the laundry local, I needed to go back to working from the office.

You still came to this office on afternoons when I could pick you up from the factory, which happened maybe three times a week, but the charts there weren't really yours anymore. You spent your time poring over printed spreadsheets of your coworkers and talking through the grievances you had filed with Jorge, who was helping you resolve them or move them through the steps of the procedure.

During this same time, the UNITE-side staff union, for which I was thinking of running for shop steward in the next round of elections, was undergoing a major push to sign up the staff from the HERE side. We were a year out from bargaining our next collective agreement with the union's leadership, and with the merger, our density had just fallen to below half of the staff. In most parts of the country, the HERE organizers were refusing to sign—the structure of their union had been such that their side's national organizing director, who had been in charge of all of the organizing staff employed by their international union, had personally trained many of them, and he was a giant in their minds, lionized to mythic proportions. He was their capital L Leader, which in the culture of their union was more important than anything. They talked about him with a sort of hushed reverence that was widely mocked among the UNITE-side organizers. If he came to dinner at one's house, or better, if one was invited to dinner at his, which was rumored to be an event of intense personal conversation and lots of booze, you were a favored member of the staff, perceived as a rising star, envied by the rest. The HERE-side organizers would not sign union cards because it would disrupt this system of loyalty and ingratiation and favor, which they had been trained to understand as the bedrock of trust on which the rest of the union was built.

But still, when the wife half of the HERE organizing team asked me to get coffee to talk, I agreed, thinking that at least I would get some time alone with her to ask her to join our staff union. Despite being told to stand down in our office, her husband was on the brink of being promoted to a level beyond the bargaining unit, into the management of the union (a prize, I thought, to placate him after the loss of his presumed subordinates: us). When I asked her if she had thought about joining the union, she scoffed, and then said with nearly the exact tone of reverence the UNITE organizers mocked, *I could never do something so disrespectful to our director* (to whom she referred by his first name), and she asked, *What signal does that send to workers—how can we ask them to trust our union leaders if we don't trust them?* And I asked, *How can we go around asking them to stand up for themselves and their coworkers if we aren't willing to do the same?* And she asked, *Stand up against what?*

We were seated at a shaky table in an old house that had been converted to a hippie coffee shop, and I kept leaning over as we talked, to stuff sugar packets under the legs. As we drank our coffee and I smoked my cigarettes, I discovered that she was much more skilled at HERE's method of asking personal questions than her husband. She had no list on her knee. She asked the questions in a way that indicated an earnest curiosity about me and my life. She did not write down my responses, which were still purposely nebulous (I knew what she was doing), though later I learned that she returned to the office and keyed them into a database they were keeping on UNITE-side staff.

Moreover, she was willing to talk about the method as a method. *You and Alma clearly have a strong bond*, she said. *She trusts you*. Which, she went on to explain, is the only purpose of the questionnaire, or "pink sheet," as HERE's system of gaining these personal stories from workers and then recording and sharing them among staff is called. The question set that apparently helps to evoke the stories had at one point been printed on pink paper. The sheets were no longer pink—at least not the ones I saw—but the questions and the method remained the same.

In theory, the pink sheet is a process for building bonds with workers, for gaining their trust in a way that is teachable and reproducible, so that organizers can be trained how to do it. She said that she imagined that I had gained your trust by sharing with you things about my life and then listening while you confided in me in return. *That's all it is*, she said, and then described with great solemnity that HERE, under the guidance of its director, has figured out how to train organizers to identify and tell their most important and compelling personal story so that workers will open up to them and share their own most important personal stories. *We record them in a database*, she said, *so that we remember them, and, yes, so we can share them with each other, so that when a campaign gets hard, we know what motivates each worker, and we can push them through their fear.*

By this point in the merger, the pink sheet had become its own kind of lore, at least among the organizers from the UNITE side of the union. The problem was that UNITE organizers had seen how this technique can play out, and in some places had even been required to participate in it. There were stories about long, tear-filled sessions among teams, wherein organizers were expected to divulge personal information to their leads under the premise that it would make them better organizers. Aside from the torment this seemed to cause, the focus on holding these drawn-out sessions also appeared to make their actual organizing move at a glacial pace. Then there was the problem that they used the same pink-sheet questions with workers they were attempting to develop as leaders among their coworkers—the ones who were eventually invited to join the organizing committees at various worksites were the ones who had most clearly demonstrated their trust for the union and its organizers by agreeing to move through the exercise.

I was disturbed by this pseudoscience, by the idea that leadership, to them, had less to do with a person's relationship to their coworkers than with their relationship to the union's staff organizers. And I was bewildered by the idea that my friendship with you, in all its urgency and grit, could be so neatly parsed, its elements and phases made rational and classifiable, that it could be learned/trained/replicated with such ease. I could understand the allure of this idea—that solidarity could be assembled and packaged, perfectly mass-produced, that a working-class movement could be efficiently built in this way—but I did not believe it.

I believed in the work we did together—and how and why we were doing it—more than I believed in anything. I believed in and was moved, driven even, by the solidarity we'd built by hand. To be confronted with the theory that I simply did not understand it, or was too naïve to realize that it was simply a skill set, changed me. I saw them unraveling what we had made, and though I knew it did not belong to me, I took the unraveling personally. I panicked, and my outrage—at their method and at them—became a new kind of drive.

They asked you out to lunch one day while I was house-calling with Mariana, and you agreed to go and did not tell me. *I didn't want to worry you*, you told me later. But I knew something had happened when you came back to the office with them and then asked Jorge for a ride home instead of me. He had a meeting with one of the airplane catering workers his local had long represented, and so I ended up taking you anyway. You sat facing away from me in the car, your shoulders soft as you looked through the window not talking. When we got to your house, I said something about not being able to tell them to go fuck themselves unless I knew what they had done.

They just kept asking about Julio, you said. *Does he support the union, and does he support me, and why does he never come to the office, and why have we not seen him at any of the cenas or the membership meetings or the rallies?* You told them that was between you and Julio but that they should not worry—he wouldn't get in the way of your work with the union. You thought they were asking if Julio might put some constraint on the time you could spend organizing, and so you reassured them that this would not be the case. But then the organizer asked why you put up with Julio's lack of enthusiasm for the union when you are such a fighter at work, why you would let someone hold you down, why don't you stand up to him. *I didn't know how to answer them*, you said, your voice small, forlorn, *because it is true*.

When we got to your house, Julio was home, so I did not go in. We hugged across the console, and I told you that I was so sorry. I was sorry that you had undergone that conversation with those near strangers, that the private space of your life had been entered into in that way. But I was sorry, too, that it took them asking you for it to come up between us, that I had never asked outright about Julio, though I had long known something was wrong. *Don't worry*, you kept saying, trying to brush the whole mess away. *It's not important*, you said. Then you quickly got out of the car and went inside.

I drove back to the union building and ripped into their office. I told them to stay away from you. I told them not to speak to you or Mariana or Dario or any member of our laundry local or any worker we were organizing, that we were not subjects for their psychological games, that if they had to be trained how to talk with people through the rote memorization of a list of questions and a script of their own personal stories then what they were building was not a union; it was a cult. And then I walked out and drove to the motel, pissed and shaky and proud, though with enough sense to know I should not be.

That night I got a call from the director, who had already heard about the incident, which had been reported to her as a verbal attack. She used the word *hysterical*, which I wrote down in my notebook and circled many times, though looking at it now, I don't know if it was her word or one that had been reported to her. She had been tasked by someone higher up to fly to Phoenix and mediate the conflict.

This seemed fair to me—the no-contact-between-teams agreement had been broken when she invited them to be part of the card-check blitz. And I guessed the organizer felt justified inviting you to talk, with his wife's help in translating, after spending three nearly silent days in a car with you. But the director was annoyed about this extra trip, and she let me know it. She was busy directing the national campaign against Angelica, which was heating up, and, mercifully, happening in a space within the union that was free from the merger clashes that were beginning to boil over in a handful of local offices across the country. She had already booked a flight, she said. She'd be there in two days. *And I have some good news*, she said.

Two days later, I sat with her at Hamburger Mary's, because I could think of nowhere else to go when she insisted on talking over food, which she did perhaps because she noticed how gaunt I had become. After our food arrived, the organizing director said that she had a few projects for me— urgent turf to run in Texas and Ohio and then a campaign in California, plus someone needed to take over and give new thought and energy to a waning campaign at a national uniform company. It was the biggest laundry corporation in the United States, all nonunion, and the heaviest drag on our ability to improve wages and safety conditions across the industry. The union had been waging a campaign in a handful of its factories for years and needed badly to win in order to continue making strides. She wanted someone who was ready to run these campaigns on their own, with their own team. I could tell that she hoped I would feel flattered, and I did.

It would mean a promotion to organizing coordinator, a position outside the staff union's bargaining unit. *Yes, you'd be management*, she said, *but it's not so bad. There are good managers, you know.* She cocked her head to the side in a comical reference to herself. I remember her saying something about growing the capacity of our national organizing team, that we had to do this in order to grow the union to be able to dictate standards for the whole industry and truly make laundries less dangerous places to work. (*We*, in this case, were two white women, eating veggie burgers in a gay diner in Phoenix, so it was hard to see exactly who she meant.)

She did not say what I assumed was also true—that the call about me taking the position had already been made at some higher level in the union. It was not really a choice. The situation in the local office was too volatile, and no one was going to ask the other organizers, who had just arrived with the understanding that they would get to be in charge, to leave. Still, she did not have to try hard to convince me. She said: *You can get out of Phoenix.* And: *It's not like this everywhere in the union.* And: *The organizers here just drank too much of the pink-sheet Kool-Aid.* And: *A lot of the big HERE-side locals don't do this stuff. In fact, most of their staff thinks it's batshit crazy.* And: *Dario and Mariana can handle Angelica, and you can fly back once a week—to see Alma and run staff meetings and do the cenas and keep things moving on the market campaign.* I didn't turn the position down. I didn't fight at all to stay.

I tried not to come off as sheepish the next day when I told Dario and Mariana that I was leaving; an urgent thing in Texas, I said, and I'll be back at the end of next week and then again two weeks after. Dario nodded along and took notes in his notebook as I walked through the files and lists and plans and where to find everything. He did not remind me of the bets they had made the year before, about when a college-educated white person like myself would be promoted.

The next day, I picked you up from the factory after your shift. I was planning to tell you on the way to the office, but I did not. I was planning to tell you at the office, but I did not. Instead, we worked together on the paperwork for a grievance you needed to file—El Mero Mero had given vacation time to one of his friends over a union member with more seniority. It was an easy grievance to win, a clear violation of the contract, but a tough one to have to file and talk about in the factory—forcing the favored woman to move around her vacation could piss off a lot of people. We put together a leaflet on the importance of seniority over favoritism and made copies on the office machine, for which you chose blue paper, because you said that it is a calming color. *Maybe it will help Las Viejas chill out*, you said.

When I drove you home that evening, you told me that you were going to take vacation, too, to visit one of your sisters in Mexico. You had been planning to take the trip on a weekend the following month, but an earlier vacation slot had opened up, and you took it, which meant that you were leaving in a couple of days. I knew that I would not see you again before you left, but still I did not tell you that I was leaving, that I would not be there when you got back. You got out of the car, and I managed to say only the things we always said, plus maybe "Have a good trip," or something of the sort. I'd be back again the following week anyway, I told myself, or the week after, at the latest, though I did not come back at all for five months and then was there for only three days, because, it turns out, it is possible to give yourself over to the intensity of union work outside of Arizona, too.

That is how I almost left without saying goodbye. I did talk with you, finally, but only by phone and from the airport. I'd taken notes about what to say, but I had carried them around in my pocket in one-hundred-plus-degree weather and I'd sweated through them, making them hard to read. The paper had said something about leverage and power and better contracts in Phoenix in the long run—a bunch of stuff that is true but also bullshit. And I knew it was bullshit, and I knew that you would know it was bullshit.

I found a quiet boarding area and dialed your number. You were still using a prepaid phone then, and I hoped it would be out of minutes, or I hoped you would not or could not answer from where you were in

Mexico. I hoped you would call me back later when I could make an excuse for not answering, and in that way I'd buy some time. I'd find a better way to talk about why I had left.

But you did answer the phone. You sang, "Polilli-i-i-ta," your voice slow and low as always, in that way that sounds both tired and unwavering. And I called you by your name, and you knew something was wrong, and then you called me by my name, and I knew that we would not call each other Polilla again and that there would be no matching moth tattoos, which we had jokingly designed, then less jokingly considered getting on our left shoulders.

12: Fires

THE *LYMANTRIA DISPAR* moths that haunted Ohio while I was growing up there were direct descendants of Étienne Trouvelot's escapees. When they first arrived, they were trapped and counted and mapped, held at bay with poison and a certain fungus. But still I knew, as everyone seemed to know, that they would eventually arrive en masse, that they would not be contained by any means.

By the time I was in high school, they had infested large portions of the state and had begun to arrive in the rural county where my brothers and I lived with our mother and stepfather. My mother, who had a difficult time maintaining a drive for caretaking, told us often—usually in wild bursts of anger—that she wished she had chosen a different life. I enrolled in every after-school activity in which I had a shred of ability, and even some in which I did not: cross-country and track, marching band, concert and pep band, drum line, the annual musical—all the nerdy stuff. Most nights I would not leave the school until nine or ten. Then, wanting to be sure my parents were asleep before returning to the house, I, sometimes along with my younger brother, would stop in the middle of one of the gravel roads that twisted between fields or along the Portage River and get out and lie down on the hood of the car or on the gravel road itself, the small stones poking sharply into the backs of our heads. We'd listen—sometimes to music blaring from the tape deck (the Violent Femmes, Dinosaur Jr., the Cranberries, the Smashing Pumpkins), sometimes to nothing. Some nights, we listened to the moth larvae as they chewed their way through the woods all around, sounding like rain.

In a 1981 *New York Times* article titled "Learning to Live with Gypsy Moths," biologist Roger Swain, who was perhaps best known as "the man with the red suspenders" and the host of *The Victory Garden* on PBS, argues that the burns and ulcers and nerve damage and other occupational injuries incurred by the generations of workers who had been tasked with containing the moths, along with the several hundred million dollars spent over the years to combat them, was all for naught. The moths, it turns out, and counter to what he says "certain people, notably the manufacturers of pesticides" claim, are not apocalyptic to forests. They weed out weak trees, compressing their mortality into fewer years, but the forests grow back. Defoliated in early summer, they are usually at full leaf again by Labor Day or certainly by spring of the next year, when the moths have ballooned themselves on to another stand of trees. And besides, he claims, there is no point in fighting them; the moths have won. No matter the tactic used against them, the moths have proliferated across every state, all the way to the West Coast. Instead of continuing on with our gases and poisons and trick pheromones, we should acquiesce to them, allow them to establish themselves, give their natural predators a chance to catch up.

Away from Phoenix and outside the repetition of our daily work, I was still endlessly busy, but I was unmoored, as if I did not really know what kind of union to build or how to build it outside the iterative tasks—folding and unfolding of the metal chairs, driving our loops through the city, knocking on doors, sitting on couches, talking and talking about how things should be better—that constituted the fabric of the *solidatious*

kinship we had manifested. Away from the "ground," where real organizing happens, away from the lives and bodies of people who worked in
danger in laundry factories every day, I was now in the "air fight," as we
called the pressure game between the union and the laundry corporations, the figuring and refiguring of how to cause enough damage to the
companies to win.

It wasn't the strategy of this game that eluded me, though I was on
a steep learning curve in that regard. It was that I was meant to win by
building a different kind of power, the kind wrested away from a boss,
rather than the kind that we built anew on the ground. I had trouble,
too, learning how to move the campaigns inside the wide union organization—with its budget and boardrooms and people in expensive suits—in
a way that could still mean something real. From this altitude, it was difficult to parse the language of the union—the *we* rarely referring to the
lives and bodies of people working in factories. These difficulties were not
a good sign. Either I was not ready to take on this work, or the practicality
it necessitated simply wasn't in my nature. I still don't know which it was.

After I canceled the first flight back to Phoenix, I called and called.
You did not answer. You called back, days later, during the nightly debrief
of the team I was leading in Texas, a time you knew I would not be able to
answer. You did not leave a message.

I heard from Mariana and Dario that the HERE-side organizers in
Phoenix offered to bring you out of the factory on union leave, to work
with them on the hotel campaigns. You accepted. I called to ask you about
it—to tell you that I understood, despite having talked you into staying in
the factory for a while a longer, until the union there was strong enough
for you to step away. I wanted to make a plan with you for electing and
training a new shop steward in your factory, someone who could keep
things running smoothly while you were away. But you did not answer.
You did not call back.

I tried again, too-early Phoenix time, after jolting awake one morning with the realization that I was no longer dreaming of the moths. I wanted to warn you with greater specificity about the organizers and their pink sheets, since I had avoided talking to you about my interactions with them in any detail. I didn't want to talk you out of working with them—I just wanted you to know. You did not answer. At that point, I'd already been gone two months.

One day, Mariana called to tell me that you were crying in the other room, in the middle of a meeting with the organizers and their team. You were in the hot seat for what she supposed was a "group push," another part of their method by which organizers were asked to self-critique in front of their teams as the leads and other organizers pepper them with questions. The point of this, I would later read in national news, was to cajole organizers into fessing up about their shortcomings and the emotional or psychological factors that—according to this method—must certainly underlie them. I asked Mariana to listen in on the meeting, to write down everything she could hear and to call me later. When we talked again, I wrote what she reported into my notebook: *Why are you resisting?* and *Why don't you follow his orders?* and *Are you committed to building the union at the hotel or not?* and *It doesn't seem that you are.* And *Don't you want to learn to be a leader?* And *What are you so afraid of?*

That night, I called you again, and you answered. Your voice sounded deeper and farther away than I remembered it to sound, as if it were coming from some recessed place inside you. You did not want to talk about it, you said. I did not push you to say anything, as was our way, though I no longer knew if this way was any good either. And, no, you said, you did not want me to call anyone about it or do anything about it. *What is there to do anyway?* you said. *I can't just get up and leave Phoenix.*

* * *

After being pushed out of the union in 1910—seven years before the rebellion inspired by Fannia Cohn's curriculum—for her own belief in the idea that women workers ought to be in charge of their own organization, Clara Lemlich did not intend to go back. She did not believe, as Rose Schneiderman did, that women's organizations focused on cross-class solidarity could be trusted to better the lives of working women—not even the ones that focused their advocacy on pro-worker legislation. And she did not believe, as Fannia did, that the union could be wrested from the control of its male leaders and bent into a proper conduit for the empowerment of women workers. So Clara dropped out of both kinds of organizations and started organizing her fellow Brooklyn housewives instead, who, under her guidance, became a truly powerful force. She led them to rent-strike and to boycott overpriced food and to demand safer housing and access to education, all of which she would later say were tools better suited to create change for working people than all of the organizations, both labor and women's, and political parties combined.

Clara Lemlich's three children grew up knowing her in this way, as a radical organizer of housewives and a devoted member of the Communist Party, not as a garment worker or a union organizer. But in 1944, Clara's husband had a stroke, so she went back to work in the garment industry for the first time in over three decades. She was fifty-eight years old. Her maiden name—Clara Lemlich—was still blacklisted, but her married name—Clara Shavelson—was not, and she was hired in a cloak factory as a hand finisher of garments. After a few months, she started to attend union meetings at a local office of the ILGWU. She had not been to a union meeting in thirty-one years. Her coworkers, who did not know she was Clara Lemlich, even as they sat together learning the origin story of the union, the lore of "the wisp of a girl" and the Uprising of the 20,000, later reported feeling surprised that such a small, elderly woman could be such a "spark plug" during the meetings after long hours of hunched-over stitching in the shop.

In 1950, the ILGWU was preparing for its fiftieth anniversary celebration, and someone on the union staff must have imagined how powerful a story it would be to locate the girl who had organized its most important local and sparked the strike that made the union what it had become, to bring her back into the fold, if even just for a few choreographed moments. The purposeful construction of this story, as with all stories (as with this story) serves to strengthen or reify, or sometimes to adjust or trouble an idea of who we are. Stories are one way to arrive at and to think about *we*. Whoever had the idea to present the ILGWU to itself on its fiftieth anniversary with an in-the-flesh appearance of a mythic Clara Lemlich must have discussed it in a planning meeting for the celebration, and then whoever was present in the meeting must have decided that the idea was a good one (and it was, wasn't it?—a hero's return always creates good vibes) and that the union should publish a query in a series of magazines across New York—"Does anyone know where Clara Lemlich is?"—because that is what they did.

In *Common Sense and a Little Fire*, Annelise Orleck quotes one of Clara's daughters about what happened next: "She went to the union and she knocked on the door. And she said, 'I understand you're looking for Clara Lemlich.' And they said, 'Yes, do you know where she is?' And she said, 'Yes.' They said, 'Where is she?' She said, 'Where is she? Here she is. She's standing right in front of you.'" By this point, Clara had been attending union meetings at the local for six years.

In the weeks that followed, union journalists interviewed her extensively, and when the fiftieth-anniversary commemorative book was published, it included a long description of Clara's role in the Uprising of 1909, which seemed to do its best to bridge the distance between telling the story of the real work that went into preparing for the strike and the union fable of courage and spontaneity her speech had become. It was only after this book's publication that the leadership in the union's headquarters realized that Clara Shavelson, the "insistent elderly woman cloakmaker who had been making trouble in her local for the past decade," was the same Clara they must have been hoping would step out of the woodwork as a quiet canvas onto which the union could project the story of its history. Upon this realization—that Clara was Clara—"they didn't want to touch her with a ten-foot pole," said Clara's daughter.

But Clara would stick around for another four years, agitating in her small shop and needling the union during membership meetings at the local to be bolder, more transparent, more democratic. When she retired at age sixty-eight, she applied for her pension, but the union denied her application—only workers with fifteen *consecutive* years of membership were eligible. But Clara needed the pension. She would not let it go, and the dispute became, according to Orleck, "a pitched battle with the union leaders who had for so long been ambivalent about the woman who sparked the 1909 uprising." Clara won, but only after having to embarrass the union by loudly reminding its leaders who she was, how important a figure to its origin and its story, its understanding of itself.

The pension allowed her to move to Long Beach, California, where her children had gone in the years before. From there, she would correspond with the graduate student to whom she wrote about "the girl" on the Cooper Union stage, reciting the lore her organizing had metamorphosed to become.

When we won the Angelica campaign, I came back to Phoenix for the contract negotiations. I had been gone nearly six months, during which we had spoken, I think, only three times; each time your voice quieter, deeper, farther away than the call before. I wanted to work with you again, and I needed your help; your experience would go a long way in guiding

the Angelica workers who had been elected to their bargaining committee. So I called the organizing director, and she called the director on
the HERE side, and then he called the HERE lead organizer in Phoenix,
who released you from the hotel team for one week and assigned you to
the bargaining team, along with one of the workers from Top Shelf—
Paloma, who was a new VO working with the HERE team on the hotel
campaign.

The day before I arrived, I called you but you did not answer. When
my flight landed, and I retrieved a rental car, I called to see if I could pick
you up at your house, but you did not answer. When I got to the local,
you were there, in the large meeting room at the center of the office space,
from which all of the smaller offices split away. You and the rest of the
hotel team were sitting in the metal folding chairs in a circle. Paloma was
there, too, and her chair indented the circle by a foot or two. Her hands
were in her lap, her shoulders heaved and shook. This was the first time
I witnessed a "hot seat" or a group push, or whatever it was they were
calling it then. The lead and his wife and two other organizers—who
had been assigned to them from the HERE local in LA—were focused on
Paloma, but you were not. You were looking at the floor, as if not wanting to witness her crying or to witness whatever it was that was making
her cry.

I walked into the meeting space and half sat on a table that was
pushed against one of its walls—I wanted you and Paloma to know that I
was there. The meeting paused, but neither of you looked up at me. I sat
there in the quiet room until the lead organizer, the one who had been
sent to take charge, said that he would continue the meeting in one of the
smaller offices, and you all got up and took the chairs into a side room
and closed the door.

When the negotiations were underway, the lead organizer told me
that he would pick you up and drop you off at the Angelica factory, where

the bargaining was scheduled to occur. That way, he said, he would be able to keep you apprised of the goings-on of the hotel campaign. To which I replied that he could easily provide you with any necessary information over the phone. To which he replied that he preferred to drive you and that he was your lead now and so it was really his decision.

The bargaining was hard work. The regional manager of the Western States Regional Joint Board had flown in from LA, and she was hell-bent on not having to schedule a second set of sessions with the company for some future time, because it had been difficult to get the company to commit to this first set of dates, so we negotiated through long, consecutive days for a solid week. When we were not in the room with the company representatives and their lawyers, we were planning and plotting with the bargaining committee, and writing and translating and printing proposals, and rushing to the factory with leaflets to deliver to the contract action team, and passing out union buttons, and holding shift meetings—all of which is to say that you and I did not have much time to talk.

The lead organizer picked you up in the morning at your house and drove you to the negotiations and then picked you up at the negotiations in the evening and drove you back to your house, until one day something happened—something to do with his family, though I can't remember what—and he had to go home instead of giving you a ride, so I got to drive you instead. On the way, you were quiet. I asked how you were doing and how things were in the factory and how your family was, questions to which you barely responded or responded to with few words. And I was frustrated at this, and I started spouting my bitterness over it as we drove into south Phoenix. *What does he think he is teaching you?* I said. *You are already a better organizer than he will ever be*, I said. And: *Alma, why are you letting them push you around?*—which was, of course, the wrong thing to say.

And you said, *Querida amiga, mira, no te preocupes por mi.* (Dear friend, look, don't you worry about me.) The *querida amiga* was delivered with pure scorn. We drove the rest of the way in silence. I could not have spoken if I had tried. I remember feeling that I had to focus very hard to continue breathing. I remember how bright the taillights of the other cars on the road seemed, how loud the turn signal in the new rental car sounded. I remember I pulled up to the curb in front of your salmon-colored house. I remember how gently you closed the car door.

In *The Dictionary of Obscure Sorrows*, an online compendium of neologisms and invented words aimed at filling holes in language where "aches, demons, vibes, joys, and urges" have gone unnamed, the word *chrysalism* is defined:

> *n.* the amniotic tranquility of being indoors during a thunderstorm, listening to waves of rain pattering against the roof like an argument upstairs, whose muffled words are unintelligible but whose crackling release of built-up tension you understand perfectly.

I would like to know how it was imagined that the chrysalis is a place of amniotic tranquility when the moth inside is digesting itself right down to its raw imaginal discs—turning itself to soup in order to grow wings.

After that car ride, we did not speak for a long time. In the spring of 2007, I was promoted to organizing director, in charge of all laundry organizing across the United States. When I was not on the road, staying in motels, I lived between an apartment in Brooklyn, which the union rented for me, and a new house in Tucson. My team of organizers was running a campaign among twenty-five thousand workers at a uniform laundry company and we were on strike with thousands of workers at another uniform laundry across California, plus we were organizing Milum in Phoenix and a few other one-off laundries in other cities. Most of my work consisted of flying around the country—to New York, to meet with union researchers and communications staff to plot the air campaigns; to California, to build strategy for the strike; and to the big HERE-side locals in Boston and Chicago and San Francisco and Las Vegas, to try to convince them to support our laundry organizing by pressuring the hotels where their members worked to move their business to union laundries. Mostly these locals were not interested in helping our campaigns—not in this or any other way. Partly because the higher-ups on the HERE side did not like the fact that the union was spending so much money organizing laundries; they were devoted to organizing the hotel industry, and the smaller-shop red-state brawls we got into with the laundry companies was a big drain—in their minds—on the union's focus and resources. Another part of their disinterest likely stemmed from the fact that merger tensions, once optimistically thought of as growing pains in a few isolated locations, were now entrenched and on the rise. In addition to the disastrous clash of organizing cultures and methods, there was a leadership election on the horizon, and the UNITE-side president was on the brink of losing his position as general president of the merged international union.

There were secret meetings and conference calls happening on both sides of the union, to plan for this election. Both sides wanted to increase their influence at the top of the union structure to be in control of its organizing priorities and resource allocation. On the UNITE side, there was a subset of secret meetings and conference calls happening, driven by organizers' growing concerns: about the methods of the HERE organizing staff, about how to protect the organizers on our teams from them as our intermingling with their teams increased over time, and how to make sure that the workers we helped to organize could avoid participating in what we had come to view as the egregious privacy violations and abusive manipulations that were foundational to the organizing method and culture of at least one faction of HERE organizers.

The position I held was high up in the organizing department, but not high enough among union executives to understand how these two wings of internal strife came together. I suspect that the UNITE-side leaders saw our complaints about pink-sheeting and hot-seating as an opening, one that, with proper steering, they could shift from a campaign to remove the HERE organizers who practiced these abusive methods to one that would result in better odds for them come the leadership election. There were long meetings in which this plan, the one that seemed to be about removing the pink-sheeting organizers, was designed and plotted on calendars and vetted and approved. I dodged most of these meetings, not because I did not want the organizers to be kicked out (I absolutely did), but because I believed that making the plan was a waste of time, that it would amount to nothing more than a point of leverage in the fight over internal institutional power, that whatever energy we put into organizing around it would be co-opted by the broader fight. I was sure that the concern would be traded away at the last minute, that the factions of higher-ups would reach a settlement, some power-sharing plan that would require us all to muddle along for another few years just as we were, pink-sheeting and hot-seating, until there was another crisis about who would go on holding the reins of the union.

So when I got the call from the joint board manager on the morning the "take-back" (as we called the plan to kick out the pink-sheeting organizers from offices of locals that belonged to UNITE-side joint boards) was scheduled to happen, I was still in Tucson, though the plan had called for me to be already arriving via the I-10 at the local in Phoenix. She was not pleased. I got in the rental car and spent the hour and half of driving time calling you and then Jorge and then you and then Jorge, knowing that if there was any way to break with the HERE organizers and keep the union whole, it would have to be alongside the two of you, but neither of you picked up. I stopped at the only rest stop between Tucson and Phoenix, which is on a plateau overlooking a wide expanse of picturesque desert. I sat there for a long while, not wanting to arrive, knowing it was going to be an absolute war.

When I got to the office, the regional manager was there, pissed because the plan had been for me to be with her when she instructed the HERE team to leave, but she had had to do it with Mariana and Dario instead of me. You weren't there, they said—it was just the couple from the Northeast and their organizers from LA, who left quickly when they were asked to, without question or argument or hesitation. The regional manager discovered, after they had gone, that the office was cleaned out; filing cabinets were empty, and office computers were scrubbed of organizing files and databases and grievance information. The take-back, which was taking place on the same morning as similar moves at two other locals, in Michigan and Florida, had not come as a surprise to HERE.

Paloma came to the office not long after I arrived. She told us that the HERE lead organizer had called a meeting at the office of another union, where he told her that she had to choose between HERE and UNITE, that she had to make her decision right then, that they were going to continue on with a meeting, but she had to get out if she was not with them. She walked out. You were there, too. You stayed.

That afternoon and all the next day, we made rounds to the union factories, where the regional manager and I took turns in the lunchrooms making the announcement that I was now the director of the Arizona District of the union, a position that Jorge had held since the merger but had vacated when he decided to go along with the HERE organizers when they were told to leave. Some of the laundries tried to deny access to us by furnishing a letter from Jorge, which claimed that he was the legal representative of the union and that they were not to allow us entry. We would stand outside and wait for the UNITE-side union lawyers to call the company lawyers to point out that it was our regional manager's signature on the company's collective bargaining agreements with the union. They let us in.

The HERE team chased us around the city. Some of the laundry managers let them into the lunchrooms as well, and then there was a lot of yelling, the absurdity and obnoxiousness of which, to workers trying to take a break during Phoenix high-season work, I cannot imagine, though the show was likely very entertaining to workers who already didn't like the union, not to mention the company supervisors.

At your laundry, La Sandra capitalized on the dueling claims of legal representation and denied access to both sides, and she found clever ways to keep denying it for months. The case there was more complex than in the other factories, because you and your coworkers weren't members of UNITE HERE. You belonged to SWU, the Big 3 union, which paid UNITE-side joint boards to "service" the membership and the contracts at the multiservice worksites.

Those first two days, I must have called you a hundred times. You did not answer. I took side trips to your house in the time between factory visits. You were not home.

The regional manager left on the second day of the take-back, and while I was dropping her off at the airport, Jorge and the HERE organizers came back to the local office. Mariana was there, and she called to tell me they were in the building. I told her to tell them they were not allowed to be there and then not to say anything else, to sit down where they could see her and take notes on everything they did, which was essentially to wander around the place and collect the few things they had apparently left behind.

That night, I called a locksmith to change the locks on the office door. It was after-hours, so I had to pay up front and double the daytime price. The keys of the HERE organizers no longer worked on the door. Your key no longer worked.

After the locksmith left, I slept in the office, along with Dario and another organizer who was among a group being sent in to help bolster what was already a wreck of an internal fight. The thermostat was preset to shut off at night, and only Jorge and Lisa knew how to change the setting. It was the cusp of winter, when the desert sheds forty or fifty degrees after the sun goes down. I curled into the footwell under one of the desks but couldn't sleep. The organizers and I took turns going out to our rental cars to warm up in the heat.

The next day, there were more confrontations at the laundries, where we were running comité meetings in parking lots, and HERE-side organizers, whose ranks were also growing as their backup arrived from Las Vegas and Los Angeles, stormed the meetings to shut them down. There was more yelling, a lot of close-proximity finger-pointing in faces, some pushing that Dario broke up before it turned into real violence. You were not there for any of these incursions, and so I kept calling you, hoping that it meant you had not decided to stay with them.

That night, the HERE side stormed the office. They could not get in because the locks had been changed, but forty people rushed the door, pounding its glass and the windows next to it. The UNITE organizers barricaded the door, fearing the dead bolt would not hold. I was behind them but could see through the chairs that made up the barricade and through the glass door, to you. And you saw me. And we stood looking at each other for some immeasurable stretch of time, and it seemed to me that we were sliding down into the still center of the storm all around.

Eventually, the HERE lead organizer led the group, and you, away.

* * *

Starting the next week, I tried to figure out how to direct a team of organizers through the business of running the two locals—Local 2732 along with Local 631, the HERE local Jorge and Lisa had long managed. We divvied up the dozen or so union workplaces and trained ourselves on the contracts, we started meeting with shop stewards about ongoing grievances, we filed new grievances, we organized shop floor actions and petitions around issues we thought we could win, we won some, and we made plans to prepare for the upcoming contract expirations at two of the shops.

A man left a message in English for me on the office phone system threatening to "fucking kill" me, and the next day, I got another call on my cell phone, from a different man, who simply recited my address in Tucson and then hung up. The joint board hired security guards to sit at the office and one to zigzag behind me as I drove through the city—office, laundries, motel, in circles. When HERE organizers followed us to our motel, we moved motels. When they followed us again, we moved again. This went on for three months, during which time the fight expanded across the entire union, in every city across the United States and Canada where it represented workers.

The HERE-side organizers distributed leaflets at union laundries—first in Phoenix, then in LA, then all across the country—attacking UNITE-side organizers, claiming that the take-backs of local offices were part of a coup, orchestrated, they believed, out of loyalty to the UNITE-side union president, a belief which may have made sense in the structure and culture of their union, but which didn't translate to UNITE, where loyalty to leaders was not foundational to our training. The leaflets called on workers to disaffiliate their locals from UNITE-controlled joint boards, which prompted us to hold a referendum across Arizona in which workers voted to stay affiliated with the UNITE-controlled joint board. These local battles escalated to the union's headquarters in New York, which HERE organizers occupied one night, locking out the UNITE-side president and his staff and then hiring guards to break into their offices and ransack their files and computers. This prompted my team to go back into union factories across Arizona and hold another vote, this time to leave UNITE HERE and form a new union, which we did.

By March of 2009, Workers United was founded, with over one hundred thousand workers, who had previously been members of UNITE HERE. The message around which this feat was accomplished was one of laundry-worker empowerment and independence: laundry workers should be in charge of their own union so that they can ensure that their dues money is used to organize the rest of the industry in which they work, and so that they can set standards with regard to factory safety and wages and health insurance and retirement plans. *Your dues money should not be controlled by a union that has no intention of continuing to organize your industry,* I said, repeating this message countless times during the month Workers United was formed. The organizers on my team practiced it during our staff meetings and repeated it hundreds of times as well.

What we were promising is not what would happen—laundry workers would *not* be in charge of their own union and have control over its resources—but we didn't know it at the time. Immediately upon its formation, Workers United merged with SEIU. The UNITE-side president joined the executive board of one of the most powerful unions in the country.

I did not see you again.

In the office of the local you had fought to build, I held daily staff meetings with a team of twenty people who had come to work for the union to help nonunion workers form unions, and I directed them to do appalling things, which we were asked to do by the UNITE-side president in order to leverage a better and less costly divorce from HERE. We bullied our way into contract negotiations among airport food-service workers. We sabotaged a hotel organizing campaign. We attempted to sabotage a second hotel organizing campaign. We planned to sabotage a third hotel organizing campaign. Most of the organizers did not want to do these things, but they did them fervently, in the belief that breaking the union apart was the only way to save it. They believed it because I told them: *Breaking the union apart is the only way to save it.* I told them that the greater the number of workers who broke away, the better and stronger the union would be, though in the tangle of locals and national locals, like SWU at your factory, and regional joint boards and international unions, I'm no longer certain to which "union" I was even referring. I was angry. I ran the team angrily. I told the organizers to get out of Phoenix if they could not do these things. I told them if they chose to stay, they were not allowed to complain. I fired an organizer for complaining.

At the same time, I could not eat. I did not sleep. My skin was turning yellow. One of the organizers from the three-day training, a person who had many decades of organizing experience and had become a kind of mentor to me, came to the office early one day and told me to go home, told me that the organizers did not want to confront me, that they had gone to him and asked him to speak to me instead. He told me to get some sleep, to go to a doctor, and not to come back until I was better.

I drove to Tucson. When I got there, I told the security guard who had followed me and was stationed in front of my house to leave. I slept for days. I did not dream. I went to a doctor who told me I was very sick, so I stayed in Tucson. I thought, *A few more days*, and then, *One more week*, as I watched the news roll in, first over union email and then media headlines, about escalations in the union divorce. There were injunctions and counterinjunctions, a frenzy of lawsuits, for which I gave statements to lawyers over the phone and then collected via fax at the Kinko's near my home and signed and faxed back. I got on conference calls with the UNITE-side president and the people leading the offensive in other cities, but from Tucson, I had nothing to report. I stopped getting on the calls, and then I stopped answering my phone, and then I stopped logging in to my email, and then I put my union-issued phone and my union-issued computer down and did not pick them up again. I returned the rental car to the Tucson airport and took the bus home.

The union knew I was done before I did. A very kind woman from the operations department of the new union, Workers United/SEIU, finally called to give me instructions for shipping back the laptop and cell phone. When I sounded surprised, she said that she'd been told I wasn't coming back to work. *Do I have that right?* she asked. And I knew that she did.

And then I did nothing. I slept. I took the dog on walks. I waited tables and bartended. I took art classes at the community college and hunted moths.

One day about two years later, I went to the University of Arizona Museum of Art to wander through its gallery, and found in the gift shop a book about an installation by Joseph Scheer, which the gallery had exhibited years previously, while you and I were still driving in circles around Phoenix, listening to 106.3 with the folding chairs in the trunk, drinking water that had gotten too hot in the car from plastic gallon jugs. The book is called *Mothing*, which is not really a word. It contains images from the installation, which Scheer subtitled *Flight, Light, and Desire*, in which photographs of moths were printed in high definition on massive sheets of paper and hung to flutter around the gallery spaces. The images in the book are interwoven with essays written by a cast of artists and scientists that provide information about moths so textured with esoteric detail they border on the mystical. In one essay, moths are miked, their sounds, amplified and enriched, turned into screams. In another essay, the moths are said to shiver, warming their muscles and drying their scales in order to take flight. In the book's final essay, the story of Psyche and Cupid is paraphrased: Psyche agrees not to look but knows she has to see, and *moth* and *soul* are the same word.

Not long after that, I saw the laundry-truck driver who used to scream "Bitches!" at us during the run-up to the union election. He had a regular stop at the bar where I was working after it started sending its towels to the nonunion laundry. That was in March of 2011—exactly one hundred years after the Triangle fire, eight years and one month after you and I met, six years after we won the card check at your laundry, five years after I left Phoenix for the promotion to organizing coordinator, two years after the union broke apart. I went to the hospital, still sick, or sick again with the same thing that had been plaguing me since quitting. I cocooned in blankets that would travel down your soil-sort line the next day.

That same March, in 2011, one of Clara Lemlich Shavelson's daughters was in New York, attending a commemoration of the Triangle shirtwaist factory fire and a ceremony in which thirty women were receiving awards named after her mother. At these events, she kept getting approached by people offering their condolences for the tragic way her mother had died—in the Triangle fire, they said—which was confusing to her since her mother did not work at the Triangle factory and, in fact, had lived a very long time. She died in her sleep in 1982 at ninety-six at the Jewish Home for the Aged in Los Angeles, where she had recently helped the staff form a union.

One survivor of the Triangle fire, Rose Cohen, stumbled, still in shock, to her family's apartment after escaping the blaze, where she fell down on her bed and cried herself to sleep. No one else was home. Her cousin had heard about the fire and was out looking for her. When he returned to the apartment, he was weeping so loudly in the kitchen over not finding Rose that it awoke her. She later stated that she "got up from the bed and began the long walk to the kitchen, passing through one room after another as in a dream." Her mother took one look at her and collapsed on the floor. For a long time after, Rose dreamed that she was screaming and either "falling" from a window or "jumping" from a window, though she wasn't sure which. In her statements about these dreams, she uses the two words interchangeably.

After

A LITTLE OVER a year after I quit the union, I began graduate school (for writing, a type of program I didn't know existed until I became friends again with the housemate I'd shared a home with years before, who is a poet). On the night before classes started, I was working at my restaurant job, and I served a table where a woman was waiting for her party to join her. She held her menu a little too close to the candle flame, and it caught fire.

The next day, I had a meeting with the associate dean of the Honors College at the University of Arizona, whose teaching assistant I was applying to be. We recognized each other immediately—she was the woman who had burned her menu the night before. I got the job, and after finishing my degree, she hired me on as an adjunct to teach a course I had helped her design. Graduate school was supposed to be a short break, a few years to think and read and sleep and recuperate before going back to the good, hard work of organizing. But I liked teaching. I liked my earnest, curious students. I liked that I could mostly sleep at night, so I stayed on, teaching at the university for six years. I had friends. I fell in love with an incredibly kind human. We made a family.

In 2018, I saw a picture of Alma on the Facebook page of an acquaintance who had started organizing for the Western States Regional Joint Board of Workers United/SEIU (its long title reflecting its precursors, as unions are wont to do). In the photo, she was among a group of workers who had gone up to Flagstaff from Phoenix to try to stop a decertification effort at the one union laundry there, which we had organized all those years ago. The laundry where, after getting to a majority on cards, I hydroplaned off the highway and rolled into a ravine.

I messaged the organizer to ask for Alma's phone number. He had no idea who she was, and I had to explain that she had founded the laundry workers' local in Arizona, that she had been fired doing it, that she had taken on a wealthy multinational corporation and won. I was in disbelief that he did not know who she was. I had to describe which person she was in the photo: the second from the left. I called the number he sent me from my new phone. No one answered, and there was no voicemail on which to leave a message. I sent a text message and waited, but no reply came.

In 2019, I was sifting through this material—the writing to Alma, and the notebooks and files, and the timeline I had made—most of which had made it into the same box as pieces of art projects involving moths. I was packing it for a move across the country, and I was thinking of Alma, and so I texted her number again. *Alma, soy Daisy. Como estas?* (My phone did not have Spanish punctuation.) She wrote back immediately: *OLA DAISY NO ESTOY MUY BIEN.* She'd been hit by a car in Mexico and was badly injured. She had returned to Phoenix after a few weeks but was unable to move around much. She felt alone, she said. She was having trouble remembering things. She was sad all the time. She was afraid. We messaged each other every day until Alma's niece moved into her house, along with her three children. She did not want to talk on the phone.

We communicate now in intensive bursts. She answers but never initiates the hours-long flurries of text messages. After five months on disability, she went back to work in the factory, but her arm was still so sore from the crash that she could not lift the sheets from the soil-sort belt. A doctor assigned a work restriction—extreme light duty—and La Sandra, who is still managing human resources in the factory, reported to her that no such thing exists in industrial laundries, and she sent Alma home, on indefinite leave, with no pay. The business agent for the union was unable—or, according to Alma, unwilling—to pursue any sort of charge against the company. They had gotten rid of her at long last.

We don't talk about the union much, but I know that the workers in her factory ended up, by virtue of the divorce settlement and not by any choice of their own, with Workers United/SEIU. I know that Alma hasn't worked with the HERE organizers since 2009. She told me that she ended her union leave and went back to work in the factory not long after we saw each other through the office door. *It was all too much pressure*, she said. She didn't want to work with that lead organizer anymore. I know that her factory was bought by another company years ago, and that the new company made all of the workers reapply for their jobs and start as new employees with fewer benefits and no seniority. I know that Alma tried to refuse signing as a new worker, tried to organize her coworkers to fight, but the union was weak, and most of the new hires over the decade since the split are Somali refugees. Alma can't speak with them. The union leaders instructed her to just do what the company said.

One day, I messaged Alma to check in, to see how she was getting along without a job, if her niece was still living with her and paying the bills in exchange for Alma's taking care of the kids, and she asked me to send pictures of my two children, and when I did, she wrote: *Que hermosos estan BELLISIMOS* (How beautiful. They are GORGEOUS). And I wrote: *Hermosos y locos, con tanta energia!* (Beautiful and crazy, with so much energy!). And she wrote: *Es k van estar fuertes como tu* (It's that they are going to be strong like you). And I wrote: *O mas como TU*

(Or more like YOU). And she wrote, *Las nuevas polillas* (The new moths). And the kids were napping upstairs, so I cried as quietly as I could on the couch in my new home in Pittsburgh.

In 2020, industrial laundry workers made $10.13 an hour on average, while the CEO of the largest laundry corporation in the United States made $9,778,369. This is a typical disparity in today's economy, in which more is owned by fewer people than at any point in US history, and in which unions have collapsed: union density has fallen to 6.4 percent in the private sector, around 11 percent overall, similar to the percentage it was in 1900, when the ILGWU was formed. These numbers form a telling equation. Since union density fell below 25 percent in 1977, income inequality has risen exponentially every year. In fact, the only years in our entire history in which the share of income held by the top 10 percent *declined* are years when union density was above 27 percent, from 1942 to 1973.

Just over a century ago, there was an explosion in US labor organizing. It happened among miners and transportation workers and garment workers. They struck wildly and militantly and founded the unions that are still the backbone of labor today: the steelworkers, the Teamsters, the ILGWU, which evolved into UNITE. All of the same conditions that led to that explosion of organizing are present today, to an almost eerie degree: union density is hovering at around 6 percent, the wealth share of the 1 percent is growing exponentially, real wages have fallen steadily over the last twenty years, and the legal right to organize, which was established in 1935 to quell the growing strife of a century ago, has been eroded back to the point of near nonexistence through decades of politicians ceding influence to corporations in exchange for campaign contributions. And just as workers on the other side of this century took aggressive action in the form of large-scale strikes, workers in three recent years (2018–20) are striking in greater numbers and winning more strikes than in the previous three decades, since Reagan broke the PATCO airline strike in 1981.

In the midst of this new wave of worker momentum, with its growing appetite for militant action, something surprising is happening. While some of the strikes have been supported by "traditional" unions and labor law, like the General Motors strike of 2019, others have been mass illegal strikes instead. Two-thirds of the striking teachers in Arizona and West Virginia in 2018 were not members of the teachers' union, and they struck, without any legal protection, even after the union told them not to. A friend of mine, who is a lead organizer for the teachers' union in Arizona, told me that reporters were calling the union's office, asking questions about their demands. She had to tell them the union didn't know what the demands were, that they were still trying to figure out who was leading the strike, which seemed to have been organized on Facebook.

This new strike wave will grow. It will spread to new states and other industries. It will grow in part because labor law in this country is broken, and just as in the early 1900s, a strike is workers' only recourse, the only way to force a company to the bargaining table. Labor-law reform and minimum-wage reform are likely coming—because the new, liberal White House knows it owes its victory to working people and, in part, to unions, and the administration of President Joe Biden, at least in its early days, has signaled support for the Fight for $15, a movement demanding a fifteen-dollar-an-hour minimum wage, and the PRO Act (the Protecting the Right to Organize Act), a set of labor law reforms championed by unions that would expand organizing rights and give the NLRB some teeth, including the power to fine bosses for breaking the law.

But even despite these reforms, the strike wave will grow (or—this is my hope—it *must*), because workers will hold on to these gains and build on them only if they stay in the streets even *after* they win them.

Dollie Robinson, an industrial laundry worker and union organizer among the mainly Black women workers of New York's "power laundries" in the 1930s, said that the workers she helped to organize started to fight back once they had "reached the peak . . . when they just couldn't exist anymore on the wages and treatment." These strikes will grow, too, because workers, increasingly, are at "the peak." They'll fight because there is no other way to exist. It's time for metamorphosis. Time to "shed that tight, dry skin, or die," as Nabokov writes of the caterpillar in its final instar.

This moment is rife with opportunity, rife with the sacred responsibility unions have to be at the forefront of the movement for justice that is already underway, to ensure that workers are at the center of defining and creating their own liberation.

When I worked for UNITE and then UNITE HERE and then Workers United/SEIU, I was taught—and so I believed—that anger is the primary emotion that drives people to fight, the only emotion strong enough to overcome fear. And anger is powerful, it's true, but care for one another is, too. And care for one another, unlike anger (or unlike anger for me), is continually renewable—it becomes both an engine for the fight and a destination for it, elemental to the new world the fight demands. (Nothing drives the moth to light if the moth *is* drive.) Care for one another functions this way mainly because it allows for hope, which is the substance of solidarity.

I think now that fighting from a place of anger is most effective in the kind of organizing that is satisfied with taking power away from the boss and calling it union. This type of organizing is top-down, more interested in cleaving the orange than in creating a new kind of sustenance that arises out of care and hope and solidarity, a sustenance that diminishes oppressive power simply by existing yet is made of a different substance.

I've come to think of solidarity, this mixture of hope and care, as a physical force or maybe a force field, and as such it invisibly acts on all things that are passing through it at all times. It's the space between bodies that are marching or singing or striking or otherwise taking action together. Maybe you've felt it, at a protest or on a picket line. I've heard people say that it feels like church. It's the way bodies, our bodies, working collectively, change the properties of the space between them. It's the most important thing.

Where do you work?

What is the pay disparity there? And what do you think about that?

If you could change one thing about your job, what would it be?

What would it take to change it?

If you went to your boss and asked for the change by yourself, what would happen?

What would happen if ten people asked for it?

How about one hundred?

How about everyone in your place of work, all together?

How about everyone in your place of work, backed by the solidatious support of thousands of other people who work in your industry?

That's a union.

If you are already a member of a union, challenge it—on every level, all the time—to be more transparent and democratic and accountable to and representative of its members.

If you are not part of a union yet, organize. Really. Right now. There are resources listed below. The next flight is emerging, and we need you.

Later, Alma and I did talk on the phone, and I told her I was doing some work with the United Steelworkers on a campaign in Pittsburgh. *Great, I'll be on the next plane. I'm coming to join you,* she joked. I told her I was thinking about going back to Workers United, to organize with laundry workers again, and she said, *You should, my friend. There is a lot of work to do.* I told her about this writing, that I wanted to write a book about the campaign and about what happened with the union, and she said, *Bueno.* I told her that part of the writing has to do with moths, and she said, *Dios mío, ¿por qué?*—she thought the long story of the campaign was already too much for ten books, and I said that I didn't know how to write it without the moths. *That's a little strange*, she said, laughing. *But you've always been a little strange.* And then she said, *Sí, está muy bien.*

ACKNOWLEDGMENTS

All books are the product of collective effort. This one was made with advice, inspiration, and thoughtful feedback from family, coworkers, friends, and mentors. I will always be grateful to Francisco Cantú, Laura Berry, Sarah Minor, Ahmer Qadeer, Mariana Padias, Jessica Friedrichs, Anne Rashid, David Hill, Belinda Theilen, Brian Callaci, Peter Jay Pitkin, Amelia Frank-Vitale, Katie Unger, Dario Almanzar, Alison Deming, Arianne Zwartjes, Richard Siken, Sarah Schoenbrun, Aisha Sabatini-Sloan, Peter Rachleff, David Chioni Moore, and Sarah Donnelly.

To my bookcraft coven: Jes, Anne, Sylvia, and Holly, thanks for getting me through. I'm honored to count you as friends.

Special thanks to Veronica Goldstein at Fletcher and Co. for your fierce support through this long process. Thanks also to Ryan Harrington and Amy Gash for your editorial wisdom and for whipping the manuscript into its proper shape. This book was also ushered into the world through the creative work of Jonathan Bush, the editorial eye of Elizabeth Johnson, and the legal rigor of Nick Jollymore.

For their help in parsing the wild, early iterations of this work, I wish to thank my Arizona cohort: Margaret Kimball, Bethany Maile, Craig Reinbold, Lawrence Lenhart, and Noam Dorr. Thanks also to the Monique Wittig fellowship board for your belief in the project's first sparks.

This book would not exist without the encouragement and unparalleled kindness of my love, Scott, and our little ones. Thanks for letting me spend so many hours in the attic.

To A, in solidarity, thank you for allowing me to tell this story.

A NOTE ABOUT SODEXO

Sodexo (which at the time of the campaign at Alma's factory was named Sodexho) did not respond to a request for comment on this book. In 2010, Human Rights Watch published *A Strange Case: Violation of Workers' Freedom of Association in the United States by European Multinational Corporations*, a 132-page report that includes a detailed description of Sodexo's reaction to our union-organizing drive in Phoenix. The company made the following statement to Human Rights Watch in advance of the report's publication:

> The circumstances at Sodexo's Commercial Linen Exchange in Phoenix, AZ, demonstrate Sodexo's respect for our employees' right to choose a collective bargaining representative and our commitment to bargain in good faith where the employees have fairly chosen a bargaining representative. On February 15, 2005, Sodexo recognized SWU as the collective bargaining representative for its employees at the Commercial Linen Exchange in Phoenix, AZ. Sodexo recognized SWU based upon the results of an agreed upon card check and neutrality process. Sodexo and the Union thereafter agreed to an initial contract, and have subsequently negotiated a renewal labor contract there.

This collaborative work between Sodexo and the Union has superseded any past disagreements that may have existed. The findings and order to which your correspondence likely refers arose out of events occurring in 2003. By order dated April 7, 2005, those findings and the order of the ALJ [administrative law judge] were vacated. . . .[T]he findings were based upon actions by supervisory personnel at a single Sodexo unit. Two of the managers involved in the allegations are no longer with Sodexo. The remaining two managers have gone through substantial subsequent training and coaching, and have in fact worked constructively with the Union over the last several years. As a result of Sodexo's collaborative work with the Union to resolve their various differences in this matter, all charges were withdrawn and the entire proceeding was dismissed on April 12, 2005.

The entirety of Sodexo's response, as well as the Human Rights Watch report itself can be found on the HRW website: www.hrw.org.

SELECTED BIBLIOGRAPHY

The following sources, along with my own files and notebooks and publicly available court documents, were instrumental in my research for this book:

1. *Common Sense and a Little Fire: Women and Working-Class Politics in the United States, 1900–1965* by Annelise Orleck

2. *Triangle: The Fire That Changed America* by David Von Drehle

3. *Of Moths and Men: The Untold Story of Science and the Peppered Moth* by Judith Hooper

4. *The Story of Silk* by John Feltwell

5. *Mothing* by Joseph Scheer

6. Cornell University's Triangle Factory Fire Archive and its Industrial and Labor Relations School's Kheel Center for Labor-Management Documentation & Archives

7. The Jewish Women's Archive, a national organization dedicated to collecting and promoting the stories of Jewish women

8. The 2005–09 reporting on UNITE HERE by *Labor Notes* and the *New York Times*

9. The Working Class History site and podcast, a project by labor historians dedicated to "those who have struggled in the past for a better world, and who continue to do so now"

ORGANIZING RESOURCES

Your Rights During Union Organizing

The National Labor Relations Board website (nlrb.gov) states:

"You have the right to form, join or assist a union. You have the right to organize a union to negotiate with your employer over your terms and conditions of employment. This includes your right to distribute union literature, wear union buttons, t-shirts, or other insignia (except in unusual 'special circumstances'), solicit coworkers to sign union authorization cards, and discuss the union with coworkers. Supervisors and managers cannot spy on you (or make it appear that they are doing so), coercively question you, threaten you or bribe you regarding your union activity or the union activities of your coworkers. You can't be fired, disciplined, demoted, or penalized in any way for engaging in these activities."

Information on How to Organize a Union at Your Workplace

Many labor unions offer basic organizing guides on their websites. The AFL-CIO's "How to Form a Union," can be a helpful place to start. Find it at aflcio.org/formaunion.

Labor Notes is a media and organizing project that has been an invaluable resource for labor activists and organizers for more than forty years. Their magazine, website, and book, *Secrets of a Successful Organizer*, are all pure gold. I find the handouts and exercises produced in connection with the book particularly helpful. Find them at labornotes.org/secrets/handouts.

For Organizing Support and to Contact an Organizer

When you are ready to organize, you can contact a union organizer through the AFL-CIO on their Form a Union site: aflcio.org/formaunion/contact.

Another way to connect with an organizer is through the Emergency Workplace Organizing project, a joint effort of the United Electrical, Radio, and Machine Workers of America and the Democratic Socialists of America. The project's website, workerorganizing.org, also offers resources and training materials.

While I am skeptical of most digital platforms aimed at helping workers organize (especially the for-profit ventures), one such tool recommended by activists I trust is coworker.org, which is not for profit and geared toward helping people build collective power in order to resolve workplace issues. You can contact their staff for support on workplace issue campaigns at coworker.org.

To File a Health and Safety Complaint

Federal law entitles you to a safe workplace. Your employer must keep your workplace free of known health and safety hazards. You have the right to speak up about hazards without fear of retaliation.

If you are concerned about health and safety at your place of work, you have the right to file a complaint and can do so anonymously through the Occupational Safety and Health Administration either on their website, osha.gov, or by phone, 800-321-6742 (OSHA).

QUESTIONS FOR DISCUSSION

1. Think about the last time you came into contact with items that were laundered at a factory like the one in *On the Line*. Did the book change the way you think about the linens you use at restaurants and hotels, or in the hospital?

2. Were you surprised to read about the dangerous conditions in these laundry factories? Why do you think this issue is so rarely reported on in the mainstream press?

3. Alma is vital to the success of the campaign, and she and Pitkin grow very close. Have you ever bonded deeply with someone because of a shared commitment? Why do you think the rift between Alma and Pitkin happened?

4. The corporation in the book and corporations throughout the country often spend multimillions of dollars to keep workers from organizing. Why do you think industries are so invested in "union avoidance," and do you see present-day examples of this?

5. Throughout the book, Pitkin highlights the historical contributions of immigrant women to the labor movement, and the ways they have

been held up as heroes on the one hand but denied real power within the unions they fought to build on the other. Do you think this is typical of the way women and certain groups have been marginalized in other struggles?

6. Storytelling is a critical part of union organizing. Pitkin was trained to frame the Triangle shirtwaist factory fire in a particular way. What did she learn about the real story there that differs from the accounts many people are familiar with? How are stories used to promote the idea of the individual actor? Are such stories beneficial to unions, or do they undercut movements based on collective action?

7. Moths play an important role in the book. How does the author use moths to guide the story about the union campaign, and what do you think the moths represent? Was this effective?

8. Pitkin describes the role of an organizer as one of helping workers form *their* union, not a union belonging to organizers who staff campaigns. There is a power dynamic inherent in the role, as the organizer often hasn't worked the jobs in the industry they are organizing or share race, gender, or even primary language with the rank-and-file members. How did Pitkin's thinking about her role shift over the course of the book?

9. We are living in a moment when union activity is surging. Why do you think there are more strikes now than in recent decades?

10. As we see the clash between two unions in the book, Pitkin offers some harsh critiques of labor organizing. What can *On the Line* teach us about what we need to do to make unions viable and powerful today?

Daisy Pitkin has spent more than twenty years as a community and union organizer, working first in support of garment workers around the world, and then for US labor unions organizing industrial laundry workers. Her essays have been awarded the Montana Prize, the DISQUIET Literary Prize, the New Millennium Award, and the Monique Wittig Writer's Scholarship. She grew up in rural Ohio and received an MFA from the University of Arizona. Pitkin lives and writes in Pittsburgh and is the national field director of the Starbucks Workers United campaign for Workers United, an offshoot of UNITE. Find her at daisypitkin.net.